ADVANCES IN SMART CITIES
SMARTER PEOPLE, GOVERNANCE, AND SOLUTIONS

ADVANCES IN SMART CITIES
SMARTER PEOPLE, GOVERNANCE, AND SOLUTIONS

EDITED BY

ARPAN KUMAR KAR, MANMOHAN PRASAD GUPTA,
P. VIGNESWARA ILAVARASAN, and YOGESH K. DWIVEDI

CRC Press
Taylor & Francis Group
Boca Raton   London   New York

CRC Press is an imprint of the
Taylor & Francis Group, **an informa** business

A CHAPMAN & HALL BOOK

CRC Press
Taylor & Francis Group
6000 Broken Sound Parkway NW, Suite 300
Boca Raton, FL 33487-2742

© 2017 by Taylor & Francis Group, LLC
CRC Press is an imprint of Taylor & Francis Group, an Informa business

Printed at CPI on sustainably sourced paper
Version Date: 20161212

International Standard Book Number-13: 978-1-4987-9570-8 (hardback)

Library of Congress Cataloging-in-Publication Data

Names: Kar, Arpan Kumar, editor.
Title: Advances in smart cities : smarter people, governance and solutions /
[edited by] Arpan Kumar Kar, M. P. Gupta, Vigneswara Ilavarasan, Ygesh
Dwivedi.
Description: Boca Raton, FL : CRC Press, [2016] | Includes bibliographical
references and index.
Identifiers: LCCN 2016032829| ISBN 9781498795708 (hardback) | ISBN
9781498795715 (e-book)
Subjects: LCSH: Cities and towns--Technological innovations. | City
planning--Technological innovations. | Urban policy.
Classification: LCC HT153 .A29 2016 | DDC 307.1/216--dc23
LC record available at https://lccn.loc.gov/2016032829

Visit the Taylor & Francis Web site at
http://www.taylorandfrancis.com

and the CRC Press Web site at
http://www.crcpress.com

Contents

Preface.. vii

Editors.. ix

Contributors... xi

1. Understanding Smart Cities: Inputs for Research and Practice 1
   Arpan Kumar Kar, Syed Ziaul Mustafa, Manmohan Prasad Gupta,
   P. Vigneswara Ilavarasan, and Yogesh K. Dwivedi

2. How Do Smart Cities Influence Governance? A Descriptive Literature Review 9
   Sumedha Chauhan and Neetima Agarwal

3. Smart People for Smart Cities: A Behavioral Framework for Personality and
   Roles 23
   Shristi Gupta, Syed Ziaul Mustafa, and Harish Kumar

4. Self-Sustainable Integrated Township: A Resource-Based Planning to
   Improve the Quality of Urban Life 31
   Sahil Singh Kapoor

5. Adoption and Acceptance of Mandatory Electronic Public Services by
   Citizens in the Developing World: Three Case Studies from India 49
   Harjit Singh, Arpan Kumar Kar, and P. Vigneswara Ilavarasan

6. Role of Manufacturing Sector to Develop Smart Economy: A
   Competitiveness Study between India and China 71
   Manoj Kumar Singh, Harish Kumar, and Manmohan Prasad Gupta

7. Concept of Smart Village in India: A Proposed Ecosystem and Framework 83
   Sheshadri Chatterjee and Arpan Kumar Kar

8. Smart City: An Integrated Approach Using System Dynamics 93
   Alok Raj and Gourav Dwivedi

9. Smart City Technologies: An Oversell Product of Global Technology
   Companies or the Ultimate Solution to the Challenges Persisting in Urban
   India 105
   Alok Tiwari

10. A Cloud-Based Mobile Application for Cashless Payments to Enhance
    Transportation Mobility in India 115
    Arunava Ghosh

11 **Financial Viability of Energy Conservation Using Natural Light in an Institutional Building in India** 127
Pooja Sharma and Dibakar Rakshit

12 **Management of Multidimensional Risk for Digital Services in Smart Cities** 149
Syed Ziaul Mustafa and Arpan Kumar Kar

13 **M-Commerce in Smart Cities: Changing Mindsets of Individuals, Organizations, and Society** 167
Himanshu Agarwal and Gaurav Dixit

14 **The Shift toward a Sustainable Urban Mobility through Decision Support Systems** 181
Valeria Caiati, Salvatore Di Dio, Francesco Ferrero, and Andrea Vesco

15 **Low-Carbon Logistics Network for Smart Cities: A Conceptual Framework** 199
Harpreet Kaur and Surya Prakash Singh

Index 213

Preface

There has been a massive focus on "smart cities," both in developed and emerging economies in recent times. Europe, the United States, and several Asian countries (e.g., Korea and Japan) have been leading smart city development. Attempts have been made to deploy an assortment of smart technologies to make a new city livable, that is, safe, more comfortable, and secure. Underneath lies a complex web of issues that keep city managers busy, and which broadly boil down to transforming a city into a sustainable city. This transformation refers to a new scenario defined by clean and surplus energy, modern living in serene surroundings, and a real-time response system to meet needs or deal deftly with emergency situations (terror attacks, natural calamities, or accidents).

Digital services, transportation, energy, and natural resource management are central themes of all smart city projects. Clean energy is a major concern all over the world. Germany, in particular, has been quite aggressive in revising its energy policy from demand to supply and in shifting from centralized to distributed generation to replace overproduction and avoidable energy consumption with energy-saving measures and increased efficiency. Smart technologies are vital in energy production and consumption as they enhance our capacity multifold to deal with the challenges. Digital services, which may provide residents access to utilities and services over the Internet, are increasingly gaining prominence.

Following these trends, other nations have also announced similar programs. Today, China and India are in focus as they deal with a variety of complex problems arising from irreversible urbanization trends across all cities. They therefore offer vast business opportunities for proven smart city solutions. The Government of India (GoI) has announced the launch of 100 smart cities across the nation to fulfil a dream of maximizing urbanization without overburdening the ecosystem that exists in major cities. However, these attempts are not greenfield projects, but are mostly brownfield projects. The focus is on whether, by using enablers such as information and communication technologies, smart technologies, sensors, process reengineering and governance, productivity, and resource utilization could be optimized for sustenance. However, there are enormous challenges in implementing the vision of restructuring and reengineering the economy within such urban settlements so that the best utilization of resources and maximization of productivity may be achieved by leveraging enablers such as technology. This edited book, titled *Advances in Smart Cities: Smarter People, Governance and Solutions*, is a compilation of studies that contribute to creating a better understanding of smart cities in terms of critical issues and concerns surrounding governance, processes, and policies, which may make such a focused effort successful.

The book is organized into 15 chapters, contributing to 4 distinct themes. First, we introduce readers to the concept and perspectives through which research and development in smart cities could be analyzed and categorized. Subsequently, readers are exposed to some of the key needs of the residents of such smart cities, and how such needs can be serviced. A lot of discussion has centered on how urban life may be improved by better understanding of needs and better governance. This is followed with discussions on the public policies and governance issues surrounding smart city planning and development. Readers are exposed to holistic insights, developed through comparative analysis of best practices and frameworks that may be adopted for governance. Furthermore, much discussion provides perspectives on the potential scope of development through smarter governance. The next section focuses on introducing readers to some of the solutions and governance of such solutions that may be needed for smarter cities. The focus of such solutions has been to leverage the best practices that are enabled through different technologies and provide extraordinary benefits across domains such as digital services, logistics and mobility, and mobile-based economic activity, among others.

To meet this objective, the editors planned a research conference for attracting the best ideas that could be converted into chapters for this book. To meet this objective, the International Conference on Smart Cities was organized at the Indian Institute of Technology (IIT) Delhi on January 22, 2016. This conference was a joint academic effort between IIT Delhi, Swansea University, and Waterford Institute of Technology, and was supported by Beyond Evolution Tech Solutions and Unnat Bharat Abhiyan. The conference was coorganized by the EU-India Cooperation Platform in Future Internet and Electronic Media project (EU-INDIA FI-MEDIA) and FIWARE Mundus. From over 34 very high-quality research presentations chosen from over 50 submissions after peer review, the editors finally chose 14 articles that contributed significantly to enriching the knowledge and understanding surrounding smart cities. On behalf of the editorial team, we take this opportunity to thank our sponsors and supporters, who made this conference—and hence the realization of this edited book—a success. The enormous support from our hosting department (Management Studies) and our colleagues cannot be expressed in words. However, we thank our esteemed colleagues in our department and in other departments/centers of IIT Delhi for making this initiative successful and for supporting us in all our stages of academic endeavors. A special mention goes to Professor Sushil (Deputy Director, Operations) and Professor Kanika Bhal (head of department) for extending their support to make this conference a major success. We also thank our conference secretaries (Vimal and Amit) and our research scholars (Harish, Syed, and Ashish) for their support during the conference; they are the driving force behind the implementation of our plans.

After the initial submissions and presentations made at the conference, each chapter in this book has undergone three to four revisions after review and further screening. We thank our reviewers and research scholars for all their hard work in supporting these activities. On behalf of the editors, a special mention goes to Mr. Nimish Joseph, who has taken on the task of interacting with the individual authors so many times after each review and has brought each chapter to its current stage. Furthermore, the team from CRC Press/Taylor & Francis has been extremely helpful in providing us with detailed reviews that have helped the editors to shape the book to its current form. Many aspects that have been added, especially many of the case studies and examples, are based on the feedback received after review. We are thankful to the reviewers for their reviews, which have helped us significantly in enhancing the content of this book.

Arpan Kumar Kar
Manmohan Prasad Gupta
P. Vigneswara Ilavarasan
Yogesh K. Dwivedi

Editors

Arpan Kumar Kar is an assistant professor at IIT Delhi. Prior to joining IIT Delhi, he was an assistant professor at IIM Rohtak. He is also a visiting professor at IIM Lucknow. He has published over 60 articles with Elsevier, Springer, Emerald, Taylor & Francis, the Institute of Electrical and Electronics Engineers (IEEE), the Association for Information Systems, Inderscience, and so on, and has presented his research at leading international conferences such as the Hawaii International Conference on System Science and the International Federation for Information Processing. He is the recipient of multiple prestigious awards and recognitions for his research. He also has prior industry experience with IBM—India Research Laboratory and Cognizant Business Consulting, besides having completed a number of prestigious projects for multiple leading organizations such as the EU and GoI. He completed his doctorate and master's studies at the Xavier School of Management Jamshedpur, and graduated in engineering from Jadavpur University (gold medalist).

Manmohan Prasad Gupta is a professor, area chair of information systems, and coordinator of the Center for Excellence in E-governance at the Indian Institute of Technology (IIT) Delhi. He is well known for his pioneering work in the area of e-governance (including 18 doctoral theses, 13 sponsored projects, the coauthored book *Government Online*, two other edited books, *Towards E-government* and *Promise of E-governance*, and 176 research papers in national and international journals/conference proceedings). He is involved in several policy-making committees on information and communications technology (ICT) at central and state government level in India. He is also on the jury of prestigious awards committees such as the Data Security Council of India, the Computer Society of India E-governance Awards, and the Web Ratna Awards.

P. Vigneswara Ilavarasan is an associate professor at the Department of Management Studies, IIT Delhi. He researches and teaches on the production and consumption of ICT, with a special focus on India. His specific research interests are ICT and development , the Indian information technology (IT) industry, and social media. Presently, he is teaching management information systems, e-commerce, social media, and market research methods. Dr. Ilavarasan is a recipient of the Outstanding Young Faculty Fellowship Award at IIT Delhi and the Prof. M.N. Srinivas Memorial Prize of the Indian Sociological Society. He is also the recipient of research grants from the International Development Research Centre (Canada), GoI, Oxford Analytica (United Kingdom), the European Commission Institute for Prospective Technological Studies, and IdeaCorp (Philippines). He has previously taught at Pondicherry Central University and the Indian Institute of Management (IMM) Rohtak. Dr. Ilavarasan is an active contributor to international journals and conferences of repute. His publications and other details are available at http://web.iitd.ac.in/~vignes.

Yogesh K. Dwivedi is a professor of digital and social media, director of the Emerging Markets Research Centre (EMaRC), and director of research in the School of Management at Swansea University, Wales, United Kingdom. His research interests are in the area of information systems including the adoption and diffusion of emerging ICTs and digital and social media marketing. He has published more than 100 articles in a range of lead-ing academic journals and conferences. He has co-edited more than 15 books on tech-nology adoption, e-government, and IS theory and had them published by international publishers such as Springer, Routledge, and Emerald. He acted as co-editor of 15 special issues; organised tracks, mini-tracks, and panels in leading conferences; and served as programme co-chair of the IFIP WG 8.6 Conference and Conference Chair of the IFIP WG 6.11 I3E2016 Conference. He is associate editor of the *European Journal of Marketing*; assis-tant editor of the *Journal of Enterprise Information Management and Transforming Government: People, Process and Policy*; and senior editor of the *Journal of Electronic Commerce Research*. More information: http://www.swansea.ac.uk/staff/som/academic-staff/y.k.dwivedi/

Contributors

Himanshu Agarwal
Department of Management Studies
Indian Institute of Technology
Roorkee, India

Neetima Agarwal
School of Management
G D Goenka University
Gurgaon, India

Valeria Caiati
Smart City Strategic Program
Istituto Superiore Mario Boella
Turin, Italy

Sheshadri Chatterjee
Department of Management Studies
Indian Institute of Technology
Delhi, India

Sumedha Chauhan
School of Management
G D Goenka University
Gurgaon, India

Salvatore Di Dio
Palermo Urban Solutions Hub (PUSH)
Palermo, Italy

Gaurav Dixit
Department of Management Studies
Indian Institute of Technology
Roorkee, India

Gourav Dwivedi
Operations Management Area
Indian Institute of Management
Lucknow, India

Yogesh K. Dwivedi
Swansea University
Swansea, United Kingdom

Francesco Ferrero
Smart City Strategic Program
Istituto Superiore Mario Boella
Turin, Italy

Arunava Ghosh
Indian Institute of Management Indore
Indore, India

Manmohan Prasad Gupta
Department of Management Studies
Indian Institute of Technology
Delhi, India

Shristi Gupta
Amar Nath and Shashi Khosla School of
    Information Technology
Indian Institute of Technology
Delhi, India

P. Vigneswara Ilavarasan
Department of Management Studies
Indian Institute of Technology
Delhi, India

Sahil Singh Kapoor
Department of Policy Studies
The Energy and Resources Institute (TERI)
    University
Delhi, India

Harpreet Kaur
Department of Management Studies
Indian Institute of Technology
Delhi, India

Harish Kumar
Department of Management Studies
Indian Institute of Technology
Delhi, India

Arpan Kumar Kar
Department of Management Studies
Indian Institute of Technology
Delhi, India

Syed Ziaul Mustafa
Center of Excellence in Cyber Systems and
    Information Assurance
Indian Institute of Technology
Delhi, India

Surya Prakash Singh
Department of Management Studies
Indian Institute of Technology
Delhi, India

Alok Raj
Operations Management Area
Indian Institute of Management
Lucknow, India

Dibakar Rakshit
Centre for Energy Studies
Indian Institute of Technology
Delhi, India

Pooja Sharma
Centre for Energy Studies
Indian Institute of Technology
Delhi, India

Harjit Singh
Department of Management
    Studies
Indian Institute of Technology
Delhi, India

Manoj Kumar Singh
Department of Management
    Studies
Indian Institute of Technology
Delhi, India

Alok Tiwari
Department of Urban and Regional
    Planning
King Abdulaziz University
Jeddah, Kingdom of Saudi Arabia

Andrea Vesco
Istituto Superiore Mario Boella
Smart City Strategic Program
Turin, Italy

1

Understanding Smart Cities: Inputs for Research and Practice

Arpan Kumar Kar, Syed Ziaul Mustafa, Manmohan Prasad Gupta,
P. Vigneswara Ilavarasan, and Yogesh K. Dwivedi

CONTENTS

1.1 Introduction 1
1.2 Smart People 3
1.3 Smart Economy 3
1.4 Smart Mobility 3
1.5 Smart Living 4
1.6 Smart Governance 4
1.7 Smart Environment 4
1.8 Connecting the Perspectives: A Unified View 5
1.9 Concluding Discussion 5
References 7

1.1 Introduction

Smart cities are envisioned as the future of technology-enabled, resilient, sustainable, creative, and livable urban human settlements in the world. It is increasingly becoming part of the vision of the national governments wherein technologies are massively used to improve the processes surrounding all dimensions of urban development, planning, and management. Various domain experts such as civil engineering specialists, information and communication technology (ICT) specialists, process consultants, private corporations, and government departments are required to work together to plan and implement how the smart city will be understood, conceptualized, designed, and maintained. On a more holistic scope, smart cities can be explored as an assemblage of ICTs, public policy, process reengineering for sustainability, urban development, and citizen participation in public life.

Since 2011, contribution in the smart city has been examined by scholars from diverse disciplines—information systems, political economy, economics, urban planning, public administration, public policy, and so on. Basically, the relationship between technology and society creates a situation like actor-network theory (Söderström et al., 2014), where technology becomes an enabler and partner in realizing many of the societal needs and process improvements, and vice versa. Several discussions have been raised in the literature related to the impact of ICTs in cities. With the increase in digital technologies, which enable urban planning, policy makers realize the connection between urban development and ICTs, and how ICTs can impact the outcome of urban development initiatives.

Literature has shown that the smart city has been represented with different concepts over a period of time, such as networked cities (Castells, 2001); techno cities (Downey and McGuigan, 1999); cyber cities (Graham and Marvin, 1999); creative cities (Florida, 2005); and digital cities (Komninos, 2009). The concept of the smart city was first introduced in academic literature in the 1990s. However, since then, no detailed definition has been standardized that can fit into all the dimensions of the city. This may stem from a lack of empirical validation of proposed frameworks, and a gap between practice and academia. This book is a modest attempt to fill this gap by bridging fundamental research at the academic space and practitioner-based standards.

An exploration into academic literature highlights that there are six important dimensions of smart cities that have been explored typically, namely smart economy, smart people, smart governance, smart mobility, smart environment, and smart living (Chatterjee and Kar, 2015; Chauhan et al., 2016). An exploration into practitioner-oriented literature on urban management (ISO 37120:2014) highlights the presence of areas surrounding economic and societal indicators; education management; energy management; environment management; financial management; emergency management, public policy and governance; health-care management; recreation facilities; safety, shelter, and housing facilities; waste management; telecommunication management; transportation and logistics management; urban planning; water resource management; and sanitation. An attempt has been made in Figure 1.1 to integrate these indicators for defining the focus areas of smart cities.

In subsequent sections, we explore what these pillars of smart cities actually entail and what could be explored for research and development, under these pillars.

Smart people	Smart economy	Smart mobility	Smart living	Smart governance	Smart environment
• Higher education • Social and ethnic diversity • Openness and cohesion • Cosmopolitan outlook • Flexible approaches in work and life • High work productivity • Entrepreneur focus and zeal • Cultural plurality	• High-full time employment • High economic productivity • Entrepreneurs hip and globalization • Idea and IP generation • High-skilled labor and jobs • Small supporting businesses • Vocationally trained workforce	• Local accessibility • International accessibility • Green transportation systems • Public transportation • Physical safety • Monitoring and control systems • Logistics and freight control • Commutation infrastructure	• Better education • Digital literacy programs • Better health care • Planned housing facilities • Cultural facilities • Sports facilities • Smart urban planning • ICT access • Low infant mortality	• Access to information • Public utilities and services • Democratic participation • Women participation • Smart policing and crime control • Urban planning support • Grievance management • Information security and risk management	• Water resource management • Smart energy management • Gas and particle pollution control • Hazardous waste management • Solid waste management • Sanitation management • Noise control
Pillars of smart cities					

FIGURE 1.1
Integration of academic and practitioner literature to define the pillars of smart cities.

1.2 Smart People

This perspective highlights the focus on issues surrounding people's education, learning, creativity, and participation in public life as some of the critical indicators to exploit the human potential of a smart city. In order to make the residents of such settlements smart, quality of life and personality should be systematically enhanced. The High Human Development Index could be considered the most important aspect of such smart people. One of the most important attributes is enrolment of graduate students to higher education and the highest level of qualification achieved, which could further lead to knowledge-driven jobs and intellectual property creation. Such smart people should have the zeal to learn lifelong as well as having high social and ethnic plurality. Open-mindedness is also one of the desired qualities of such people residing in smart cities. Flexibility to adapt to the changes in the environment as well as sufficient creativity to contribute to the knowledge economy would be of paramount importance. Such smart people would also be expected to possess a democratic nature and participate in public life as well.

1.3 Smart Economy

It may be envisioned that a smart economy can be achieved by securing investment, jobs, businesses, and talents. According to Lombardi et al. (2012), focus areas for a smart economy could be indicators such as public expenses on education, research grants, research and development (R&D), and percentage of gross domestic product (GDP) per head of city population. Some factors, such as GDP per head of the city population, average annual household income, the unemployment rate, percentage of the project funded by civil society, average annual household income, business activities, financial intermediation, and commercial services, also contribute to the smart economy. A smart economy is driven by innovation and would be expected to be supported by best-in-class universities, providing an ecosystem to nourish the entrepreneurial spirit of the people in the society. The economy of the should create an economic image globally, and have a trademark as well. Productivity and a flexible labor market should be provided by the city administrative authority. The economy should have international branding as well as generate a highly diversified economy.

1.4 Smart Mobility

A smart city would need smart mobility systems and an infrastructure to address the needs of the residents within the city. In this context, a smart mobility simulation analysis may help policy makers plan for smart cities in a better way. Smart mobility requirements would also entail that the city have national and international accessibility. Also it would be important to ensure that ICTs have been used widely during the development and management of related infrastructure, such as bridges and national highways, monorail and metros. Intelligent transportation systems should provide last-mile connectivity for both citizens and organizations. Transportation systems should take care of the daily and occasional commuters, as well as logistical needs within and outside the city.

1.5 Smart Living

Literature highlights (Lombardi et al., 2012) that indicators of smart living may be considered within smart cities when there are areas for leisure use: cinemas, sports arenas, public libraries, and multiplexes. People need to be exposed to industrial training and international standards while developing such infrastructure. Diverse cultural facilities for different religions and ethnicities should be made available, whether they belong to minor or major communities. Both primary and higher education facilities should be given high priority. Further development of world-class universities with a focus on both knowledge creation and dissemination should also have high priority. Moreover, a city should have world-class hospitals with state-of-the-art treatment facilities and infrastructure. Cities should have provisions for good-quality housing and a related supporting ecosystem, so that citizens can contribute positively to their city's development.

1.6 Smart Governance

A smart city will be able to develop and maintain only if focus is brought into developing policies for smart governance. It is not only about making the right policy choices but also about implementing those policies. Accessing public information should be made easy for the general public. This should not breach privacy or security, nor risk misuse of the information assets, opportunities for which may be created when all of the key processes and entities are digitized. Electronic governance and its maturity would play a critical role in such a smart city. Public participation in democracy and policy-making would be expected in such cities. For example, in India, platforms such as MyGov facilitate a citizen's participation in public policy and urban governance. As per Lombardi et al. (2012), smart governance may be enabled for a citizen by the use of e-governance. Sharing of information, transparent decision making, and stakeholders' participation for improving the government services would play a critical role in achieving smarter governance. Lee et al. (2014) highlight that public–private partnership and citizen participation would be an important element of smart city governance.

1.7 Smart Environment

A smart city should have a high focus on the sustainability issues of the environment. Smart energy management schemes may be adopted, such as the conversion of natural light for use in institutional buildings, homes, hotels, and so on. Since carbon emissions and other pollutants affect the environment of a city, low-carbon logistics networks should be used to reduce the carbon footprint. According to Lombardi et al. (2012), smart environment management constitutes the management of green gas emissions, achieving high-energy efficiency, conservation of electricity, treatment and conservation of water resources, and management of green spaces. A comprehensive policy would be required to improve and monitor environmental performance and air pollution. With respect to civil society: the percentage of people using public transport, efforts to use clean transport, and engagement in sustainability oriented activity could be indicators to focus on. With respect to industry: the percentage of energy derived from renewable sources, the proportion of recycled waste as a ratio of total waste produced, the management of gas emissions, and the management of buildings and infrastructure could be some of the key indicators assessed in terms of sustainability. For achieving and maintaining a smart environment, focused initiatives need to be started to monitor the carbon footprint and preservation of natural resources such as water, greenery, and air.

1.8 Connecting the Perspectives: A Unified View

The studies in this book touch upon many of these pillars of smart cities, and provide a futuristic direction for deliberation and development of public policy to address these concerns. Each of the perspectives in isolation adds little to enhance the understanding on smart cities. A broader perspective needs to be developed by focusing on studies that contribute to enriching the understanding across these perspective in unison rather than in isolation. This is what the individual chapters in this book strive to contribute to and enrich the existing literature on smart cities. By utilizing interdisciplinary and mixed-research methodologies, perspectives of addressing key issues in smart cities are discussed. Figure 1.2 highlights the potential areas that would need special focus in terms of policies and exploration, as touched upon by subsequent chapters in this book.

The scope of understanding smart cities would remain incomplete without bringing in perspectives from multiple facets of public policy, engineering, process management, and urban governance. Many of the experts working on these domains often work in isolation, which is why the knowledge created has limited scope for dissemination through proper platforms and channels.

1.9 Concluding Discussion

While there has been significant focus on developing smart cities for over a decade, the scientific literature is still at a rather nascent stage. Although empirical validations for the purpose of generalizability are difficult in many of the explorations, this book highlights many examples that provide real-life cases for developing a deeper understanding of smart city literature. Since the literature is still at an infancy stage, this book contributes significantly in strengthening the understanding of different interdisciplinary issues in smart cities. Readers will be exposed to different areas of deliberation and solutions, which contribute to a unified view of the smart city as the ultimate solution of the future

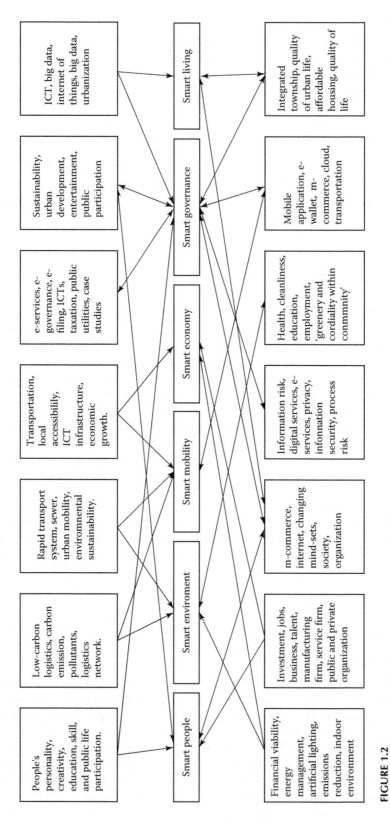

FIGURE 1.2
Relationship between different factors with the dimensions of smart cities.

for urbanization and the improvement of human settlements, not only in metropolitan cities, but also in smaller cities.

References

Castells, Manuel. 2011. *The Rise of the Network Society: The Information Age—Economy, Society, and Culture*. Vol. Wiley.

Chatterjee, Sheshadri, and Arpan Kumar Kar. 2015. Smart Cities in developing economies: A literature review and policy insights. *Advances in Computing, Communications and Informatics (ICACCI), 2015 IEEE International Conference on*, 2335–2340.

Chauhan, Sumedha, Neetima Agarwal, and Arpan Kumar Kar. 2016 Addressing big data challenges in smart cities: A systematic literature review. *Info* 18, no. 4: 73–90.

Downey, John, and Jim McGuigan, eds. 1999. *Technocities: The Culture and Political Economy of the Digital Revolution*. London: Sage.

Florida, Richard. 2005. *Cities and the Creative Class*. New York: Routledge.

Graham, Stephen, and Simon Marvin. 1999. Planning cybercities: Integrating telecommunications into urban planning. *Town Planning Review* 70, no. 1: 89.

ISO. ISO37120: Sustainable development of communities—Indicators for city services and quality of life. http://www.iso.org/iso/catalogue_detail?csnumber=62436 (Accessed 01-07-2016).

Komninos, Nicos. 2009. Intelligent cities: Towards interactive and global innovation environments. *International Journal of Innovation and Regional Development* 1, no. 4: 337–355.

Lee, Jung Hoon, Marguerite Gong Hancock, and Mei-Chih Hu. 2014. Towards an effective framework for building smart cities: Lessons from Seoul and San Francisco. *Technological Forecasting and Social Change* 89: 80–99.

Lombardi, Patrizia, Silvia Giordano, Hend Farouh, and Wael Yousef. 2012. Modelling the smart city performance. *Innovation: The European Journal of Social Science Research* 25, no. 2: 137–149.

Söderström, Ola, Till Paasche, and Francisco Klauser. 2014. Smart cities as corporate storytelling. *City* 18, no. 3: 307–320.

2

How Do Smart Cities Influence Governance?
A Descriptive Literature Review

Sumedha Chauhan and Neetima Agarwal

CONTENTS

2.1 Introduction..9
2.2 Smart City and Its Role in Governance 10
2.3 Research Methodology 11
2.4 Results of Classification 11
    2.4.1 Benefits 15
        2.4.1.1 Sustainability...15
        2.4.1.2 Urban Development...15
        2.4.1.3 Entertainment..15
        2.4.1.4 Public Participation...16
    2.4.2 Challenges..16
        2.4.2.1 Political Issues..16
        2.4.2.2 Human Issues 16
        2.4.2.3 Security Issues 17
        2.4.2.4 Technological Issues 18
2.5 Discussion and Conclusion 18
2.6 Future Directions...19
References..20

2.1 Introduction

Advances in the field of information and communication technologies (ICTs) have contributed vitally in enhancing the effectiveness of electronic governance (e-governance). E-governance refers to the intensive use of ICTs for timely provision of public services, government information, information access without bureaucracy, improvement of managerial effectiveness, and promotion of democratic values (Stemberger and Jaklic, 2007). Today, the concept of smart cities has gained popularity in city associations and governmental institutions (Van den Bergh and Viaene, 2015). Cities were once merely considered as part of local government but they are now the centers of governmental innovation (Lee and Lee, 2014). The importance of developing cities in a sustainable manner is dramatically rising because of population growth and urbanization trends. The urban population is estimated to grow by 2.3 billion in the next 40 years, while around 70% of the world's population will reside in cities by 2050 (Theodoridis et al., 2013). This increasing population growth will lead to a rise in the consumption of resources, which will pose a challenge to the quality of life. A wide range of problems can be tackled by exploiting ICTs in a smart city. As ICTs play a critical role in designing smart cities, a significant part of city investment is utilized in developing new ICTs (Perboli et al., 2014).

Smart city is a newly introduced and ambiguous term. Nevertheless, it can be used to describe a city that uses ICTs to enhance the quality of life of its citizens and promotes sustainable development (Chourabi et al., 2012). Smart city initiatives have attracted the attention of policy makers and researchers, as they can address issues related to either e-government, economy, mobility, environment, energy, or a combination of these (Caragliu et al., 2011). Several smart city initiatives target the development of ICTs to augment the effectiveness, efficiency, accountability, and transparency of communications and transactions between citizens and government (Perboli et al., 2014). Though the smart city and e-government initiatives might differ from each other in the context and characteristics of specific projects, there is still much commonality between them. This is because many smart city initiatives are driven by governments with the objective to serve the citizens in a better way. ICT-based governance is also known as smart governance. The research firm Forrester has stated that smart governance is fundamental to smart city initiatives (Chourabi et al., 2012).

On the other hand, researchers have also put forth negative aspects of the smart city. Martinez-Balleste et al. (2013) argued that the collection and management of huge amounts of data would lead to a "Big Brother" effect, that is, a lack of privacy due to which citizens may abstain from availing of smart city services. Thus, the rapid growth of smart cities, along with these contrasting claims, makes it an exciting area to research on. As smart city initiatives and governance complement each other, gaining an understanding of the hitherto sparsely studied impact of smart cities on governance underscores the importance of conducting this research. In light of the aforementioned view, we raise our research question: How do smart cities influence governance? This research intends to answer this question by conducting an in-depth literature review to find and classify the benefits and challenges faced by governance in a smart city. Most importantly, given the contemporary relevance of this subject, we also provide key insights for future researchers and policy makers.

2.2 Smart City and Its Role in Governance

The concept of the smart city is related to many other concepts, such as the information city, the intelligent city, the digital city, the ubiquitous city, and the knowledge city. Though there might be differences in the wordings, these concepts mainly focus on the use of ICTs in urban management (Lee and Lee, 2014). The indicators for managing the smart city should follow the SMART (specific, measurable, achievable, relevant, and time-bound) principle (Carli et al., 2013). Though the concept of the smart city is still blurry, several researchers have provided different definitions for this term. Roscia et al. (2013) defined a smart city as a city with increased connectivity, automation, and coordination among consumers, providers, and networks, in order to make the most of data transmission and distribution. A smart city is required to develop and manage various innovative services that deliver information related to all aspects of life to its citizenry, through Internet-based and interactive applications (Kuk and Janssen, 2011). Caragliu et al. (2011) articulated that a city is smart "when investments in human and social capital and traditional (transport) and modern (ICT) communication infrastructure fuel sustainable economic growth and a high quality of life, with a wise management of natural resources, through participatory governance."

A smart city facilitates the government in monitoring, understanding, analyzing, and subsequently planning the city in order to improve equity, efficiency, and quality of life (Carli et al., 2013). Caragliu et al. (2011) stated that within the concept of the smart city, e-governance acts as a tool through which the current structures, processes, and practices of government can be improved. Thus, it aims to realize the social inclusion of citizens in public services. Good governance in the context of smart administration also refers to the use of new channels of communication for the citizens, for example e-governance or e-democracy. Smart governance consists of aspects related to political participation, services for citizens, and the functioning of administration (Giffinger et al., 2007). Further, ICTs play a crucial role not only in enhancing the efficiency and transparency of government, but also help in facilitating the democratic practices by improving the collaboration between citizens and government. ICTs enable government institutions and citizens to voluntarily share knowledge, stimulate innovation, and nurture new knowledge (Gil-Garcia, 2013).

2.3 Research Methodology

The particular goal of a literature review is to conceptualize research areas and synthesize prior research. The firm foundation of advancing knowledge can be created through an effective review of existing literature (Webster and Watson, 2002). In order to achieve the research objective, a comprehensive descriptive literature review was conducted. A descriptive review reveals an interpretable pattern from the existing body of literature (Guzzo et al., 1987). It involves the systematic process of searching, filtering, and classifying research papers.

The research papers for this review were selected via a computerized search in seven prominent databases—ProQuest (ABI/INFORM), Elsevier (ScienceDirect), EBSCOhost, JSTOR, INFORMS, IEEE, and Google Scholar. The relevant research papers were identified by querying these scholarly databases using a combination of keywords such as "smart city," "smart cities," and "e-governance." The papers considered for this research were published on or before August 2015. The initial search resulted into a total of 101 hits, which were subsequently filtered in two steps.

The first step of the filtration process involved the manual scanning of the titles of all the papers so that the irrelevant ones could be removed. This resulted in the exclusion of duplicates and opinion articles. The second step involved reading the abstract and complete text, if required. In this step, we removed papers that didn't discuss smart cities and e-governance as the central concept, but merely mentioned them in the text. After the second step, we were left with only 32 peer-reviewed research papers addressing the concepts of the smart city and e-governance together.

The reviewed research papers enabled us to classify the benefits and challenges into four major categories of each. These categories were further classified into subcategories that were further broken down into sub-sub-categories. The next section elaborates the results of classification of benefits and challenges of smart cities in e-governance context.

2.4 Results of Classification

Table 2.1 depicts the classification of reviewed research papers. Figure 2.1 classifies the benefits of smart cities, while Figure 2.2 classifies the challenges of smart cities in an e-governance context.

TABLE 2.1

Classification of Reviewed Research Papers

Category	References
Sustainability	
Quality of life	Kourtit et al., 2012; Lee and Lee, 2014; Roscia et al., 2013; Capdevila and Zarlenga, 2015; Awaluddin, 2014; Theodoridis et al., 2013; Carli et al., 2013; Chourabi et al., 2012
Environment	Perboli et al., 2014; Albino et al. 2015; Sivarajah et al., 2014; Roscia et al., 2013; Delponte and Ugolini, 2011
Urban Development	
Transport and logistics	Delponte and Ugolini, 2011; Lee and Lee, 2014; van Geenhuizen and Nijkamp, 2009; Roscia et al., 2013
Infrastructure	Capdevila and Zarlenga, 2015; Tranos and Gertner, 2012; Van den Bergh and Viaene, 2015; Albino et al., 2015; Martinez-Balleste et al., 2013; Roscia et al., 2013; Lee and Lee, 2014; Kourtit et al., 2012; Mainka et al., 2015
Entertainment	
Tourism	Roscia et al., 2013; Kourtit et al., 2012
Leisure and recreation	Roscia et al., 2013; Kourtit et al., 2012
Public Participation	
Social media	Khan et al., 2014; Mainka et al., 2015; van der Graaf and Veeckman, 2014; Van den Bergh and Viaene, 2015; Przeybilovicz et al., 2015; Sandoval-Almazan et al., 2015
Crowdsourcing	You et al., 2014; van der Graaf and Veeckman, 2014
Political Issues	
Leadership Issues	Lee and Lee, 2014; Awaluddin, 2014; Van den Bergh and Viaene, 2015
Human Issues	
Social issues	Awaluddin, 2014; Sandoval-Almazan et al., 2015; Theodoridis et al., 2013
Cultural issues	Kourtit et al., 2012; Lee and Lee, 2014; Delponte and Ugolini, 2011; van Geenhuizen and Nijkamp, 2009; Carli et al., 2013; Roscia et al., 2013; Albino et al., 2015; Vakali et al., 2013
Communication issues	Veeckman and van der Graaf, 2014; Mainka et al., 2015; Thomas et al., 2010; Syväjärvi et al., 2015; Przeybilovicz et al., 2015; Martinez-Balleste et al., 2013; Cano et al., 2014; Gil-Garcia, 2013; Khan et al., 2014; Chadwick and May, 2003
Behavioral issues	Nam and Pardo, 2013; Thomas et al., 2010; Lee and Lee, 2014; Sandoval-Almazan et al., 2015
Security Issues	
Crime and disaster issues	Sandoval-Almazan et al., 2015; Przeybilovicz et al., 2015; Martinez-Balleste et al., 2013; Cano et al., 2014; van der Graaf and Veeckman, 2014; Syväjärvi et al., 2015
Privacy issues	Bartoli et al., 2011; Veeckman and van der Graaf, 2014; Martinez-Balleste et al., 2013; van der Graaf and Veeckman, 2014; Syväjärvi et al., 2015
Authenticity issues	Van den Bergh and Viaene, 2015; Albino et al., 2015; Martinez-Balleste et al., 2013; Roscia et al., 2013; Lee and Lee, 2014; Kourtit et al., 2012; Mainka et al., 2015
Technological Issues	
Hardware and software incompatibility	Roscia et al., 2013; Delponte and Ugolini, 2011; Przeybilovicz et al., 2015
Lack of know-how	Veeckman and van der Graaf, 2014; Mainka et al., 2015; Thomas et al., 2010; Syväjärvi et al., 2015; Przeybilovicz et al., 2015; Martinez-Balleste et al., 2013; Cano et al., 2014; Gil-Garcia, 2013; Khan et al., 2014; Delponte and Ugolini, 2011; Odendaal, 2006

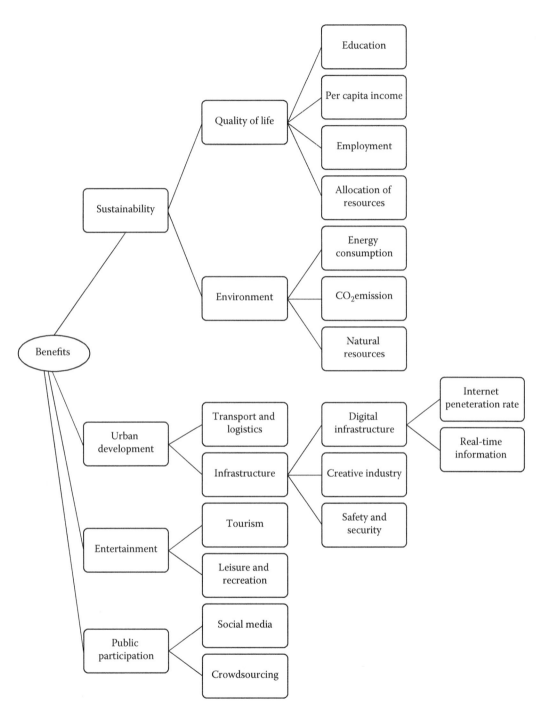

FIGURE 2.1
Benefits of smart cities in an e-governance context.

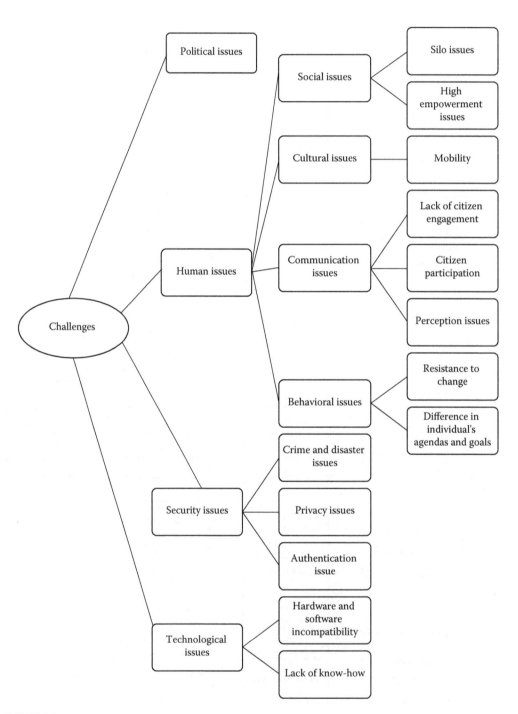

FIGURE 2.2
Challenges of smart cities in an e-governance context.

2.4.1 Benefits

2.4.1.1 Sustainability

Sustainability refers to a harmonious relationship between humans and the environment. It ensures that human needs can continue to be met in the long run through conservation and allowing the regeneration of the natural environment (Keirstead and Leach, 2008; Alberti and Susskind, 1996). This category refers to the urban population's basic needs and quality of life, which includes the measures of individual income, poverty, income distribution, unemployment and training, housing conditions, health, security, and work satisfaction (Kourtit et al., 2012; Awaluddin, 2014).

2.4.1.1.1 Quality of Life

This subcategory includes the topics that cover the basic dimensions of socioeconomic sustainability, such as population or demography (Carli et al., 2013); economic activity; per capita gross domestic product (GDP) or personal income; rates of change in employment, education, and culture (Awaluddin, 2014; Capdevila and Zarlenga, 2015). In other words, good governance in smart cities should ensure the physiological, safety, social, economic, and esteem needs of every individual.

2.4.1.1.2 Environment

This subcategory specifically addresses environmental sustainability indicators, such as greenhouse gas emissions, rise in GDP, modal split of transport, urban air quality, and municipal solid waste landfilled or incinerated (Perboli et al., 2014; Sivarajah et al., 2014; Roscia et al., 2013).

2.4.1.2 Urban Development

This category contains the research papers that provide a general view of urban development with an aim of providing an understanding of how smart city development can provide equitable growth opportunities to the following two subcategories (Lee and Lee, 2014; Mainka et al., 2015).

2.4.1.2.1 Transport and Logistics

This subcategory refers to the topics that examine how the evolution of smart cities would improve transportation facilities (Van Geenhuizen and Nijkamp, 2009). Further, few research papers proposed the detailed classification of info-mobility, intelligent transport systems (ITS), smart mobility, and logistics (Roscia et al., 2013).

2.4.1.2.2 Infrastructure

This subcategory contains the research papers discussing infrastructure development (Capdevila and Zarlenga, 2015; Tranos and Gertner, 2012). Smart cities should lead to growth of significant infrastructures, such as roads, bridges, tunnels, railways, subways, airports, seaports, communication infrastructure, water, power, and major buildings. In smart cities, the entire infrastructure should be constantly monitored for maximizing services such as the security of residents, while optimizing the use of these resources (Van den Bergh and Viaene, 2015; Albino et al., 2015).

2.4.1.3 Entertainment

This category includes the research papers that discuss how smart cities would lead to an effective management of resources and time. This would in turn encourage tourism, leisure, and recreation. Thus, the brand equity and prosperity of the country and its citizens would improve (Kourtit et al., 2012; Su et al., 2011).

2.4.1.3.1 *Tourism*

This subcategory examines how smart city tourism would apply useful databases capable of acquiring various kinds of tourism information such as tourism resources, tourism economy, tourism activities, and tourism participants. The real-time tourism information would be obtained through mobile Internet or Internet terminal equipment (MacKay and Vogt, 2012; Roscia et al., 2013).

2.4.1.3.2 *Leisure and Recreation*

This subcategory inspects how the availability of digital gadgets, timely information, and a conducive environment in an ICT-enabled city would expedite and reduce the complexity of tasks. As a result, it would provide freedom for individuals to be creative and enable them to spend quality time with friends and family (Roscia et al., 2013; Kourtit et al., 2012).

2.4.1.4 **Public Participation**

This category scrutinizes the topics related to public participation. In a smart city, ICTs would strengthen the freedom of speech and improve access to public information and services via social media and crowdsourcing (Khan et al., 2014; Sandoval-Almazan et al., 2015). Citizens prefer online participation and discussion because of the absence of nonverbal politics in an online environment (Veeckman and van der Graaf, 2014).

2.4.1.4.1 *Social Media*

This subcategory discusses how the use of social media would increase public participation in government policies and various other issues (Khan et al., 2014; Mainka et al., 2015). Social media analytics enables the measurement of public sentiments with real-time data mined from Twitter, blogs, and other social networks (Przeybilovicz et al., 2015).

2.4.1.4.2 *Crowdsourcing*

Crowdsourcing refers to the user collaboration and engagement that would foster public participation in the smart city governance process. Crowdsourcing leads to the sharing of knowledge among the citizens and citizen participation, which facilitates the smart city to utilize the wisdom of the crowd. Moreover, virtual communities launch communication channels across residents, government, and relevant business stakeholders (You et al., 2014).

2.4.2 Challenges

2.4.2.1 *Political Issues*

This category discusses various political issues that would be faced by an ICT-enabled government functioning in smart cities. Some of the political issues are lack of horizontal and vertical integration across various government and urban initiatives, leadership issues, and a relatively low level of interest shown by many national authorities working together (Van den Bergh and Viaene, 2015).

2.4.2.2 **Human Issues**

This category discusses several issues such as social issues, cultural issues, communication issues, and the behavioral issues that may occur in smart cities.

2.4.2.2.1 Social Issues

This subcategory includes research papers that mention the silo and high-empowerment issues (Awaluddin, 2014; Theodoridis et al., 2013). The advent of smart cities would create an isolated environment in which people would be detached from their immediate surroundings. Excessive use of digital gadgets could turn citizens into highly empowered robots, with all modern facilities but lacking friends and family (Sandoval-Almazan et al., 2015). Ease of access to information and use of public domains in which people can freely express their views could lead to conflict between them and government bodies (Lee and Lee, 2014; Awaluddin, 2014).

2.4.2.2.2 Cultural Issues

This subcategory includes research papers that discuss high-mobility issues in smart cities (Delponte and Ugolini, 2011; van Geenhuizen and Nijkamp, 2009). The stability quotient would be low, and people would live nomadic lives. There would be more footloose firms and businesses with an amoebic operational style (Carli et al., 2013; Roscia et al., 2013).

2.4.2.2.3 Communication Issues

This category discusses citizen engagement, participation, cognitive, and perception issues (Veeckman and van der Graaf, 2014). Citizens in a smart city could easily come across all facts and figures, but sometimes too much information is also dangerous (Mainka et al., 2015). The decision-making process in smart cities would not be too easy, as generating citizens' interest in public policies and government activities would be a challenging task (Syväjärvi et al., 2015). Furthermore, people may have mixed perceptions about smart cities (Cano et al., 2014; Gil-Garcia, 2013). They may be unable to adjust to the changes (Khan et al., 2014) if they carry the horn effect (Chadwick and May, 2003).

2.4.2.2.4 Behavioral Issues

This category articulates that the inherent nature of human beings is to resist changes that are outside their comfort zone (Nam and Pardo, 2013). Therefore, it would be a challenge to change their views and style of living (Thomas et al., 2010). Furthermore, if there is a misalignment between government's mission and vision, a conflicting situation may arise (Sandoval-Almazan et al., 2015). This would pose a challenge in aligning the individuals' goals with the goals of the smart city (Gil-Garcia, 2013).

2.4.2.3 Security Issues

This category includes research papers that discuss security issues in smart cities. Smart cities require access to cost-effective, high-performance security services, along with sophisticated control systems that would allow better control and higher network reliability.

2.4.2.3.1 Crime and Disaster Issues

This subcategory mentions that the digital infrastructure of smart cities would be in private hands, which may lead to information theft and thus increase cybercrimes. Theft of private information may also lead to an increase in terrorist activities and other disasters (Martinez-Balleste et al., 2013; Cano et al., 2014).

2.4.2.3.2 Privacy Issues

This subcategory includes research papers that discuss privacy issues in smart cities. Privacy-preserving mechanisms should be the key concern to achieve the trust and acceptance of smart cities. Continuous tracking programs can cause unnecessary and unwanted surveillance, which invades the privacy of citizens (Sandoval-Almazan et al., 2015). This may lead to an increase in personal data thefts and the crime rate (van der Graaf and Veeckman, 2014).

2.4.2.3.3 *Authenticity Issues*

Authenticity refers to the verification of the credentials of an individual with the existing database of authorized users (Bartoli et al., 2011). The authenticity issue may arise when an attacker (third party) attempts to gain electronic access to and misconfigure or manipulate a component and report a false condition or alarm. Smart city protocol designers must ensure that proper care and attention is given to this threat during protocol development (Su et al., 2011).

2.4.2.4 Technological Issues

This category includes research papers that discuss hardware and software incompatibility and the lack of know-how related to digital platforms and gadgets used by citizens in smart cities.

2.4.2.4.1 *Hardware and Software Incompatibility*

One of the biggest challenges would be hardware and software incompatibility. Everything in smart cities would be automated, and any fragmentation may lead to serious failures and accidents (Gil-Garcia, 2013).

2.4.2.4.2 *Lack of Know-How*

This subcategory represents the citizens' lack of technical skills, because of which they would be unable to properly utilize the government information-sharing initiatives (Gil-Garcia, 2013).

2.5 Discussion and Conclusion

This research paper explains the influence of smart cities on governance by conducting an in-depth review of the literature on topics such as ICT-enabled urban planning, policy-making, and the government's role in sustainable city development (Syväjärvi et al., 2015). Currently, many countries are in the early stages of e-governance. Europe, the United States, and other Westernized countries, such as Australia and Singapore, have begun to reap the benefits of e-governance. In the next couple of years, developing countries and their citizens could also benefit from e-governance (Backus, 2001; Sivarajah et al., 2014).

This research paper is an attempt to explore the benefits and challenges that can be faced in governing a smart city, an evolving concept. The comprehensive descriptive literature review provided detailed classification of benefits and challenges. Through this research, we found four major categories of benefits and challenges. The four major categories of benefits were further divided into 8 subcategories and 10 sub-sub-categories. Similarly, categories related to challenges were further divided into nine subcategories and eight sub-sub-categories.

We proposed four major benefits of smart cities on governance: sustainability, urban development, entertainment, and public participation. The literature has largely stated that the emergence of smart cities would lead to sustainability and urban development. Existing papers in the "sustainability" category mostly focused on how smart cities would enable the government to improve the quality of life of citizens and the environment in which they live. The category of "urban development" included papers primarily focusing on how the emergence of smart cities would result in robust infrastructure that is crucial for the development of any city. Further, it has been claimed that the availability of real-time information and a high-Internet-penetration rate would make citizens more informed. In a smart city, citizens would be able to participate extensively in public activities via social media and crowdsourcing. In other words, the smart city would provide a safe dwelling place equipped with digital infrastructure and creative industries. At the same time, very few research papers mentioned how smart cities would affect the tourism, leisure, and recreational activities of any country. Though the existing research papers are informative, they lack substantial discussion on existing cases of smart cities and e-governance together. Therefore, it can be difficult to visualize the situation. This limitation is attributed to the newness of the smart city concept.

In addition to benefits, we discovered four major challenges posed by smart cities on governance: political issues, human issues, security issues, and technological issues. Human and technological issues have been the primary area of focus in the existing literature. Under the "human issues" category, the subcategories of cultural and communication issues are the fundamental issues discussed in the research papers. Researchers have extensively mentioned that the emergence of smart cities would result in the creation of an isolated environment for citizens. They would have high access to information, which may sometimes lead to conflicts of interest. The establishment of smart cities would bring a large change, which citizens may resist. The category of "technological issues" mostly discussed authenticity issues and issues arising from a lack of technical know-how, and hardware and software incompatibility.

The capabilities offered by smart cities can save citizens time, make them more informative, and enable them to raise their voice through various channels of public participation. Additionally, the skills and capabilities of the crowd can also be leveraged through crowdsourcing. Various existing and upcoming technologies, such as radio-frequency identification (RFID) and the Internet of things are contributing to making cities smarter (Su et al., 2011; Roscia et al., 2013). Technologies have reshaped the existing systems and resulted in a paradigmatic change. Similarly, smart cities are bringing various sophisticated technologies together in an innovative way, and we are yet to see the actual results.

2.6 Future Directions

The findings of this research provide many research opportunities to future researchers. Smart cities can lead to a paradigmatic shift and therefore influence every aspect of governance from policy-making to its implementation. Currently, many issues of high relevance deserve rigorous academic examination. The contradictory claims made by researchers also deserve academicians' attention. For example, Roscia et al. (2013) and Kourtit et al. (2012) articulated that smart cities could enable citizens to spend time with kin because of lack of complex tasks. However, at the same time, Sandoval-Almazan et al. (2015) argued that smart cities could socially isolate its citizens. Additionally, many questions need to be answered: Which issues deserve immediate attention? How do we prioritize each issue and in which order? What are the potential remedies to these issues? How do we utilize the benefits in order to make governance smarter? What are the critical factors for successful governance in a smart city? Mainstream journals or conference papers could encourage discussion and exploration in these areas.

References

Alberti, M., and Susskind, L. 1996. Managing urban sustainability: An introduction to the special issue. *Environmental Impact Assessment Review* 16:213–221.

Albino, V., Berardi, U., and Dangelico, R. M. 2015. Smart cities: Definitions, dimensions, performance, and initiatives. *Journal of Urban Technology* 22:3–21.

Awaluddin, M. 2014. The partnership between business and government towards sustainable city development. In *International Conference on ICT for Smart Society (ICISS)*, Bandung, Indonesia (pp. 131–138). IEEE.

Backus, M. 2001. E-governance and developing countries: Introduction and examples. *International Institute for Communication and Development (IICD), The Netherlands*, Research Report No. 3. April.

Bartoli, A., Hernández-Serrano, J., Soriano, M., Dohler, M., Kountouris, A., and Barthel, D. 2011. Security and privacy in your smart city. In *Proceedings of the Barcelona Smart Cities Congress*, Barcelona. December.

Cano, J., Hernandez, R., and Ros, S. 2014. Distributed framework for electronic democracy in smart cities. *Computer* 47:65–71.

Capdevila, I., and Zarlenga, M. I. 2015. Smart city or smart citizens? The Barcelona case. *Journal of Strategy and Management* 8:266–282.

Caragliu, A., Del Bo, C., and Nijkamp, P. 2011. Smart cities in Europe. *Journal of Urban Technology* 18:65–82.

Carli, R., Dotoli, M., Pellegrino, R., and Ranieri, L. 2013. Measuring and managing the smartness of cities: A framework for classifying performance indicators. In *International Conference on Systems, Man, and Cybernetics (SMC)*, Manchester (pp. 1288–1293). IEEE.

Chadwick, A., and May, C. 2003. Interaction between states and citizens in the age of the internet: "e-government" in the United States, Britain, and the European Union. *Governance-An International Journal of Policy and Administration* 16:271–300.

Chourabi, H., Nam, T., Walker, S., Gil-Garcia, J. R., Mellouli, S., Nahon, K., Pardo, T. A., and Scholl, H. J. 2012. Understanding smart cities: An integrative framework. In *45th Hawaii International Conference on System Science (HICSS)*, Maui, Hawaii (pp. 2289–2297). IEEE.

Delponte, I., and Ugolini, P. 2011. Patterns of local development as a roadmap towards urban transport sustainability. *Procedia Engineering* 21:526–533.

Giffinger, R., Fertner, C., Kramar, H., Kalasek, R., Pichler-Milanović, N., and Meijers, E. 2007. *Smart Cities: Ranking of European Medium-Sized Cities*. Vienna, Austria: Centre of Regional Science (SRF). available at: www.smart-cities.eu/download/smart_cities_final_report.pdf (accessed 1 November 2015).

Gil-Garcia, J. R. 2013. Towards a smart state? Inter-agency collaboration, information integration, and beyond. *Information Policy* 17:269–276.

Guzzo, R. A., Jackson, S. E., and Katzell, R. A. 1987. Meta-analysis analysis. *Research in Organizational Behavior* 9:407–442.

Keirstead, J., and Leach, M. 2008. Bridging the gaps between theory and practice: A service niche approach to urban sustainability indicators. *Sustainable Development* 16:329–340.

Khan, Z., Ludlow, D., Loibl, W., and Soomro, K. 2014. ICT enabled participatory urban planning and policy development: The UrbanAPI project. *Transforming Government: People, Process and Policy* 8:205–229.

Kourtit, K., Nijkamp, P., and Arribas, D. 2012. Smart cities in perspective: A comparative European study by means of self-organizing maps. *Innovation: The European Journal of Social Science Research* 25:229–246.

Kuk, G., and Janssen, M. 2011. The business models and information architectures of smart cities. *Journal of Urban Technology* 18:39–52.

Lee, J., and Lee, H. 2014. Developing and validating a citizen-centric typology for smart city services. *Government Information Quarterly* 31:S93–105.

MacKay, K., and Vogt, C. 2012. Information technology in everyday and vacation contexts. *Annals of Tourism Research* 39:1380–1401.

Mainka, A., Hartmann, S., Stock, W. G., and Peters, I. 2015. Looking for friends and followers: A global investigation of governmental social media use. *Transforming Government: People, Process and Policy* 9:237–254.

Martinez-Balleste, A., Perez-Martinez, P., and Solanas, A. 2013. The pursuit of citizens' privacy: A privacy-aware smart city is possible. *IEEE Communications Magazine* 51:136–141.

Nam, T., and Pardo, T. A. 2013. Building understanding of municipal service integration: A comparative case study of NYC311 and Philly311. In *46th Hawaii International Conference on System Sciences (HICSS)*, Maui, Hawaii (pp. 1953–1962). IEEE.

Odendaal, N. 2006. Towards the digital city in South Africa: Issues and constraints. *Journal of Urban Technology* 13:29–48.

Perboli, G., De Marco, A., Perfetti, F., and Marone, M. 2014. A new taxonomy of smart city projects. *Transportation Research Procedia* 3:470–478.

Przeybilovicz, E., da Silva, W. V., and Cunha, M. A. 2015. Limits and potential for eGov and smart city in local government: A cluster analysis concerning ICT infrastructure and use. *International Journal of E-Planning Research (IJEPR)* 4:39–56.

Roscia, M., Longo, M., and Lazaroiu, G. C. 2013. Smart city by multi-agent systems. In *International Conference on Renewable Energy Research and Applications (ICRERA)*, Madrid (pp. 371–376). IEEE.

Sandoval-Almazan, R., Cruz, D. V., and Nunez Armas, J. C. 2015. Social media in smart cities: An exploratory research in Mexican municipalities. In *48th Hawaii International Conference on System Sciences (HICSS)*, Kauai, Hawaii (pp. 2366–2374). IEEE.

Sivarajah, U., Lee, H., Irani, Z., and Weerakkody, V. 2014. Fostering smart cities through ICT driven policy-making: Expected outcomes and impacts of DAREED project. *International Journal of Electronic Government Research (IJEGR)* 10:1–18.

Stemberger, M. I., and Jaklic, J. 2007. Towards E-government by business process change: A methodology for public sector. *International Journal of Information Management* 27:221–232.

Su, K., Li, J., and Fu, H. 2011. Smart city and the applications. In *International Conference on Electronics, Communications and Control (ICECC)*, Ningbo, China (pp. 1028–1031). IEEE.

Syväjärvi, A., Kivivirta, V., Stenvall, J., and Laitinen, I. 2015. Digitalization and information management in smart city government: Requirements for organizational and managerial project policy. *International Journal of Innovation in the Digital Economy (IJIDE)* 6:1–15.

Theodoridis, E., Mylonas, G., and Chatzigiannakis, I. 2013. Developing an IoT smart city framework. In *4th International Conference on Information, Intelligence, Systems and Applications (IISA)*, Piraeus, Greece, 1–6. IEEE.

Thomas, C., Samuels, D., Kanu, M., and Mbarika, V. 2010. Facilitating better governance through government initiatives: Successful case in Sub-Saharan Africa. *International Journal of Business and Public Administration* 7:71–85.

Tranos, E., and Gertner, D. 2012. Smart networked cities?. *Innovation: The European Journal of Social Science Research* 25:175–190.

Vakali, A., Angelis, L., and Giatsoglou, M. 2013. Sensors talk and humans sense towards a reciprocal collective awareness smart city framework. In *IEEE International Conference on Communications Workshops (ICC)*, Budapest (pp. 189–193). IEEE.

Van den Bergh, J., and Viaene, S. 2015. Key challenges for the smart city: Turning ambition into reality. In *48th Hawaii International Conference on System Sciences (HICSS)*, Kauai, Hawaii (pp. 2385–2394). IEEE.

van der Graaf, S., and Veeckman, C. 2014. Designing for participatory governance: Assessing capabilities and toolkits in public service delivery. *Info* 16:74–88.

van Geenhuizen, M., and Nijkamp, P. 2009. Place-bound versus footloose firms: Wiring metropolitan areas in a policy context. *Annals of Regional Science* 43:879–896.

Veeckman, C., and van der Graaf, S. 2014. The city as living laboratory: A playground for the innovative development of smart city applications. In *International ICE Conference on Engineering, Technology and Innovation (ICE)*, Bergamo, Italy (pp. 1–10). IEEE.

Webster, J., and Watson, R. T. 2002. Analyzing the past to prepare for the future: Writing a literature review. *Management Information Systems Quarterly* 26:iii–xiii.

You, L., Motta, G., Liu, K., and Ma, T. 2014. A pilot crowdsourced city governance system: CITY FEED. In *17th International Conference on Computational Science and Engineering (CSE)*, Chengdu, China (pp. 1514–1519). IEEE.

3

Smart People for Smart Cities: A Behavioral Framework for Personality and Roles

Shristi Gupta, Syed Ziaul Mustafa, and Harish Kumar

CONTENTS

3.1 Introduction..23
  3.1.1 Overview of Smart Cities...24
    3.1.1.1 Smart Economy 24
    3.1.1.2 Smart Mobility...25
    3.1.1.3 Smart Environment 25
    3.1.1.4 Smart Living 25
    3.1.1.5 Smart Governance...25
    3.1.1.6 Smart People 25
3.2 Literature Review..25
3.3 Research Methodology 26
3.4 Findings and Discussion 26
3.5 Conclusion 28
References 29

3.1 Introduction

Creative, sustainable, and livable are some of the key features of the smart city. Developing a smart city may involve various domain experts such as consultants, corporations, marketing specialists, and city officials to frame how the smart city could be conceptualized, understood, and planned.

A smart city may be considered as an assemblage of technologies such as information and communication technologies (ICT), infrastructure, smart transport, and e-governance to increases competitiveness and administrative efficiency, as well as social inclusion.

Since 2011, contributions to the smart city have been critically scrutinized from different viewpoints, such as science and technology, politics, economy, government mentality studies, and ideological critique. In general, smart cities create a relation between technology and society. This process is related to the actor-network theory (ANT), which focuses on the making of sociotechnical networks and how certain actors try to create for their interest.

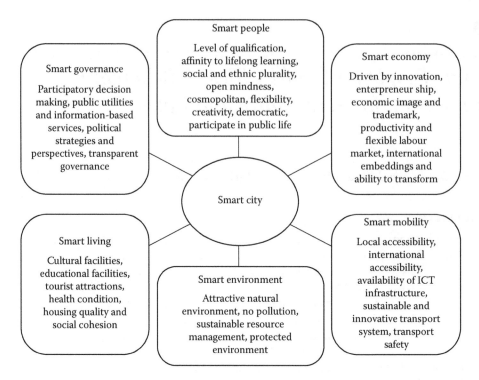

FIGURE 3.1
Dimensions of the smart city. (Adapted from Kumar, T. V. *E-governance for Smart Cities*, Springer, Singapore, 2015.)

3.1.1 Overview of Smart Cities

Various theoretical and marketing conceptualizations have been introduced, such as techno cities (Downey and McGuigan, 1999), creative cities (Florida, 2005), cyber cities (Graham and Marvin, 1999), digital cities (Komninos, 2008), sentient cities (Shepard, 2011), and networked cities (Castells, 1996).

The concept of the smart city originated from various definitions, such as the information city, the intelligent city, the digital city, the knowledge city, and the ubiquitous city. Smart cities represent a conceptual urban development model of human resource utilization and usage of technological capabilities (Angelidou, 2015).

The major dimensions of the smart city are smart economy, smart people, smart environment, smart living, smart mobility, and smart governance (Kumar, 2015). These dimensions are shown in Figure 3.1.

3.1.1.1 Smart Economy

Smart economy is driven by innovation and supported by universities, which provide an ecosystem to grow the entrepreneurial spirit of the people in a society. The economy of the city is such that it creates an economic image globally, and will also have a trademark. Productivity and a flexible labor market should be provided by the city administrative authority. The economy should have international branding and generate a highly diversified economy.

3.1.1.2 Smart Mobility

Smart mobility means that the city should have national and international accessibility, using information and communication technologies (ICTs) to ensure that technology has been used widely during the design of national highways and bridges. Metros, monorails, and an intelligent transport system should be used for daily commuters. The urban design should be such that it gives importance to last-mile connectivity. The transport system should be sustainable and innovative. It should also take care of the safety of daily and occasional commuters within and outside the city.

3.1.1.3 Smart Environment

Smart environment refers to an attractive natural environment with no pollution. Importance should be given to the carbon footprint and the natural resources available. It should have greenery in almost every part of the city. It should have waste management systems as well as natural resource management. The city should also have systems to protect the existing greenery of the city from any external factor.

3.1.1.4 Smart Living

Smart living is characterized by diverse cultural facilities available to all kinds of religions, whether they belong to major or minor communities. Education facilities should be provided by establishing world-class colleges and universities. It should also have tourist attractions as well as world-class hospitals with all the latest technology-enabled devices and equipment to allow a healthy lifestyle for every resident. Good-quality housing as well as social cohesion should be provided to citizens of the city.

3.1.1.5 Smart Governance

Smart governance is an advanced form of e-governance. It is about making the right policy choices and the implementation of same. The knowledge society should give a set of elements for smart governance that is open to sharing information and its use, transparent decision making, collaboration and participation of stakeholders, improvement in government services, and operation through the use of intelligent technologies.

3.1.1.6 Smart People

The Human Development Index is considered to be the most important aspect. The next most important attribute is the graduate enrolment ratio. The third most important attribute is the level of qualification. Smart people should have a lifelong zeal to learn, and there should be social and ethnic plurality. Open-mindedness is another quality of smart people, as is having the flexibility to adapt to changes in the environment, as well as the creativity to contribute to education. Smart people possess a democratic nature and participate in public life.

3.2 Literature Review

The big-five factor representation was introduced by Tupes and Christal in 1961. This was on the basis of a reanalysis of various datasets using bipolar variables given by Cattell in

1957. The five factors are listed as (1) agreeableness; (2) surgency (or extroversion); (3) emotional stability (versus neuroticism); (4) consciousness (or dependability); and (5) culture, intellect, or openness. Norman (1963) selected four variables after the analysis of Tupes and Christal (1961). These four factors have the highest factor loading on each of the five factors. These 20 variables have been used as big-five markers in later studies carried out by Norman, as well as Guthrie and Bennett (1971). Since the variables have some inherent limitation as markers of the big-five structure, only four variables have been included in each of the domains. The Neuroticism-Extraversion-Openness Personality Inventory (NEO-PI) developed by Costa et al. (1991) was the major alternative set of big-five markers. It provides scales to measure five domains, such as neuroticism extraversion (factor I), agreeableness (factor II), conscientiousness (factor III), emotional stability (factor IV), and openness (factor V).

3.3 Research Methodology

Personality traits describe an individual's behavior, such as the way a person interacts with others and reacts to any situation. A person could be evaluated on a series of factors. Factors such as the five-factor model (FFM), which is also known as the big-five personality traits, cover all the characteristics of an individual and explain the major significant variations in human personality. These five factors are extroversion, conscientiousness, openness to experience, agreeableness, and emotional stability, as shown in Table 3.1.

These attributes are powerful predictors of people's behavior. In this chapter, the relationships between personality dimensions and job performance have been studied. The findings show how people should behave and work smartly in a smart city in order to live a high-quality and luxurious life.

3.4 Findings and Discussion

Previous research has shown that individuals who are reliable, responsible, good planners, hardworking, organized, persistent, and have positive attitudes tend to have higher job performance in most occupations. Those with higher levels of job knowledge and problem-solving skills perform better in their jobs. Level of qualification, affinity to lifelong

TABLE 3.1

Five Personality Traits

Factor	Explanation
Extroversion	Shows the sociable, gregarious, and assertive nature of a person
Agreeableness	Describes someone who is cooperative, good-natured, and trusting
Conscientiousness	Indicates persistent, dependable, responsible, and organized nature of a person
Emotional stability	Shows self-confident, calm, secure (positive) versus depressed, nervous, and insecure (negative) traits of a person
Openness to experience	Characterizes someone in terms of sensitivity, curiosity, and imagination

learning, creativity, flexibility, participation in public life, and good decision making are some essential qualities that make people smart (Giffinger et al., 2007) and increase their work performance.

The extroversion dimension captures people's comfort level with relationships and social life. Extroverts tend to be social and assertive, enjoy the company of others, live a happier life, have more positive emotions, perform better in all types of work, are willing to make changes, and participate actively in decision processes. The people in a smart city should be extroverts rather than introverts, who are usually reserved, timid, and quiet.

The agreeableness dimension refers to highly agreeable people who are cooperative, warm, happy, romantic, organizational team members, and are more satisfied in their jobs. This personality trait is required for interpersonally oriented jobs such as customer service. Superior organizational ability leads to greater efficiency in an employee, an artist, a student, a business owner, or a celebrity. People with this attribute may contribute to the enhancement of the living environment of a smart city by engaging citizens in various city activities.

The conscientiousness dimension is a measure of reliability. A highly conscientious person is less distracted and more organized, responsible, dependable, interested in new learnings, and persistent. These types of people generally live longer since they take care of themselves in better ways. Paying attention to what happens in their surroundings and acting accordingly are key factors for the success of smart people in a particular smart city. This personality dimension can create a safe, secure, corruption-free, crime-free, and healthy environment in a smart city.

The emotional stability dimension is mostly related to job satisfaction, life satisfaction, and low stress levels. Such people are calm, self-confident, optimistic, and not vulnerable to the psychological and physical effects of stress. Hope for the best possible scenario and preparing for the worst indicates the far vision of smart people. People with good emotional stability have a better way of overcoming their obstacles and finding the solutions to compensate for their shortcomings. This dimension of personality can lead to a frustration-free life environment in a smart city.

Extremely open people are curious, creative, and artistically sensitive. Creativity is important to leadership, as open people are more likely to be effective leaders, and more comfortable with change and ambiguity. This quality makes people compatible when exposed to a new environment or experience. The situation could be controlled and negative impacts on lives could be prevented if a person learns from his or her mistakes. Smart people always view a situation from every possible angle in order to find the best solutions. People with this personality trait don't lose the opportunity to broaden their experience. Openness may provide good acting leaders who identify new opportunities in a smart city and also participate in order to change situations according to the citizens' needs, future growth, and prosperity. Table 3.2 shows the relationships among the personality traits, people performance, quality of smart people, and the roles of people in a smart city's development.

Smart people understand the importance of people in their surroundings to get support, opportunities, and to make a healthy environment. Smart people can generate a pleasant city environment and a positive workforce. Making smart decisions in different situations leads people to face reality and judge themselves honestly to overcome problems. Being smart is not just about intelligence, critical thinking, logical reasoning, and scientific approaches, but it is also about constantly working to improve the capability for various tasks with the use and understanding of technology. A person may have a brilliant mind and an outstanding intelligence, but without the five factor traits, a person cannot be one

TABLE 3.2

Relations among the Five-Factor Model and Smart People Traits

Personality Dimensions	People Performance	Quality in Smart People	Roles of People in Smart Cities
Extroversion	Better interpersonal skills, willing to take changes, participate actively in decision processes.	Enhanced leadership, better teamwork, motivated to take up new projects.	Increase in work performance, better and smarter utilization of new ICT infrastructure and services.
Agreeableness	Cooperative, warm, happy, romantic, organizational team members, more satisfied in jobs and trusting.	Creation of a happier and more positive atmosphere, harmony in the city, cooperativeness toward development.	Creation of a more felicitous city, city may flourish because of the harmonious, warm, and happy atmosphere.
Conscientiousness	Less distracted and more responsible, organized, dependable, interested in new learnings, and persistent.	Such people have more success in their work because they are more organized and always follow a plan to meet their professional goals.	Less chaos, processes and activities are better organized and always go according to plan, the city will grow successfully.
Emotional stability	Life satisfaction, job satisfaction, and low stress levels, calm, self-confident, optimistic.	Better control over emotions at work, calm and optimistic attribute helps mitigate disasters efficiently.	Smart city will be able to cope up with obstacles easily because of the optimistic, calm, and stress-free characteristic of its citizens.
Open to experience	Creative, curious, and artistically sensitive.	Creative and flexible attitude, more successful and higher-quality research, open to new ideas, innovation.	Increase in innovation, development of technologies, make smart cities more sustainable.

of the smart people. Unless people are smart enough within a city to make good use of ICT technology and create a healthy, happy city environment, the development and sustainability of the smart city seem questionable. The framework of smart people to develop a smart city is shown in Figure 3.2.

3.5 Conclusion

The concept of the smart city varies from city to city and country to country. However, one thing that remains common in all definitions and characteristics of a smart city is citizen engagement. Hence, human factors and human development in smart cities is a very important domain to analyze. This chapter has attempted to provide a base to establish attributes that are important for people to be characterized as smart people. The big-five personality traits are powerful predictors of human behavior. Although they are mostly used in an organizational setup to recruit and hire people, these traits are equally beneficial in defining attributes of smart people. In a smart city, its citizens need to possess nearly all the attributes described in this study to become the smart people. Smart people can lead to the sustainable growth and development of smart cities.

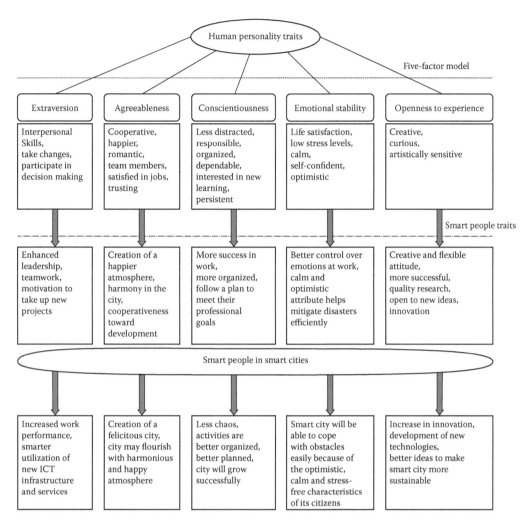

FIGURE 3.2
Behavioral framework of smart people for the development of sustainable smart cities.

References

Angelidou, M. 2015. Smart cities: A conjuncture of four forces. *Cities*, 47: 95–106.

Castells, M. 1996. *The Rise of the Network Society. Vol. 1 of the Information Age: Economy, Society and Culture*. Oxford: Blackwell.

Cattell, R. B. 1957. *Personality and Motivation Structure and Measurement*. Yonkers, NY: World Book Company.

Costa, P. T., McCrae, R. R., and Dye, D. A. 1991. Facet scales for agreeableness and conscientiousness: A revision of the NEO Personality Inventory. *Personality and individual Differences*, 12, 9: 887–898.

Downey, J., and McGuigan, J., Eds. 1999. *Technocities: The Culture and Political Economy of the Digital Revolution*. London: Sage Publications.

Florida, R. 2005. *Cities and the Creative Class*. New York: Routledge.

Giffinger, R., Fertner, C., Kramar, H., Kalasek, R., Pichler-Milanovic, N., and Meijers, E. 2007. Smart cities. Ranking of European medium-sized cities, Final Report, Centre of Regional Science, Vienna UT.

Graham, S., and Marvin, S. 1999. Planning cybercities: Integrating telecommunications into urban planning. *Town Planning Review*, 70, 1: 89–114.

Guthrie, G. M., and Bennett, A. B. 1971. Cultural differences in implicit personality theory. *International Journal of Psychology*, 6, 4: 305–312.

Komninos, N. 2008. *Intelligent Cities and Globalization of Innovation Networks*. London; New York: Routledge.

Kumar, T. V. 2015. E-governance for smart cities. In *E-governance for Smart Cities* (pp. 1–43). Singapore: Springer.

Norman, W. T. 1963. Toward an adequate taxonomy of personality attributes: Replicated factor structure in peer nomination personality ratings. *Journal of Abnormal and Social Psychology*, 66, 6: 574.

Shepard, M. 2011. *Sentient City: Ubiquitous Computing, Architecture, and the Future of Urban Space*. MIT Press.

Tupes, E. C., and Christal, R. E. 1961. *Recurrent Personality Factors based on Trait Ratings*. No. ASD-TR-61-97. Lackland Air Force Base, TX: Personnel Research Laboratory.

Zipf, A. Live cities and urban services: A multi-dimensional stress field between technology, innovation and society.

4

Self-Sustainable Integrated Township: A Resource-Based Planning to Improve the Quality of Urban Life

Sahil Singh Kapoor

CONTENTS

4.1   Introduction 32
4.2   Concept of Integrated Township 32
4.3   Principles of Integrated Township Planning 33
4.4   Approach to Sustainable Development 34
4.5   Literature Review 34
    4.5.1   Case Study of Magarpatta City 35
    4.5.2   Case Study of Bhartiya City Integrated Township 36
    4.5.3   Diverse State Integrated Township Policies 36
4.6   Concept Development and Methodology 37
    4.6.1   Zoning in the Proposed Township 38
    4.6.2   Residential Area 38
    4.6.3   Commercial Area 39
    4.6.4   Mixed-Use Development Area 39
    4.6.5   Public and Semi-Public Buildings 39
    4.6.6   Recreational Areas 40
    4.6.7   Roads 40
    4.6.8   Supporting Infrastructure 41
        4.6.8.1   Sustainable Water Management 41
        4.6.8.2   Decentralized Wastewater Treatment System 41
        4.6.8.3   Integrated Solid Waste Management System............ 41
        4.6.8.4   Solar Energy Generation 42
        4.6.8.5   Transportation Facilities 42
4.7   Township Modeling 42
    4.7.1   Layout Plan and 3-D Model 42
    4.7.2   Mobility Plan 44
4.8   Sustainability Indicators 44
    4.8.1   Environmental Indicators 45
    4.8.2   Social Indicators 45
    4.8.3   Economic Indicators 45
4.9   Conclusion 45
4.10 Acknowledgment.. 46
References 46

4.1 Introduction

India is one of the fastest growing and largest emerging economies (World Bank Group 2016) in the world. It has the largest rural population (857 million) in the world, but this is expected to lessen by 52 million people as urban areas anticipate an increase in population. Nearly half of the total population in India will be living in cities by 2050 (World Urbanization Prospects: 2014 Revision); the proportion is currently almost one-third. The recent pace of urbanization in India is driven by the augmentation of the service sector, which has led to unplanned and informal growth of urban areas. Urbanization in India is confronted with typical challenges and unique opportunities. Urban expansion of traditional Indian cities, with a compact built-up form (KPMG 2013) and low-rise development, means cities have run out of land, water, and energy, and are sprawling, making them difficult to manage logistically. Contemporary Indian cities depict an amalgamation of traditional and colonial compositions, sprawling with a lack of systematic city and regional planning that leads to unplanned suburbs. Urban planning in India from independence up to the early twenty-first century has not been able to envisage long-term planning or understand how inhabitants and the surroundings will interact as a whole in the future. Agricultural areas surrounding cities are adversely affected by advancement in urban lifestyles. On the other hand, integrated townships can be a potential solution to the excess pace of urbanization through a focus on sustainable urban development.

The concept of smart cities envisages private townships (Ministry of Urban Development 2015b) as sustainable urban centers offering economies of scale in providing employment opportunities close to residential areas. Integration of site-sustainable infrastructure such as water, sewage, and waste management systems can address numerous environmental problems.

Jawaharlal Nehru Urban Renewal Mission (JNNURM), launched in 2005–2012 by the Government of India (GoI), has continued under the new name Atal Mission for Rejuvenation and Urban Transformation (AMRUT) and, along with the Smart Cities and Housing for All missions, facilitates a modern emphasis on integrated planning and development. The integrated township exemplifies the approach of integrated planning through micro-level planning, maximizing short-term actions, and considering long-term sustainability. Township development is a paradigm shift to urban land-use planning focusing on mixed-use development and the integration of land use with transportation (Schoeman, 2015) for better urban mobility and resource efficiency.

UN-Habitat (2014) suggests five principles with three key features, namely, compact, integrated, and connected to address rapid urbanization issues such as urban sprawl, traffic congestion, pollution, mobility challenges, urban poverty, and social inequality. The five principles, namely, high density, mixed land-use character, social mix, limited land-use specialization, and adequate space for road networks together achieve the objective of sustainability and sustainable development.

4.2 Concept of Integrated Township

An integrated township can be defined as combined clusters of housing, commercial business, education, and health-care facilities with the related physical infrastructure of water, sewage, roads, and power. Traditional Indian cities are facing typical problems, namely, urban sprawl, affordable housing shortage, access to public transport, and lack of equitable access to basic services that adversely impact productivity, mobility, and quality of urban life. At the same time, integrated townships (Hitest and Padhya 2015) with minimal land area, multiple housing, employment opportunities, open areas, and associated infrastructure can be the possible solution to prevent accelerating urbanization. The basic core of any city is examined through supporting physical and social infrastructure, recreational facilities, and economic generation ability. Integrated townships are conceptualized to the economic, infrastructure, and geographic needs of sprawling metropolitan cities (McKinsey 2010). The objective of integrated townships (Rai 2012) is the creation of self-sustained and integrated urban settlements by having planned communities, social infrastructure, and lifestyle amenities in the same place. Building a planned community that contains heterogeneous housing options (KPMG 2014) with lower rents and workplaces within short distances offers high productivity at work with a low cost of living and better lifestyle. Furthermore, a planned community has access to social infrastructure such as hospitals, schools, and educational institutes, offering high literacy rates and better health-care facilities. Residents working, living, and relaxing within a particular area will make urban spaces efficient and sustainable.

4.3 Principles of Integrated Township Planning

Some of the directing principles of township planning are as follows:

1. Housing: Provision of multiple housing options with supporting urban services for all sections of society is essential. To reduce overall energy consumption and housing stress in the township area, low-rise, high-density housing is suggested by the National Sustainable Habitat Mission (NSHM). Such low- and mid-rise apartment buildings are affordable, with equitable access to basic urban services.

2. Zoning: Land-use zoning divides the township into various zones, such as commercial, residential, mixed use, and so on. The buildings in each zone relate to one another or the surrounding functional buildings, to optimize urban land use and minimize land requirements.

3. Green spaces: Township planning should consider providing adequate and equitable access to green spaces for recreational purposes (IGBC Rating System Reference 2010). By providing a green belt along the fringe of the township, reductions in noise levels from the surrounding area are possible.

4. Recreational centers: Providing dedicated land area for developing recreational centers is an integral part of township planning and serves as a magnet for residential development. Community recreation centers need to be located close to residential buildings and within walking distance for daily access.

5. Road system: The road system will connect most parts of the township and needs to have sufficient width for effective carrying capacity.

6. Transport facilities: The provision of affordable and effective transport facilities should be implemented in the township to reduce traveling time between home and another place.

7. Public buildings: Public buildings need to be located in a decentralized manner across the township area to provide amenities for all sections of society. The centralized concentration of public amenities at certain defined places of the township needs to be avoided.

8. Commercial buildings: Commercial buildings are meant to create employment opportunities for economic generation. They need to be physically accessible from all parts of a township.

4.4 Approach to Sustainable Development

The former definition of sustainable development is found in the Brundtland Commission Report of 1987. The focus of sustainable development is on the creation of "sustainable space," as the region where the economic, environmental, and social spheres overlap. Applied to the background of township planning and development, the vital fundamental elements of sustainability are energy efficiency, renewable energy, integrated waste management, public transport, and water management (Seth et al. 2010). Sustainable development achieves stability between social and economic development by bringing equity to the provision of basic services, housing, employment, social infrastructure, and transportation. Solar energy (renewable energy source) technology options such as rooftop photovoltaic (PV) cells and water-heating systems can meet some energy demands of electricity, transport, and heating. The generated solar energy can power the batteries of electric and hybrid vehicle technology to minimize air and noise pollution. Integrated solid waste management (ISWM) incorporates the full circle of waste management and reuse. Collected solid and horticultural waste can be treated in decentralized units such as organic waste composting units or plastic waste-to-fuel conversion and pellet-making plants to generate end products or energy.

4.5 Literature Review

Earlier models of townships in India after independence came with the establishment of industrial towns such as Bhilai, Rourkela, and Jamshedpur. Thereafter, the emergence of Delhi's satellite towns, including Noida, Faridabad, and Gurgaon, came in the interstate regional planning concept of the National Capital Region (NCR). Soon, subcities with planned townships such as Navi Mumbai came up with divergent designs with the growth model different from city planning but with the administration and governance in the hands of the local government. With the buzzing concept of smart cities along the Delhi Mumbai Industrial Corridor (DMIC), various greenfield integrated townships (Knight Frank 2016) are on board. Several upcoming greenfields private townships are planned on the basis of a compact development pattern (Kotharkar and Bahadure 2012). A township can vary in physical area from 25 to 2500 acres, while areas of 20 acres or above are cited as ideal areas for integrated townships since, apart from residential facilities, commercial and lifestyle facilities are within township physical limits. Furthermore, these townships can be allocated as planned cities where residents can benefit from better basic services and a healthy environment.

4.5.1 Case Study of Magarpatta City

Magarpatta City is envisaged as an integrated township model (Gupta et al. 2012) with an impetus on integrated development and self-sustainability. The planning of an integrated township allows residential neighborhoods, schools, hospitals, hotels, restaurants, commercial spaces, and recreational areas to have a work-home-leisure lifestyle in the same place. Magarpatta City is spread over 430 acres of land, which originally belonged to nearly 120 farmer families in the village of Hadapsar, a suburban area of Pune City. The farmer families came together to convert their land to develop the city, realizing the value-added land benefits and higher quality of life. Nearly 30% (120 acres) of Magarpatta City area is reserved as natural green cover with added trees and plantations to preserve the area's natural ecology. Magarpatta City has a 25 acre round-shaped garden in the center, along with discrete gardens ranging between 0.5 and 2 acres in individual neighborhoods. The city is developing sustainable infrastructure (Pundir 2016) using rainwater harvesting, solar water-heating systems, garbage segregation, and ISWM through a biogas plant, vermicomposting, and a plant nursery. To ensure rainwater collection along roadsides, the storm water drainage collection system has soak chambers and trench drains. Interlocking paved blocks and cutout grass concrete pavers are used in open areas to prevent the inundated overflow of rainwater from roads and fields. Recharge bores and mounds have been placed along the open spaces to collect rainwater, enhance subsoil water, and preserve topsoil. An artificial lake, spread over 1.25 acres, harvests rainwater by channeling water from terraces to recharge groundwater levels. Recycled wastewater from sewage treatment plants is used in gardens through drip irrigation, ensuring water conservation and minimizing the temperature in adjacent areas. Other uses of recycled water are in the air-conditioning cooling towers and for flushing in commercial buildings. Rooftop solar water-heating systems in residential buildings meet the hot water demands for bathing and reduce electricity consumption, along with lessening heat effects on the top floors. Fly ash bricks made from dangerous waste produced by thermal power plants have been used in the construction of the project. Compared with traditional bricks, these bricks save the energy required for making cement, offer greater compressive strength with less wastage, and are cost-effective. The segregation of solid waste into biodegradable and nonbiodegradable garbage is done at the waste generation source, with garbage containers not required in the city. Biodegradable organic waste is handled through an organic waste converter (OWC), biogas plant, and vermin-composting. However, part of the nonbiodegradable waste goes for land filling (nonrecyclable) or is sold to vendors (recyclable). The city has a nursery for plants with vermin-composting and a biocompost pit, and manure compost generated from biodegradable segregated garbage is used for sustaining plants and saplings. Magarpatta City has divided residential blocks with courtyard planning, buildings encompassing central open spaces to encourage social interaction. To ameliorate the living standards of residents, recreational facilities and sports activities have been provided close to residential buildings. The sports complex provides a gym, swimming pool, tennis courts, cycling and jogging tracks, meditation centers, and an amphitheater. Access to the educational system for school-going children is envisioned by having preprimary to high-level schools within walking distance of residential buildings. Further, there is the Institute of Management and Technology with an emphasis on postgraduate education. An information technology (IT) park called Cybercity has been established in Magarpatta City, with nearly 6 million square feet of modular office space to offer a wide scope of employment opportunities. Provided with the large space available, companies can lease space, develop business centers, and have scalability options for future expansion. The office space in Cybercity has an uninterrupted power supply and 100% power backup through diesel generator (DG) sets. Besides Cybercity, GoI has approved a special economic zone (SEZ) with an area of nearly 11.98 ha proving electronic hardware and software services. There are two more commercial centers, Megacenter and Pentagon, offering office space for employment and business. Megacenter has five floors of small office areas with food courts, cafeterias, 100% power backup, and sufficient parking. Pentagon has five 8-storied towers, developed as a business center with strict security, 100% power backup, adherence to fire safety requirements, and abundant parking space. To meet residents' shopping and leisure time needs, Magarpatta City has a number of food courts, restaurants, and shopping locations. The mall, comprising an area of 12 acres, envisions renting carpet area to national and international retail giants and has a 15-screen multiplex cinema, hypermarket, and sizable parking. As a part of the medical needs, a multispecialty (with 250 beds) and tertiary care hospital provides treatment for all types of diseases and ailments. In addition, Magarpatta City has a petrol station, power substations, and a library for its residents. The city also has closed-circuit television (CCTV) cameras for security needs, Internet connectivity, and allied facilities.

4.5.2 Case Study of Bhartiya City Integrated Township

An integrated private township, located on 125 acres of land at the periphery of Bengaluru City, Bhartiya City is an inclusive and sustainable development with integrated work spaces, a hospital, schools, parks, and retail and residential spaces. Residential land use includes high-rise residential apartments along with recreational facilities such as sports facilities, a jogging track, and parks. A hospital, along with a community center for social advancement, is close to the residential apartments. The residential apartments offer a wide range of housing options such as one, two, three, and five BHK (bedroom, hall, and kitchen) units. Mixed land use is interconnected with residential areas through accessible walkways, and comprises buildings such as a five-star hotel, convention center, and shopping center. Adjacent to the mixed land use area is an area allocated under SEZ, offering small business establishment, independent office spaces, and a center of IT. Mixed-use spaces with markets, schools, residences, and community spaces offer opportunities for social interaction.

4.5.3 Diverse State Integrated Township Policies

Overcrowding of urban areas and shortage of land around cities for future expansion and development have caused town planners and policy makers to come up with new or revised integrated township polices with a focus on integrated township. Many states in India have now integrated township policies as a guiding development tool (Ministry of Urban Development 2015a) for establishing infrastructure in the peripheral areas beyond traditional city limits. State government integrated township policy is allowing private real estate developers to develop new townships (Gujarat International Finance Tec-City 2009) as smart and intelligent urban centers with a focus on technological innovation and sustainable development. Different states have defined varying land-use distributions and land requirements for building integrated townships. States with fast-growing cities are likely to have an increase in the number of integrated townships with demand-oriented housing as a dominant factor guiding the development of projects. Table 4.1 lists the variations among integrated township policies of several states, to ease and guide the development of integrated township projects.

TABLE 4.1

State-Integrated Township Policies

Description	Gujarat Integrated Township Policy 2008	Uttar Pradesh Revised Integrated Township Policy 2014	Rajasthan Integrated Township Policy 2007
EWS housing	Minimum 10% of residential land area for EWS housing.	Construction of minimum 10% of total housing units for EWS housing.	Minimum 7.5% of residential land use for EWS housing.
Residential land use	15%–30% of the developed land area	Maximum 40% of land area	Maximum 50% of land area
Commercial land use	5%–10% of the developed land area	Maximum 8% of land area	Maximum 5% of land area
Mixed land use	Not applicable	Maximum 12% of land area	Not applicable
Floor area ratio (FAR) of the gross area	As per building bye-laws	As per building bye-laws	1

Source: Government of Gujarat. Gujarat integrated township policy. January, 2008. Retrieved from http://credai. org/assets/upload/state/resources/gujarat-integrated-township-policy-january-2008.pdf; Government of Uttar Pradesh. Integrated township policy (license model-revised), Presentation by Housing & Urban Planning, Department Government of Uttar Pradesh, 20 December, 2013. Retrieved from http://awas. up.nic.in/Revised%20Integrated%20Policy%20(Draft).pdf; Government of Rajasthan. Rajasthan integrated township policy, Urban Development & Local Self Department, Government of Rajasthan, 2007. Retrieved from http://virtual.jaipurjda.org/pdf/others/notificationForIntegratedTownship2007.pdf.

4.6 Concept Development and Methodology

To develop an enduring concept of integrated township planning, demographic and socioeconomic analysis has been carried out to predict the demand for necessary physical infrastructure and, accordingly, the provision of public services. Diverse population characteristics (Bauer 2009), such as the population distribution by sex and age range, have an effect on employment composition. The total population of a proposed township is 12,500 people. Through a comparative assessment of population distribution by age group in urban areas, obtained from Census of India (the national commission on population) and United Nations (UN) data (United Nations 2014), assumptions have been considered for township planning. Table 4.2 describes the population distribution of defined age ranges to understand the possible distribution of educational and occupational characteristics. Furthermore, Table 4.3 describes the gender composition distribution of township populations.

TABLE 4.2

Population Distribution According to Age Range

Description of Age Range	Possible Percentage Range	Average Figure Assumed Out of Total Population
0–4	1–3	250
5–9	12–14	1,625
10–14	17–19	2,250
15–59	63–67	8,125
60–99	1–3	250
Total		12,500

TABLE 4.3

Gender Composition of Urban Population

Gender Composition (Urban)	Possible Percentage Range	Average Figure Assumed Out of Total Population
Male	51–53	6,500
Female	47–49	6,000
Total		12,500

TABLE 4.4

Population Distribution According to Income Group

Income Group	Monthly Per Capita Expenditure (Rupees)[a]	Percentage Range of Total Population	Population Assumed
EWS	0–3,300	10–15	1,875
LIG	3,301–7,300	30–35	4,375
MIG	7,301–14,500	40–45	5,625
HIG	14,501 and above	0–5	625
Total			12,500

[a] Report of the technical group on estimation of urban housing shortage (11th Five-Year Plan: 2007–2012).

Table 4.4 describes the population distribution of various income groups: higher income group (HIG), medium income group (MIG), lower income group (LIG), and economically weaker section (EWS).

4.6.1 Zoning in the Proposed Township

The area of the proposed township is 500 ha (5 km^2) with outer dimensions of 2500 × 2000 m. Furthermore, an area reserved for future development is 150 ha, with an actual working area of 350 ha. Building zoning regulates various land uses such as residential, commercial, mixed use, public and semi-public, and green space. Township planning understands the various needs of different sections of society to carry out their activities in a routine manner. (Shirsagar and Srinivas 2014)

4.6.2 Residential Area

Residential area distribution has been done based on the income group distribution of the population. Residential area development caters for the requirements of all sections of society, namely HIG, MIG, LIG, and EWS. The percentage of the working area for residential development is nearly 45%. The LIG and EWS housing area will have a high density, ranging from 400 to 600 persons per hectare (ppha); MIG housing density ranges from 200 to 400 ppha, and the HIG area will have a low density of less than 200 ppha. The objective of proposing different income group housing categories is to realize the integrated socio-economic development of townships. Plotted development is meant exclusively for HIG, along with access to daily basic services such as retail shops, parks with walking tracks, schools, dispensaries, and community centers. In order to enjoy a lavish lifestyle, the HIG is located away from other sections of society. LIG and EWS housing is located within walking distance of the HIG residential area, to offer daily routine services to this group. High-rise apartments with multiple housing options offering one, two, and three BHK

TABLE 4.5

Suggested Carpet Area of Dwelling Units for Different Income Groups.

Income Group	Dwelling Unit Carpet Area (Square Meters)	Proposed Residential Development
EWS	21–27	Affordable housing
LIG-A	28–40	Group housing
LIG-B	41–60	Group housing
MIG	60–80	High-rise apartment
HIG	80–95	Individual plot

units are meant for housing MIG. Furthermore, MIG housing offers access to social facilities such as education, recreational, and health care, accessible within walking distance. Parks offering recreational spaces are developed around high-rise apartments, ensuring the safety and security of children of resident families. Group housing and affordable housing with a maximum of three floors are meant for LIG and EWS. The ingress of social infrastructure such as education, health care, and parks is a subset of group and affordable housing. Table 4.5 lists the range of dwelling unit (DU) carpet areas for different income groups according to the revised affordable housing scheme guidelines.

4.6.3 Commercial Area

Commercial areas have been allotted within the township on three major scales: a central business center (CBC), subcommercial buildings, and commercial shops. The percentage of the working area for commercial purposes is nearly 8%. A range of commercial activities such as offices, wholesale, retail, restaurants, hotels, rental spaces, and shopping centers is allowed in the CBC. CBC buildings are positioned at the center of the township, with access through a main arterial road (24 m wide). The floors at the bottom of CBC buildings are meant for retail shops, while upper-level floors offer office spaces for lease. Subcommercial building uses include centers, banks, and hospitality, which comprises hotels and restaurants, cinemas, and banquet halls. Moreover, subcommercial buildings are provisioned among different income group needs at various places in the township. Lastly, commercial shop uses include automated teller machines (ATMs), shopping, and informal activities along the road. Mixed-use facilities allow the productive use of commercial buildings. Commercial buildings will have courtyard planning for maximizing access to daylight and encouraging casual interaction. A multistorey car park building is located close to the commercial buildings, within walking distance for private vehicle visitors coming from outside the township.

4.6.4 Mixed-Use Development Area

Mixed-use development areas consist of micro, small, and medium enterprises (MSME), non-polluting household industries, and other similar small-scale livelihood-sustaining activities. Instead of carrying out these activities in residential buildings, specially dedicated mixed-use land is located close to LIG and EWS housing in order to optimize employment opportunities and minimize trip length. Necessary employment, especially for unskilled and semiskilled workers with low education levels, is envisioned to be generated close to their living areas. The percentage of the working area for mixed-use development is nearly 5%.

4.6.5 Public and Semi-Public Buildings

Public and semi-public buildings include educational, community, health-care facilities, and institutions. They include uses such as educational buildings, hospitals and health

TABLE 4.6

Planning Standards Considered for Various Facilities

Standard No.	Type of Facilities	Planning Standard Range Considered (Square Meters per Person)
1	Educational	1.5–2.5
2	Health	0.75–2.5
3	Community	0.50–1.50
4	Infrastructure utilities	1.5–2.5

centers, libraries, police stations, community centers, and government offices. Educational buildings will provide educational facilities including kindergartens, primary and secondary level schools, and colleges. The building form with a courtyard area is encouraged to maximize open spaces and outdoor activities. In the evening, educational buildings can be used by nearby residents for recreational purposes. Health centers will provide healthcare facilities by having a dispensary, dental clinic, maternity home, and test center in the same place to maximize the daily utilization of the building. Educational buildings and health centers are located in a decentralized manner across the township, according to the needs of various income groups. There will be one multispecialty hospital of 100 beds on 1 ha, having intraconnectivity within the township and intercity connectivity with nearby urban centers. Emergency connectivity to hospital is ensured through a closed loop system to minimize the speed of vehicles and maximize building visibility. A comparative review of planning standards and guidelines established in the Urban and Regional Development Plans Formulation and Implementation (URDPFI), Guidelines (Ministry of Urban Development 2014) a master plan of Chandigarh and international standards, includes the standards described in the following sections—which have been considered in Table 4.6—for reserving space for various facilities. The percentage of the working area for public and semipublic buildings and areas is nearly 15%.

4.6.6 Recreational Areas

Anticipated recreational areas consist of open spaces, a green belt along the township boundary, gardens, and playgrounds around residential settlements. In addition, recreational facilities are offered in a sports complex, multipurpose ground, and stadium. A green belt of 15 m along the boundary of the township is for minimizing surrounding noise pollution and protecting natural drainage flow. In addition, one large pocket of 150 ha for regional recreation has been suggested to offer city-level recreational activities. The area held in reserve for regional recreational is 30% of the total township area. Nearly 15% of the working area is under recreational areas.

4.6.7 Roads

The road system has been divided into main arterial, primary, and internal roads, to support circulation across the township (Jurong Consultants 2011). The main arterial road has 24 m of right of way (ROW), with a cross section having a dedicated bus carriageway in the center and segregated bicycle and pedestrian tracks along the carriageway. A green strip of 10 m wide on both sides of the main arterial road is proposed to reduce the effects of air pollution from road traffic on the surroundings. The main road network exhibits curved road planning to maintain appropriate speed limits, establish visual contact with buildings, and allow emergency access. The primary access roads connecting to the main road will have 15 m of ROW with dedicated bicycle and pedestrian tracks. Internal roads for access to residences have 6–9 m of ROW, depending on the residing income group. The percentage of the working area for roads is nearly 18%.

4.6.8 Supporting Infrastructure

Supporting physical infrastructure facilitates scaling urbanization on the township scale (Sahasrabuddhe et al. 2012). The township is expected to provide basic urban services that can be optimized through innovative techniques and creative ideas.

4.6.8.1 Sustainable Water Management

Residential buildings will have a dual water supply and a distribution system with individual potable and recycled water supply lines. Potable water will be distributed to residents through a separate line and recycled water, after adequate treatment, will be sent for watering gardens and landscapes, firefighting, toilet flushing, groundwater recharge, and other nonpotable purposes. All buildings are proposed to have rainwater-harvesting systems, depending on the roof area. In MIG, EWS, and LIG housing buildings, the recharge trench water harvesting system is proposed as installation costs (5,000–10,000 rupees) are minimal. For individual HIG plots, gravity head recharge wells are suggested as installation costs (50,000–80,000 rupees) are high. In commercial and public buildings, recharge shafts will be used, with installation costs varying between 60,000 and 85,000 rupees per unit. The construction of artificial recharge wells, approximately 1 m in diameter and 6 m in depth, will be carried out in lawns by increasing the slope of surrounding areas. The catchment area of rainwater-harvesting structures will be demarcated, and clearing of vegetation will be done on a regular basis. To collect excess rainwater along the street, sumps with sand traps shall be constructed at regular intervals to improve the groundwater table.

4.6.8.2 Decentralized Wastewater Treatment System

A decentralized wastewater treatment system (DEWAT), offering a conventional treatment approach, will be used for treating wastewater. The process followed will be pretreatment, grit and screening, primary treatment, oil/fat removal in an oil separator, a baffled tank reactor, secondary treatment, anaerobic, and plant filtering. Decentralized wastewater systems will be set up for treating wastewater effectively in a decentralized manner, based on wastewater generated per day in various areas of the township.

4.6.8.3 Integrated Solid Waste Management System

Household segregation of solid waste into organic and inorganic waste (recyclable and non-recyclable waste) will be achieved by providing separate bins for disposal. Electric battery vehicles will be used to collect segregated organic waste and deliver it to compost-making plants. Electronic waste will be collected separately, once a week. A compost-making plant, using the composting process, is a simple way to turn organic waste into manure for plants. Organic waste is initially processed in an OWC followed by curing, with manure as the product. Adequate land will be provided in open areas for setting up compost plants and the collection of organic waste from households. Horticultural waste from parks and landscaped areas will be collected and sent to grass-shredding machines. This is followed by heating, drying, and finally treatment in a pellet-pressing machine. The output is a coal-like substance with a high calorific value. Residential buildings will have one or more waste chutes, preferably near staircases or lift lobbies, from where waste will terminate at ground level with an automated waste-handling amenity. Litter bins will be placed on streets and in public spaces, parks, markets, and other focal points. A plastic waste-to-fuel machine is proposed to convert plastic waste into fuel oil, based on the pyrolysis process for thermal degradation of plastic waste in the absence of oxygen at very high temperatures.

4.6.8.4 Solar Energy Generation

In every building, the installation of a solar rooftop PV system is mandatory to minimize the use of conventional electricity sources. Maximum rooftop utilization for setting up solar rooftop PV systems is permissible in residential buildings. The solar power generated will be sent to the grid and taken back as per daily requirements. In other buildings, the installation of solar rooftop PV systems will be done for captive uses. The proposal of installing light emitting diode (LED) streetlights with polycrystalline silicon solar panels will offer high efficiency, work off the grid without line voltage, and have minimal maintenance costs with an automatic daylight sensing facility. Solar streetlights can be used along internal roads and within parks and commercial and public buildings. At least 10% of the overall electricity demand will be met from solar power generation.

4.6.8.5 Transportation Facilities

Public transport ensures the reliable commutation of people within and around the township for employment opportunities. Bus terminals with interchange facilities are suggested at focal points, with passenger information signage and fare collection using an electronic card. Low-floor buses for public transport can ease accessibility for the physically challenged, with a positive effect on ridership and revenue generation. Electric battery vehicles will be used for short-distance commuting to reduce air and noise pollution from roads.

4.7 Township Modeling

For the current study, AutoCAD software (2012 version) was used for designing and drafting all of the building units and land planning. The layout plan, showing the placement of various buildings in the proposed township, is drawn to scale. Another plan, showing mobility planning to reach various areas across the township, is also drawn to scale. The 3-D view of the proposed township is also designed to scale.

4.7.1 Layout Plan and 3-D Model

Developing the 3-D model and layout plan are some of the main parts of the study. The 3-D model represents residential area segregation based on income group distribution. The plotted development area with individual plots for HIG housing is located toward the lower right corner of the proposed township, around ample open spaces. On the lower left corner, high-rise apartments for MIG housing are proposed, close to commercial buildings. A concentration of commercial buildings is proposed at the center of the township with accessibility from the main road. A large pocket of green area in the upper left corner of the township is reserved for regional recreational activities and future development. The upper right corner area of the proposed township is intended for housing LIG and EWS together. A mixed-use development area is located within walking distance of LIG and EWS housing to minimize daily travel time. Figure 4.1 illustrates a conceptual 3-D view of the proposed township. The segregation of residential areas based on income group and the location of nonresidential buildings and areas is shown in Figure 4.2.

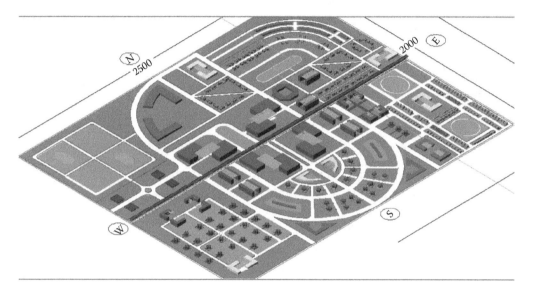

FIGURE 4.1
Three-dimensional view of the proposed township.

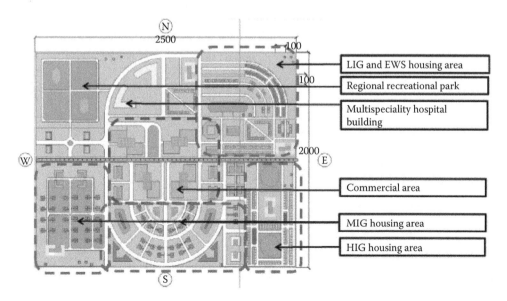

FIGURE 4.2
Layout plan of the proposed township.

4.7.2 Mobility Plan

Mobility planning envisages achieving adequate road connectivity across the township and looks for efficient sustainable transport systems. For the purpose of mobility planning, three mobility zones are proposed, considering the distance from the center of the township. A rectangular inner mobility zone varies from 200 to 300 m in walking distance, for providing access to commercial buildings located at the center of the township. A middle mobility zone varies between 300 and 500 m from the center of the township where transportation will be done through electric battery vehicles. The outer mobility zone falls beyond 500 m, where transportation will be by bus and private vehicle. Figure 4.3 describes the mobility plan for the proposed township.

4.8 Sustainability Indicators

Sustainability indicators are performance measures of sustainability (Chavan and Sarnaik 2013) that can be qualitative or quantitative. In a township planning context, indicators help evaluate whether principles adopted to guide township planning, design, and management have the desired effects. For the current study, the selection of sustainability

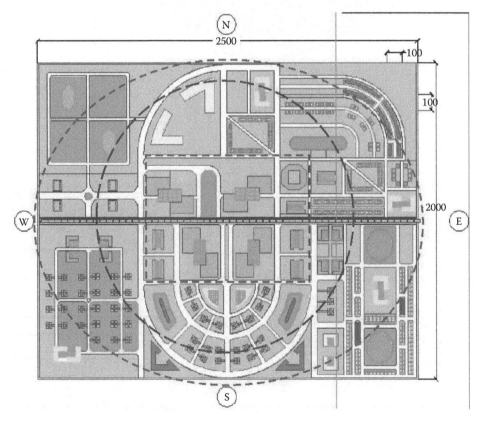

FIGURE 4.3
Mobility plan for the proposed township.

indicators has been adopted from township case studies, with a focus on enhancing sustainability. Finally, sustainability indicators have been classified as social, environment, and economic indicators for general analysis.

4.8.1 Environmental Indicators

Environmental indicators reflect the outcome of human activities in the form of development concerned with environmental problems. They include factors that are responsible for shaping the environmental conditions of a township. The environmental indicators are

- Rainwater harvesting
- ISWM
- Use of passive technologies to minimize load on conventional energy
- Green spaces occupied by parks
- Building courtyard form

4.8.2 Social Indicators

Social indicators compute the social well-being that depends on the social conditions of the township. The social indicators include

- Provision of religious gathering places and worship areas
- Multicultural society, with residents from different cultures
- Provision of community centers and banquet halls
- Meeting places for senior citizens
- Access to shopping centers and local markets within the premises of residents
- Health-care and education services within the township

4.8.3 Economic Indicators

Economic indicators define the economic setup of the township. The economic indicators include

- Provision of heterogeneous housing for distinct income groups
- Affordable housing for EWS and LIG, with cost-minimizing construction
- Use of passive technologies to bring down overall costs and earn credits
- Local retail shops and small microenterprises for generating local jobs
- Commercial and individual office spaces for business establishment

4.9 Conclusion

Since the focus is on urbanization, fast-changing aspirations in the urban areas have made the integrated township concept more viable from economic, social, and environment aspects. The municipalities are facing challenges in providing basic infrastructure and services in the perpetually growing existing cities. From the current study, it is concluded that the integrated township concept can provide residential, employment, and recreational opportunities in the same place, with a high standard of living and a healthy environment.

4.10 Acknowledgment

I would like to acknowledge Mohit Sharma (junior research associate) and Rudresh Kumar Sugam (junior research associate) at the Council of Energy, Environment, and Water (CEEW), New Delhi, for realizing the potential of the study. Their continuous efforts and insightful comments have rendered support to the study.

References

Affordable Housing in Partnership Scheme Guidelines. *Ministry of Housing and Urban Poverty Alleviation*. http://mhupa.gov.in/writereaddata/AHP-Guidelines.pdf. December 2013.

Bauer, J.W., Jacrim, L. and Katras, M.J. 2009. Children's birthday celebrations from the experiences of low-income rural mothers. *Journal of Family Issues*, 30(4): 532–553.

Chavan, D. and Sarnaik, R. 2013. Self-sustainable township. *International Journal of Innovations in Engineering and Technology (IJIET)*, 2(1): 387–390.

Government of Gujarat. 2008. Gujarat integrated township policy. January. Retrieved from http://credai.org/assets/upload/state/resources/gujarat-integrated-township-policy-january-2008.pdf.

Government of Rajasthan. 2007. Rajasthan integrated township policy. Urban Development & Local Self Department, Government of Rajasthan, 2007. Retrieved from http://virtual.jaipurjda.org/pdf/others/notificationForIntegratedTownship2007.pdf.

Government of Uttar Pradesh. 2013. Integrated township policy (license model-revised), Presentation by Housing & Urban Planning, Department Government of Uttar Pradesh, 20 December. Retrieved from http://awas.up.nic.in/Revised%20Integrated%20Policy%20(Draft).pdf

Gujarat International Finance Tec-City (GIFT). 2009. Presentation at Regional Best Practices Seminar at Manila, Philippines, April 29–30. https://faculty.washington.edu/jbs/itrans/gift-city.pdf

Gupta, A., Dalal, S., Basu. D., and Joseph, A. Magarpatta City: Farmers Direct Investment (FDI). Indian Institute of Management, Bangalore. Working paper No.: 384. http://www.iimb.ernet.in/research/working-papers/magarpatta-city-farmers-direct-investment-fdi. November 2012.

Hitest, G. and Padhya, H. Sustainable integrated industrial township. *Journal of Emerging Technologies and Innovative Research*, 2(3): 454–457. http://www.jetir.org/view?paper=JETIR1503008. March 2015.

IGBC Green Townships Rating System Reference guide. https://igbc.in/igbc/html_pdfs/abridged/IGBC%20Green%20Townships%20-%20Abridged%20Reference%20Guide%20(Pilot%20Version).pdf. November 2010.

Integrated Township Policy. 2007. Urban Development and Local Self Department. State Government of Rajasthan. https://www.jaipurjda.org/pdf/others/notificationForIntegratedTownship2007.pdf

Jurong Consultants. 2011. Master plan report 2008–2031. Mullanpur Local Planning area. Greater Mohali Region Punjab (India). http://puda.gov.in/img/approved_masterplan_files/Mullanpur_rpt_2011.pdf

Knight Frank. 2016. Global cities: The 2016 report. http://www.knightfrank.com/resources/global-cities/2016/all/global-cities-the-2016-report.pdf. Accessed on April 10, 2016.

Kotharkar, R. and Bahadure, P. 2012. Compact city concept: It's relevance and applicability for planning of Indian cities. Paper presented at the 28th International PLEA Conference. Opportunities, Limits & Needs Towards an environmentally responsible architecture Lima, Perú, November 7–9, 2012. http://www.academia.edu/15531346/Compact_City_Concept_It_s_Relevance_and_Applicability_for_Planning_of_Indian_Cities

KPMG. 2013. *Compact Cities: A Solution to Bulging Cities.* https://www.kpmg.com/IN/en/IssuesAndInsights/ArticlesPublications/Documents/Compact-Cities-Low.pdf

KPMG. 2014. Decoding housing for all by 2022. https://www.kpmg.com/IN/en/IssuesAndInsights/ArticlesPublications/Documents/Decoding-Housing-for-all-2022.pdf

McKinsey. 2010. Global Institute report. India's urban awakening: building inclusive cities, sustaining economic growth. http://www.mckinsey.com/insights/urbanization/urban_awakening_in_india

Ministry of Urban Development. 2014. Urban and regional development plan formulation and implementation guidelines. 2014. Ministry of Urban Development, Government of India. http://moud.gov.in/URDPFI

Ministry of Urban Development. 2015a. Draft model building bye-laws. Town and Country Planning Organisation, Ministry of Urban Development. http://www.indiaenvironmentportal.org.in/files/file/Draft%20MBBL-2015.pdf

Ministry of Urban Development. 2015b. Smart Cities mission statement and guidelines. Ministry of Urban Development, Government of India. http://smartcities.gov.in/writereaddata/SmartCityGuidelines.pdf. June.

Pundir, M. Environmental sustainability initiatives in master planning: A case of large-scale township projects in India. *International Journal of Modern Engineering Research*, 6(2): 24–32. February 2016.

Rai, P. 2012. Townships for sustainable cities. Paper presented at the International Conference on Emerging Economies: Prospects and Challenges (ICEE-2012). Symbiosis School of Economics, Symbiosis International University (SIU), S.B. Road Campus, Pune 411004, India, January 12–13, 2012.

Revised Integrated Township Policy. 2014. Uttar Pradesh Housing and Development Board. State Government of Uttar Pradesh. http://www.upavp.com/pol_planning.htm

Sharma, R. *Integrated Townships in India—Today and Tomorrow The Hindu*, April 20, 2013. Accessed March 16 2016.

Sahasrabuddhe, H., Bhole, A. and Deshpande, N. Application of green building concept for an integrated township project: A case study. *International Journal of Civil Engineering and Technology*, 3(1): 67–81. June 2012.

Schoeman, I. 2015. Determination and ranking of integration measures for land use and transportation applications. Paper presented at the 21st International Conference on Urban Transport and the Environment, Valencia, Spain.

Seth, S., Walia, A., and Rawal, R. Developing an energy conservation building code implementation strategy in India. Energy Conservation and Commercialization (ECO-III). http://eco3.org/wp-content/plugins/downloads-manager/upload/Developing%20an%20ECBC%20Implementation%20Strategy%20in%20India-%20Report%20No.1028.pdf. May 2010.

Shirsagar, J. and Srinivas, R. 2014. Town planning and development laws: Evolution and current amendments. Town and Country Planning Organization. Ministry of Urban Development. Government of India. http://spa.ac.in/writereaddata/tcpo.pdf

UN-Habitat. Urban Planning. Discussion Note 3. A New Strategy of Sustainable Neighbourhood Planning: Five Principles. Available at http://unhabitat.org/wp-content/uploads/2014/05/5-Principles_web.pdf. May 2014. Accessed March 20, 2015.

United Nations. Department of Economic and Social Affairs. Population Division. 2014. World Urbanization Prospects: The 2014 Revision, Highlights. http://esa.un.org/unpd/wup/Publications/Files/WUP2014-Highlights.pdf

World Bank Group. 2010. A World Bank Group flagship report. Global economic prospects: Divergences and risks. June. Retrieved from http://pubdocs.worldbank.org/en/842861463605615468/Global-Economic-Prospects-June-2016-Divergences-and-risks.pdf

5

Adoption and Acceptance of Mandatory Electronic Public Services by Citizens in the Developing World: Three Case Studies from India

Harjit Singh, Arpan Kumar Kar, and P. Vigneswara Ilavarasan

CONTENTS

5.1   Introduction..49
5.2   Literature Review...52
    5.2.1   Smart City...52
    5.2.2   Electronic Government and Electronic Transaction..........................53
    5.2.3   Barriers and Challenges to E-Government Adoption 54
    5.2.4   Adoption Models of Information Systems and E-Governance.........55
        5.2.4.1   Understanding the Stages of E-Government Growth 56
5.3   Research Gap, Contribution, and Scope 57
    5.3.1   Objectives...57
    5.3.2   Scope of Study 57
5.4   Research Methodology 58
5.5   Study of Systems 59
    5.5.1   Ministry of Finance (Income Tax Department)..............................59
        5.5.1.1   Different Studies on E-Government Initiatives in Taxation
                Organizations 59
    5.5.2   What Is E-Filing and E-Filing Systems?...59
        5.5.2.1   E-Filing of Tax Returns through the Portal of the Income Tax
                Department of India 59
        5.5.2.2   Compliance Functionality for Citizens: Mandatory through
                E-Filing Portal Only 62
        5.5.2.3   Other Statutory Documents Mandatory to be Filed through
                E-Filing Portal Only 63
    5.5.3   Other Mandatory E-Services by Government of India 63
        5.5.3.1   Passport Seva Project by the Ministry of External Affairs 63
        5.5.3.2   MCA21 Project by the MCA 65
5.6   Discussion and Conclusion 65
References..67

5.1 Introduction

Information and communication technology (ICT) worldwide is rapidly spreading across all spheres of society. The Internet is one of the major innovations of modern human history, and is giving the impression that the world has shrunk. The impact of ICT can be seen in all spheres of activities, especially in economic and social areas. Governments across the world are developing and consolidating various capabilities of service delivery for their citizens (e-service). ICT has a valuable potential to help governments deliver good governance to their stakeholders. However, this potential has largely remained unexploited in developing countries. Government operations means all back-office processes, internal and external business processes, and intergovernmental interactions within the entire government body (central, state, and local bodies). The electronic aspect of e-service means ICT-enabled systems, especially the use of the Internet, as a means of enhancing the delivery of government services to its stakeholders. A stakeholder of an initiative can be a group or an individual who is affected by or can affect the achieving of the aims of that initiative (Rowley, 2011). Governments use different technologies to interact with citizens of the nation and with other stakeholders. These are businesses (commerce), their employees, and other government agencies. Any e-government system is classified depending on the role or involvement of the stakeholder in the initiative. These classifications are G2C (government-to-citizen), G2B (government-to-business), G2E (government-to-employee), and G2G (government-to-government). A particular stakeholder that communicates and interacts with the government establishment is emphasized in each of these classifications.

With the aim of providing institutional mechanisms for e-governance, and to ensure resources for their development and implementation, the Indian government released a list of projects of national importance. These projects were termed *mission mode projects* (MMPs), and include e-governance projects at the center, state, and integrated service levels to create a citizen-focused and business-focused environment for e-services. Beginning with 27, there are now 31 MMPs in a list that includes income tax (CBDT), MCA21, and passport projects. In late 2014, the Government of India released a program called "Digital India." The vision of this program is to focus on transforming India into a digitally inspired society and a nation with knowledge. Digital India is based on the concept of the "umbrella objective"—a complete and bigger picture, wherein each element of the mission has its own scope. Nine focus areas have been conceptualized, and are called the "Nine Pillars of Digital India." A list of India's MMPs is one of the nine focus areas of Digital India. Providing public e-services on a sustainable basis is a process that requires continued political commitment for all resources and constructive interaction among different governments and private and public sector organizations. E-services at all levels of government can be a prominent tool for improving the quality of life of citizens. The focus of governments is to make all public services available as e-services to their citizens and use this as a channel to promote economic development and effective as well as efficient governance. The government has to ensure that there is end-to-end enablement of the government business processes and citizen services as e-services. We can see that e-services are becoming an integral part of its citizens' day-to-day life. Figure 5.1 explains this endeavor.

In 2015, the Indian government announced a progressive new initiative, "Smart Cities Mission," to push growth in India, especially economic growth, and also to enhance citizens' quality of life, by facilitating a focus on regional development and using technology as a way to ensure the final outcome: a "smart outcome" for citizens. The plan is to develop 100 smart cities across India in phase I of this initiative. The guidelines mention that in phase I, the focus should be on the satellite towns of metropolitan cities, and modernizing the existing mid-size (tier II) cities. A list of 98 cities has already been released, which includes 24 capitals of different states.

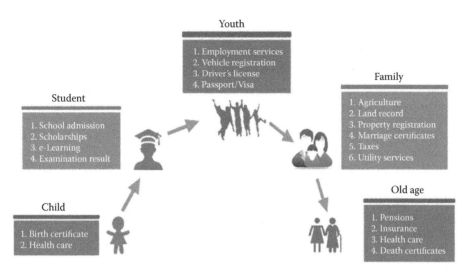

FIGURE 5.1
e-Services for citizens.

There are different versions of the definition of the term *smart city* in the literature. The concept of a smart city diverges from country to country and from state to state within a country, and even among cities within a state, subject to the level of development, the availability and quality of resources, the inclination to change and reform, and the ambition of residents of the area (adopted from: http://smartcities.gov.in/writereaddata/SmartCityGuidelines.pdf). A smart city would have a different meaning in a developing country such as India than it would in a developed country (such as the United States, or an EU country). The strategic constituents of area-based development are the improvement, renewal, redevelopment, and extension of the city, in which the new smart solutions would be applied, covering most parts of the city. One of the focuses of the Indian smart city is to build governance in a citizen-centric, friendly, and cost-effective manner, including use of e-services (online services) to convey transparency as well as accountability. Building any smart city involves a smart strategy to tackle the problems that are being created due to the growth in population in urban areas and hasty (very fast and unplanned) urbanization. There is no clear or uniform understanding of these terms among different stakeholders, including academia. However, use of ICT and governance are always an integral part of these terms. *Smart governance*, and more specifically *smart cities*, are the new terms being talked about in India in different discussions of digital government services.

The Income Tax Department (ITD) of India has reached an advanced level of maturity in its implementation of ICT systems for its business functionality and transacting with stakeholders, including providing services to taxpayers (one of the MMPs of the National e-Governance Plan [NeGP]). This integrated ICT ecosystem is one of the biggest and most complex ICT systems in comparison with other national taxation organizations in the world. Other central ministries, such as the Ministry of External Affairs (MEA) and the Ministry of Corporate Affairs (MCA), are also not far behind in providing smooth and reliable e-services to Indian citizens.

Technology adoption is important because it is a tool that allows most people to participate in a rapidly changing world where technology has become pivotal in our day-to-day life. Factors responsible for and influencing the adoption of e-services could be different for developing countries than developed countries, as the priorities and ecosystem for execution are entirely different. The strategy and approach for the distribution of e-services to the citizens with minimum resources in developing countries such as India would also be different from the practices in developed countries. However, the governments of developing countries can adapt and build on the lessons learned and the best practices of the countries that have already succeeded in e-government implementations.

This chapter consists of seven sections. The first section provides the background, definitions, and context of different terms used in this chapter. The second section covers the findings from the literature reviewed for this study, with a focus on the adoption of mandatory e-service relationships with established information systems (IS) adoption models and their relevance to smart cities. The third section tells about the research gaps, objective, and scope of this study based on the literature reviewed. The fourth section gives information about the research methodology used and the scope of the information gathered in this study. The fifth section covers the details of the case study of the e-filing system of the ITD of India. The sixth section provides the findings and recommendations, including the limitations of this research chapter, and the future research that could take findings of this case study as its basis. The final section contains a list of the research articles and studies referenced in this chapter.

5.2 Literature Review

5.2.1 Smart City

Several governments have benefited from the development of ICTs, as they have contributed to the improvement of governance. This ICT-based governance (Chourabi et al., 2012) is also known as *smart governance*. It broadly signifies an assembly of technologies, people, processes, resources, and information that perform together to support the governing activity. Many definitions of smart city (Chourabi et al., 2012) have been given in literature by different authors, which are adopted for use in the academic field as well as practical areas, such as "a city connecting the physical infrastructure, the IT infrastructure, the social infrastructure along with the business infrastructure to leverage the combined and optimum intelligence of the city." There is no unique global definition of the smart city (Neirotti et al., 2014), and therefore the current tendencies and progression patterns of any individual smart city depend more on local factors than global or macro factors. In order to make suitable strategies for their smart cities, it is suggested that policy makers try to understand each of these factors in depth, and in a holistic manner, including dependencies of these factors in the local context. It is observed that the use of ICT in governance is an integral part of almost all definitions of smart cities. It has emerged (Chourabi et al., 2012) that there are a lot of commonalities between smart city initiatives and e-government initiatives, because most smart city initiatives are driven by governments and leveraged by the exhaustive use of ICTs to serve their citizens, and the use of technology indirectly or directly affects all other success factors of a smart city framework. Since ICT-based governance is the core of smart cities initiatives (Belissent, 2011; Giffinger et al., 2007), the combination represents the most important factor for smart city initiatives. Although (Chatterjee and Kar, 2015) there will be a financial and skill-related requirement, the digital literacy of the users (citizens) of e-services is an important prerequisite for the success of smart cities in developing countries such as India. The availability and quality of the ICT infrastructure (including wireless infrastructure) are important components for smart cities

(Giffinger et al., 2007). Therefore e-government technological barriers (Chourabi et al., 2012) are referred to as barriers to smart cities initiatives as well, as both are similar in terms of their use of ICT for governance.

The objective of India's Smart Cities Mission (retrieved from: http://smartcities.gov.in/writereaddata/SmartCityGuidelines.pdf) is to encourage cities to provide essential infrastructure and give a good quality of life to citizens, a clean and sustainable environment, and the application of "smart" solutions. E-governance and citizen services are the first component of this smart solution. The mission is to cover 100 cities, and will initially run for a term of 5 years. The mission may be continued after an assessment is carried out by the Ministry of Urban Development (MoUD), including the best practices and lessons learned to be carried forward into the new mission.

5.2.2 Electronic Government and Electronic Transaction

In the literature, many different definitions of e-government are available (Palvia and Sharma 2007), and these may vary by different agencies/organizations/sources. However, there is a commonality across these definitions in terms of the use of ICT, especially the Internet and improving the delivery of government services to its stakeholders. E-government enables the citizens and users to interact and communicate to receive services from the central, state, or local government on a 24/7 basis. An e-transaction (of a government e-service) could be a transaction delivering a public service using ICT tools with the condition that the required service is requested through electronic means, including electronic mobile devices, all workflow and approvals being done using ICT systems, a database is used to store data in electronic form, and the service delivery is electronic.

It has been established in many different studies (Korpelainen, 2011) that ICT investments are helpful in improving performance and productivity (throughput). Having said that, it is also true that organizational and individual changes are always needed to successfully implement any ICT system. Ensuring acceptance and adoption by users as well as optimum use of ICT systems is a challenge in any organization. In an e-government initiative (Rowley, 2011), we need to understand and represent the relationships among different stakeholders of the initiative. The development and integration of a strong supporting back office is an essential factor in achieving the best of the front-end portal of an e-government initiative. Weak or nonexistent back-end support leads to failure of any e-government initiative (Klievink and Janssen, 2009; Theocharis and Tsihrintzis, 2013; Goldkuhl and Rostlinger, 2014). While planning an e-government initiative, a change-management package must be built in (Gupta et al., 2004). When the road map/blueprint is being drawn for any e-government initiative in any organization, there are no ready-made, common, or "one size fits all" e-governance solutions available (Hachigian, and Kaplan, 2002). Every country, at each level of government within that country, has a distinctive combination of conditions, priorities, and resources. The role of intermediaries (Weerakkody et al., 2013), particularly for developing countries, is vital for the success of e-government initiatives, as they implement their own infrastructure to bridge the digital divide and technology gap. There are also significant differences while measuring the use of e-government services by the citizens when accessed through intermediaries or via direct online access. It is empirically validated (Wang and Shih, 2009) in the perspective of the unified theory of acceptance and use of technology (UTAUT) that performance expectancy, effort expectancy, and social influence have a significant positive influence on behavioral intentions to use information kiosks and intermediaries. These kiosk operators and intermediaries are partners of the government in supporting e-services.

In the Indian governmental sector, a strategic shift is being observed (Chakrabarty, 2008). Instead of acquiring hardware and software, the governments in India (central and state) have now started buying ICT services. Most of these ICT procurements are managed services projects under the public–private partnership (PPP) model, which allows the governments to focus on critical value–adding business/activities (which only governments can do best), and transferring the technology-related requirements to information technology (IT) professionals (IT partner), usually a private organization, taking advantage of the matured Indian IT services industry. However, successful implementation of a PPP is not easy to implement in the e-governance sector in India. It requires (Sharma, 2007) the adoption and intelligent use of key best practices and lessons learned (from mistakes) from earlier PPP implementation experiences in e-government, and this is especially useful for developing countries, where there is already a scarcity of resources in terms of finances and technical skills.

E-government research touches many other research domains, such as IS, public administration, management, and political science. In a literature review, it is observed that in every e-government study or research, some of the literature cited is definitely from IS or e-business concepts modified in some way to fit into a public administration perspective. Representation of literature and ideas in e-government research from economics and sociology is rare, despite the fact that these domains have contributed significantly to informatics and governance research (Heeks and Bailur, 2007). We should not consider e-government as a one-step process, or as a single project (Jayashree and Marthandan, 2010). Instead, we should conceptualize it as evolutionary and progressive, involving multiple stages or phases of execution. We find that clear vision and goal definition, along with excellent leadership, are essential for any e-government initiative.

5.2.3 Barriers and Challenges to E-Government Adoption

Different factors influence the adoption and acceptance of e-government, and not only positive factors, but also negative factors of adoption are to be considered (Rowley, 2011). That is, we not only need to know what encourages expected users to use e-government, but we also need to know what discourages them from doing so. The implementation of ICT systems is impacted by a defined set of factors (Ebrahim and Irani, 2005), and these can be grouped as IT infrastructure, security and privacy, and implementation/ operational costs. It is observed that many of the e-government initiatives in developing countries were abandoned very soon after implementation, or that major goals were not attained (Dada, 2006). Generally, this could be due to the divergence between the current system and future systems. This mismatch could arise as a result of the gap in the physical, cultural, or economic perspectives between the software development and the place in which the system is being implemented. Many times, with the passage of time (the time when the system was conceived and the time when the system is being implemented), large changes are encountered in the circumstances, functional contexts, and business environment. The study (Savoldelli et al., 2014) compared issues encountered during three periods—1994–2004, 2005–2009, and 2010–2013—and it was observed that while few of the barriers to e-government adoption remained in all sections of these periods, others varied with time according to the environment and expectations from e-government initiatives of that period. The acceptance and usage rates (Heidemann et al., 2013) of e-services projects for citizens still lag behind expectations in many countries, especially developing countries. Hence, it is also important that we understand the reasons for nonuse of these services by citizens, as well as actions to be taken to overcome these reasons and barriers. The focus on awareness of e-services and training on e-services could be important actions to increase e-services usage (Heidemann et al., 2013).

5.2.4 Adoption Models of Information Systems and E-Governance

The existing body of knowledge/research (Alryalat et al., 2012) was analyzed on e-government-related issues in developing countries. It was observed that theories generally cited are the theory in the research area of acceptance and adoption of technology. Most theories of e-government adoption and acceptance focus at a time on any of the individual theory as TAM, TRA, TPB, or UTAUT.

The variables of success of adoption in IS are system quality, information quality, use, user satisfaction, individual impact, and organizational impact (DeLone and McLean, 1992). Service quality is included as an additional aspect of IS success (DeLone and McLean, 2003), assigning different weights to system quality, information quality, and service quality, depending on the context and scope of the project. Perceived ease of use was an important determinant factor of perceived usefulness (Venkatesh and Davis, 1996). Experience and voluntariness are the controlling factors of subjective norm (Venkatesh and Davis, 2000), and external variables affect perceived usefulness. However, UTAUT, which touches upon the impact of intervention, has four key constructs, performance expectancy, effort expectancy, social influence, and facilitating conditions. These constructs impact the behavioral intention to use a technology (Venkatesh et al., 2003). Most of the studies on technology adoption used modified versions of the TAM (Turner et al., 2010) rather than the original model, and the results were influenced by other variables that were introduced when using any of the modified versions of the TAM models.

Interventions impact both determinants of technology adoption: perceived ease of use and perceived usefulness (Venkatesh and Bala, 2008). Therefore, interventions have direct implications for two types of decision making in an organization. First, employees' technology adoption decisions and managerial decisions for managing the ICT implementation process. By implementing the right interventions, we can minimize resistance to new systems and maximize effective utilization of the ICT systems implemented. It was observed in the literature review (Sharp, 2007), that most of the studies related to technology acceptance/adoption were done in the voluntary settings. However, in the involuntary environments, where the users have no option but to use a specific technology to perform their activities, the observed results were different. It signaled that perceived usefulness could be a strong determinant of behavioral intention, and on the other hand the perceived ease of use was not significant.

The functional attributes and technological complexity of different levels and maturities of the e-service offerings are fairly different (Shareef et al., 2011), hence governments should recognize that the requirements of stakeholders for using those different service levels are different, and awareness is a significant aspect of using e-service. For mandatory adoption of any e-service (Chan et al., 2010), importance is to be given to eight external variables in influencing the three core technology adoption factors of UTAUT (performance, expectancy, facilitating conditions, and effort expectancy) and impacting the user satisfaction, and hence the impact on the adoption of a mandatory e-service. The satisfaction measure should reflect the overall efficiency and effectiveness of the e-service (Osman et al., 2013), and providers can actively participate in contributing to the improvement of users' satisfaction and e-service effectiveness. Also, the citizen's trust in technology and previous experiences with government online services (Shareef et al., 2011; Chen et al., 2015) have a meaningful effect on perceptions for the new ICT-based government system. Trust in government (Chen et al., 2015) positively influences trust in public sector e-services, and hence the adoption of an ICT project.

5.2.4.1 Understanding the Stages of E-Government Growth

The development of e-government is an evolutionary process. An e-government initiative can grow over time to include a variety of features, functions, and services. The most-used e-government maturity model (eGMM) is by Layne and Lee, and is composed of four stages: publication of information, interaction/transaction, vertical integration, and horizontal integrations.

An ICT government project progresses through four stages of development (Layne and Lee, 2001), with an increase in their integration, technological, and organizational architecture complexities. Figure 5.2 shows how MMPs of central government are mapped, with different stages mentioned in Layne and Lee's model of e-government development stages (Yildiz, 2007). These may not follow each other directly in a sequential way, especially in developing countries, as these countries get the opportunity to learn from the mistakes and successes of the developed countries. The developing countries also have a shorter learning curve, and they can attain all stages practically at the same time.

Strategy–technology–organization–people–environment (STOPE) is the development profile (Bakry, 2004) used to explore the transition to e-government and to support its continuous improvement. It describes the basic processes, and emphasizes the potential benefits. ICT systems were implemented in government organizations in India, but use of the system was only moderate (Gupta et al., 2007). The bigger organizations have better results for IT effectiveness, and user satisfaction had significantly positive results. The factors that are mainly impacting the effectiveness of e-government (United Nations, 2014) are strong political drive and collective leadership, along with new charters/concepts of governance to help and manage the citizen-focused service delivery models. There is a

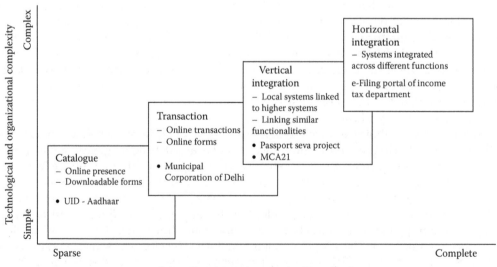

FIGURE 5.2
Layne and Lee Stage Maturity Model and mapping on MMPs. (Adapted from Layne, K., and J. Lee. *Government Information Quarterly*, 18, no. 2, 122–136, 2001.)

need to have a national-level, inclusive, and holistic ICT policy, and a strategy to include ICT in government. Also needed are to strengthen institutions/organizations and build the capacities of public servants.

In the literature, few researches related to TAM3 and UTAUT have discussed the adoption of mandatory use of IS implemented in an organization. In the literature, there is no evidence of significant research or studies on the adoption and acceptance of mandatory e-services in the context of developing economies and countries. It is also observed in the literature review that much research on e-government limited the analysis of study to a government organization implementing an ICT-based government application. On the other hand, certain methodological selections using primary data, along with the triangulation of findings (Yildiz, 2007), are very few in the literature on e-government. A combination of data and findings using different data sources and methods that were collected from multiple areas and sites increases the strength of the studies. General topics of current research (Zhang et al., 2014) are "the influence of e-government expansion on government agencies and employees," and "the relationships between ICT infrastructures and the expansion of e-government."

5.3 Research Gap, Contribution, and Scope

E-governance research can be seen as a crossroads between a number of other research domains, such as IS, public administration, and political science. Although e-government literature citation in most of the research/studies is of an IS or e-business, most of the contexts of the studies are public administration, and the cited IS-related ideas are being adapted in some way to fit the government administration context. Significant research has been done in the IS field on the adoption and acceptance of technology. However, there is hardly any study in the literature that focuses on adoption and acceptance of mandatory use of e-services provided by governments. The finding of this study will contribute to the body of knowledge and narrow this gap. Most of the services of the newly envisaged smart cities of India will provide e-services of local government as mandatory e-services; hence the findings of this study will be very helpful in providing direction to the planners of these services.

5.3.1 Objectives

- To extract the best practices and lessons learned for the acceptance and adoption of mandatory e-services and their implications for building effective smart cities.
- To explicate the best practices and lessons learned in the context of the technology adoption theories/models, with a specific focus on the mandatory use of the services.

5.3.2 Scope of Study

The scope of this exploratory research was to conduct a focused study work guided by the availability of resources and time. We studied three citizen-focused e-government initiatives providing e-service that, according to Government of India notifications, have to be mandatory e-service (there is no alternative manual service allowed for these services). These are the e-services provided by the ITD, the MEA, and the MCA.

State and central governments in India have made huge investment in the implementation of ICT systems (e-government projects), which are impacting the citizens of India. It is important to study e-government systems from the point of view of the adoption and acceptance of these systems by the users. The coverage of the study will include:

- The study of e-services of citizen portals of the ITD (e-filing portal), the MEA (Passport Seva Project), and the MCA (MCA21 project).
- The focus of the research is to explore the relationship of e-services with citizens, with the perspective of the compulsory/mandatory use of e-service.

5.4 Research Methodology

Case study–based quantitative research methods have been used in this research. Three cases have been studied to validate the results across different categories of e-services across different ministries of the Government of India and different categories of citizens. These cases involve the Ministry of Finance (the ITD), the MEA, and the MCA. It was preferred that we collect information from those stakeholders who are close to the day-to-day activities of the systems. It was considered to be more likely that we would get information from important stakeholders while discussing the ICT systems, which the person (government official) may otherwise not be comfortable in sharing, especially through e-mail. An interview is a good method to extract the incidents that are significant for (dis)satisfaction with the service.

This type of study (Venkatesh et al., 2013) helps acquire deep insights into various views of importance that otherwise may not be completely understood using a quantitative method. We collected information from multiple sources (interviews, system databases, reports/documents available in public domains), which was covered in great detail and aimed at corroborating the findings (Yin, 2013). Multiple sources of evidence basically provide multiple measures of the same phenomenon. We carried out a focused literature review (researches and case studies) of e-government initiatives in taxation organizations. We conducted interviews with personnel who had worked or were working on key positions on the project, to collect data from both service providers and sponsors (civil servants) in order to gather views from both sides. When these stakeholders were interviewed, the focus was on their specific knowledge for the system. Interviews were semistructured. We prepared a list of questions for each type of stakeholder interview, and on a case-by-case basis, we also deviated from the format to track important issues that came up during the conversation, and shifted focus to other relevant points that were not previously included in the interview outline. As part of the second phase, we had a focused discussion with different interest groups and intermediaries (e.g., law firms, chartered accountants) on their expectations and experience of these systems. In parallel, we collected data from documents available in the public domain, including relevant information regarding portal usage on different parameters. Based on these inputs, we did the analysis using critical factor analysis and human factor analysis. The outcome of this analysis became the basis for the findings and recommendations of this study.

5.5 Study of Systems

5.5.1 Ministry of Finance (Income Tax Department)

5.5.1.1 Different Studies on E-Government Initiatives in Taxation Organizations

Singapore Revenue Authority (Teo and Wong, 2005) leveraged its relationship with trade groups, professional bodies, nongovernmental organizations (NGOs), and corporations to educate taxpayers on tax matters. Easy Internet access for taxpayers (kiosks and community clubs) helped to promote e-filing of tax returns. The relationship between the automation of business and e-government systems, and the efficiency and quality of service delivery for the UK revenue department (Nisar, 2006), showed that automation is leading to improved efficiency by saving time and cost, and the detection of frauds has improved by using ICT to automate the system. Any high-end ICT-based government system (Chatfield, 2009) is not sufficient to ensure the effectiveness of public service reform through the use of e-government; it also needs to utilize the internal resources of government, particularly the employees, to own and implement the changes. Both compatibility (COMP) and personal innovativeness in information technology (PIIT) strongly influence BI (Ojha et al., 2009). The direct significant effect of perceived ease of use (PEOU) on behavioral intention (BI) supports that PEOU directly affects BI. To improve the system, information quality (Chen et al., 2015) must be the priority, especially in the case of taxation systems and e-filing, where every piece of information must be accurate. e-Enablement of the service delivery process for citizens is the key factor for achieving the real effectiveness of an e-government initiative. Effectiveness is dependent on the reach of the infrastructure to the remotest locations to use the available service.

5.5.2 What Is E-Filing and E-Filing Systems?

Different versions are available to explain e-filing and its usage in different e-governance initiatives. The e-filing system (Fenwick and Brownstone, 2002) is making it possible to transmit information electronically using the Internet as stakeholders and government change the use of basic infrastructure to interact with one another. Use of designated e-filing systems mandated by law to submit information electronically is known as electronic filing (e-filing).

5.5.2.1 E-Filing of Tax Returns through the Portal of the Income Tax Department of India

The e-filing portal of the ITD (https://www.incometaxindiaefiling.gov.in/) provides many facilities to taxpayers and has been extended to the electronic filing of other statutory forms and reports as prescribed in the Income Tax Rules. This portal is a single window interface to different categories of users such as individuals, beneficiary trusts, businesses, corporations, intermarries (ERIs), internal departmental users, and external agencies (banks and other government agencies) for information flow and communication through role-based secured access systems. A 24/7, dedicated service desk has been provided for the stakeholders of this system. Provision is there for online feedback and grievances from users and subsequently after analysis, tracking to closure. Important functionalities are being added continuously, and some of the existing functionalities are being upgraded, based on the experiences of the stakeholders and also from the analysis of the online feedback received through the portal. With state-of-the-art systems in place and realizing the potential of the use of the Internet, the department desires that taxpayers who file paper tax returns be encouraged to shift to e-filing. This system has an interface with both a dedicated facility for a jurisdiction-free bulk processing for income tax returns (ITRs), and with core application systems for information flow for assessing officers (AO) and other department officials. There are service-level agreements with all service providers to ensure the timely completion of end-to-end activities. Figure 5.3 shows the end-to-end process of ITRs.

The intimation of the final result of ITR processing is sent through e-mail as well as through Short Message Service (SMS) to the concerned stakeholders. From the financial year 2015–2016, the new functionality/facility has been introduced by the department to give optional alternatives to ITR-V. Instead of ITR-V, "Aadhaar"-based authentication or taxpayer's authentication through a bank (empanelled) database are being used to verify the e-filing of an ITR (e-signature). The trends of adoption of this facility show signs of success. For the users of this facility, the department was able to process their returns and send refunds within a few days of filing, to the bank accounts (ECS) of eligible taxpayers. This was a record, and a delightful development for the taxpayers as well as for the department. Figure 5.3 shows the end-to-end process of e-filing the ITR and information flow through the tightly coupled integration with back-end systems until the tax refund is received by the taxpayer.

To ensure that users derive maximum benefit from this e-government initiative, in the last few years, there has been a further push by the department to focus on awareness and education of taxpayers, steady inclusion of more taxpayers' categories as compulsory e-filing of ITR, involvement of intermediaries and tax return preparers (TRPs) to encourage the e-filing of ITRs, and include/shift more business services of the department to e-services through this portal. For the FY 2015–2016, more than 43 million ITRs were filed as e-returns on the e-filing portal. More than 52 million are registered users of this system (retrieved from: https://incometaxindiaefiling.gov.in/in April 2016). Figure 5.4 shows the summary of growth trends of different activities of e-filing systems of the ITD.

After the success and acceptability of this portal, coupled with the growing expectations of the citizens, it has become a single window of interaction with the department for all external stakeholders, including the taxpayers who are filing their ITRs in paper format, who are also being given many services through this portal. Observing the success of the new e-filing facility of the department, many new categories of taxpayers were added to the compulsory e-filing. This has led to faster processing of most of the filed returns and more satisfied taxpayers. The year-wise development in this direction (Table 5.1) was as follows:

New facilities (after going live) that have been added on the portal in the last couple of years are

- Option to capture the response of the taxpayer to his or her outstanding tax demand (arrears).
- Facility to capture any grievances related to processing ITRs and functionality for feedback mechanism for grievances logged.
- Audio Captcha–enabled portal.
- Compliance functionality for taxpayers.
- e-Filing and net banking integration.

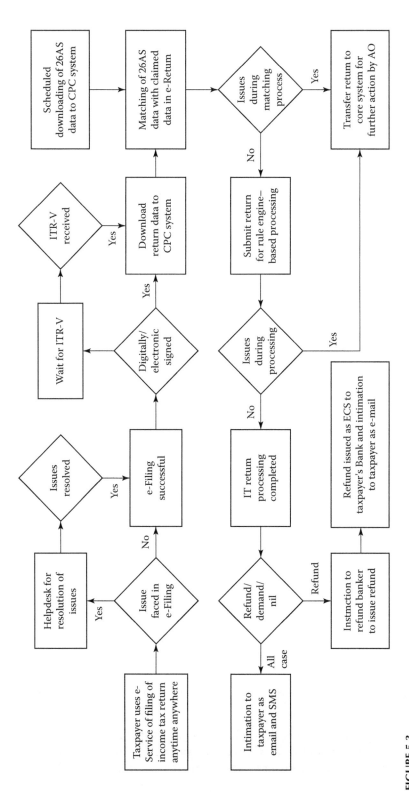

FIGURE 5.3
e-Filing of ITR.

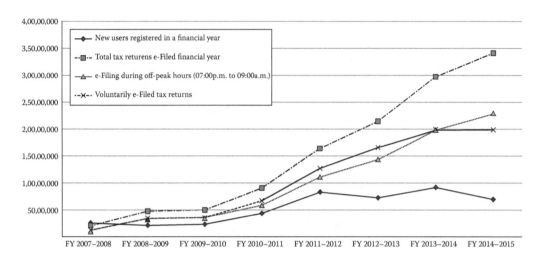

FIGURE 5.4
Year-on-year trend of actives on e-filing portal. (Source: Reports of ITD on portal.)

TABLE 5.1

Development in Respect of Inclusion of Income Tax Forms for Compulsory e-Filing

Assessment Year (AY)	Category Added for Mandatory File the Income Tax Return (ITR) Electronically (e-Filing) for the Relevant Assessment Year
2006–2007	For all those companies that require statutory audit u/s 44AB
2007–2008	For all those companies and businesses/firms that require statutory audit u/s 44AB
2010–2011	Digital signature is mandatory for e-filing of ITR for all those companies and businesses/firms that as per Income Tax Rules, require mandatory e-filing of ITR
2011–2012	It was made mandatory to file ITR-5 or ITR-4 electronically using digital signature for all businesses/firms or individual/Hindu undivided family (HUF) covered u/s 44AB
2012–2013	If the total annual income for an individual or a HUF exceeds INR 1 million, e-filing of ITR is mandatory. However, digital signature will not be compulsory for these taxpayers to e-file their ITRs.
2013–2014	If the total annual income for an individual or a HUF exceeds INR 0.5 million, e-filing of ITR is mandatory. However, digital signature will not be compulsory for these taxpayers to e-file their ITR.
	Also covered for mandatory e-filing of ITRs are the individual/HUF, being Indian residents, and having assets located outside India.
2014–2015	If a taxpayer is required to furnish a report of audit specified under different sections of the Income Tax Act, shall furnish the said reports and ITR electronically.
2015–2016	e-Filing of ITR is compulsory if refund is claimed by the taxpayer (other than above covered taxpayers).

Source: Notifications issued by the ITD from time to time.

5.5.2.2 Compliance Functionality for Citizens: Mandatory through E-Filing Portal Only

5.5.2.2.1 Filing of Income Tax Return

The ITD has released a list of nonfilers who have not filed ITRs. In this context, the ITD wants to set up a provision for the nonfilers to update the required data. This functionality in the e-filing portal will help the user to update the reason for nonfiling. The nonfiler will receive a notice from the ITD. This will contain the details of nonfiling and instructions on the various steps needed to address the issue will be communicated. Based on this notice, the taxpayer will log on to the e-filing portal and respond on the portal.

5.5.2.2.2 *Return Information Mismatch*

The ITD has introduced a new initiative called "e-Sahyog." This initiative is in line with the government's commitment to work in an e-environment and to e-enable public services for the benefit of the stakeholders, especially the citizens. This has been done with the aim to reduce compliance cost, especially for small taxpayers, and to reduce the need for the taxpayer to physically visit tax offices. It is a complete, end-to-end e-service using the e-filing portal. Related to this functionality, the taxpayer will be able to track his or her updated status on the e-filing portal.

5.5.2.3 **Other Statutory Documents Mandatory to be Filed through E-Filing Portal Only**

Certain other specified reports and notified documents related to deductions claimed by the taxpayers, international taxes are mandatory to be filed only electronically. These are

- Reports related to various deductions u/s 80 (Form No. 10CCB, 10CCBA, etc.)
- Form 3CA, 3CB, and 3CD—audit reports related to tax audit u/s 44AB
- Reports related to any remittance made to nonresidents or any international transactions

5.5.3 **Other Mandatory E-Services by Government of India**

5.5.3.1 **Passport Seva Project by the Ministry of External Affairs**

Indian passports (and some other travel documents such as identity cards for Tibetan refugees, emergency certificates, police clearance certificates, and line of control travel permits in Jammu and Kashmir) are issued by the MEA, through the Central Passport Organization and passport offices all over India. This network has Passport Seva Kendras (PSKs—the passport centers) functioning under a PPP. The functions of the MEA also include the issuance of passports and other related documents through its Indian missions/offices across the world for Indians living abroad.

The passport management by all stakeholders in India is mandatory to come through e-services (http://passportindia.gov.in). The PSP online system functionality includes broader reach, usefulness, ease of use, and greater transparency, with the availability of the information on passport services including real-time tracking of status. The system serves as an interface with the key stakeholders: citizens, internal users of the MEA, Indian missions and posts/immigration checkpoints, and the Indian police.

Citizens use the system for

- 24/7 access to up-to-date information on passport services
- Online application filing
- Making online payments in a safe and secure manner
- Appointment booking
- Real-time status tracking

5.5.3.1.1 Internal Users

Ministry officials, including from passport and visa divisions, use the application for verification and final granting of permission to issue a passport. They also get online dashboards and reports that give the health of the passport services across the passport offices. The data helps in effective governance and timely decision making, and has helped bring in greater accountability.

5.5.3.1.2 Indian Police

The passport system provides an online real-time digital interface for verification of an applicant's personal particulars. This has brought in transparency to the process, brought in greater accountability on the part of the police, and significantly reduced the time taken for police verification.

5.5.3.1.3 Call Center

A grievance redressal system is in place as a 24/7 centralized call center (help desk) through a toll-free number, operating in 17 languages to cater to supplying information to citizens regarding various services and the handling of grievances, including citizen feedback. The online portal also provides the interface for call center executives to access information on passport services/application status/any other information.

5.5.3.1.4 Indian Missions and Posts/Immigration Checkpoints

The portal provides 24/7 secured access to online, up-to-date, complete information of all passport holders, and can be accessed from worldwide Indian missions, the offices of the MEA and posts, as well as from different immigration checkpoints.

The growth in the number of passports being issued is phenomenal, and crossed 10 million in the year 2015. Table 5.2 shows the year-on-year growth achieved in issuing passports.

The mPassport Seva mobile app is being provided on different platforms, such as Android, Windows, and Apple iOS. This app is being used on different types of mobile gadgets, such as smartphones, in order to access different information relating to the passport issuance process. This includes the location of a PSK, different fees applicable, the mode of submission, and tracking a passport application status.

The e-migrate system of the Ministry of Overseas Indian Affairs has been integrated with the PSP system. It validates passports submitted by prospective workers seeking employment abroad online from the passport database. This has resulted in increased security and reduced risk of passport misuse/identity theft. In accordance with the recommendations of ICAO to include biometric data in machine-readable travel documents, India has agreed to upgrade the existing passports to electronic passports (e-passports). These e-passports provide greater protection against fraudulent practices and tampering. They also prevent issuance of multiple passports to a single person, thus ensuring a high level of security in passport issuance. The department is planning to start issuing e-passports to new applicants in the near future.

TABLE 5.2

Year-Wise Number of Passports Issued in India

Year	2009	2010	2011	2012	2013	2014	2015
No. of passports (in millions)	5.1	6.2	6.5	6.7	7.3	8.7	10.4

Source: MEA published annual reports. (HYPERLINK "http://passportindia.gov.in/AppOnlineProject/pdf/Annual_report.pdf" http://passportindia.gov.in/)

5.5.3.2 MCA21 Project by the MCA

With the beginning of the twenty-first century, as e-governance initiatives in India started taking place, the MCA took a decisive step in implementing the "MCA21 Project." This was to provide easy-of-use, secure, and transparent access to business functionalities and services to corporations and different business professionals, as well as to other stakeholders including citizens of India. This project is conceptualized for complete automation (end-to-end) of business processes related to implementation and compliance of the statutory provisions under different clauses and sessions of the Indian Companies Act. The front-office operations are handled through the front-office portal (http://www.mca.gov.in/MCA21/). The entire back-office operations have been fully automated for internal users to accomplish the objectives of optimum use of the ICT environment. The MCA21 portal is based on a single window or single point of interaction concept. All stakeholders access this system for MCA-related services, available 24/7 through the Internet (e-services). Corporations, professionals, financial institutions, and banks, as well as governments, citizens, and employees of the corporate ministry are the stakeholders of this system. The MCA21 Project provides the following services:

- Registration and incorporation of any new company.
- Registrations of directors (eligible) and allocation of a unique number: Any person intending to become a director in a company is required to apply to the ministry for allocation of a unique identification number, known as a director identification number (DIN). It is meant to be a permanent number allocated to any eligible director.
- Filing of annual returns and balance sheets: Portal facilitates mandatory e-filing of various forms and applications.
- e-Filing of forms for any modification/update/change of names/address or directors' details.
- Applications/forms related to different legal/statutory services.
- Facility to view documents of corporations online (including digitized and migrated records), and request for certified copy of same, also online.
- Facility for public to view company's master data and directors' data.
- Digital signature–based governance: Ensures validity of documents in a court of law.
- Extensive MIS and operational reporting system made available to ministry officials.
- Grievance redressal, including investor complaints and tracking of status of same.

5.6 Discussion and Conclusion

It has emerged during this study that there is no unique global definition of a smart city, and that the current tendencies and progression patterns of any individual smart city depend more on local factors than global or macro factors. City policy makers are advised to try to understand these factors in order to make appropriate strategies for their smart cities. However, the use of ICT and governance are an integral part of almost all definitions in the literature. There is a lot of commonality of smart city initiatives with e-government initiatives. The effectiveness of smart city implementation development depends on strong political will, collaborative leadership, and new governance frameworks to support and manage a citizen-centric service delivery model, including an ICT policy and strategy. The Smart Cities Mission of the Government of India aims to develop 100 smart cities as satellite towns of larger cities and by modernizing the existing mid-sized cities, to drive economic evolution and improve the quality of life of people by enabling local development and exploiting ICT to generate smart outcomes for the citizens of the cities. Internet and telephones (Chatterjee and Kar, 2015) will be important parameters in ensuring e-services are available to every citizen in these smart cities. Most of the services provided by the government in these smart cities are being provided as mandatory e-services to the citizens. Hence, the elements and dimensions determining the adoption and acceptance of government e-services would also be applicable to smart cities.

The findings showed differing variables in the mandatory situation compared with voluntary adoption and acceptance of e-services. The increase in citizens' trust can lead to further participation and hence to the adoption of e-services. We find that for improving the performance in the adoption of policy-making process, the participation of the citizens is an important factor. For citizens, service maturity levels and trust in government are important factors for the adoption of a mandatory e-service. For mandatory e-services, it is important to know the reasons why citizens are hesitant or resistant to use e-services and evaluate different actions that governments could take to increase e-services usage. The maturity levels (Layne and Lee, 2001) of the government's e-services and more importantly concerning e-government initiatives and organization are to be considered. It requires the engagement of all stakeholders from an early stage of the project, and that a prerequisite to that engagement is a shared understanding of the interests, perspectives, value dimensions, and benefits sought from e-government by the various stakeholders. Being citizen-centric systems, their reliability and availability have to be given priority. Social networking and other trends of the Internet are also to be exploited for training and awareness of citizens. The implementation of these e-services should be in a sustained manner, with the effectiveness (adoption) of each stage being measured before shifting to the next stage of maturity of e-services. However, the plan of a sustained release of e-services should be different across identified smart cities based on the local setup and conditions.

The e-services provided by the ITD through the e-filing portal are on a par with the e-services provided by the taxation organizations of developed countries through their portals. Observing the success of the e-filing system of the department, many new categories of taxpayers are being added in the compulsory e-filing of ITRs every year. With the addition of many other e-services to the citizens though this portal, this e-filing portal of the ITD is now an e-interaction portal of the department (one-stop shop—single window). Most of these e-services are mandatory e-services. Stakeholders (citizens) have to interact with the department through the portal only. The users of the passport project are across all categories of citizens. Compulsory e-application, e-payment, and e-appointment to report to a PSK has provided convenience to citizens and a boost to governance transparency. In the Indian context (a developing country), awareness, affordability, and accessibility are the basic and core factors that impact the adoption and acceptance of any e-service or digital service, irrespective of the maturity stage/level. Considering the penetration/diffusion of mobile technology in India, it is observed that these e-services are being made available on mobile platforms (m-services).

Although it was not part of the scope of our study, and was also not an objective of this research, important factors have emerged during the study, which explain the significance of the roles of intermediaries, kiosks, back office, other interfacing ICT systems (upstream ICT systems), and internal users of the organization for the success of a mandatory e-service, especially in respect of electronic services in smart cities. However, each of these needs to be further studied in this context, and could be another path to further studies and researches.

References

Alryalat, M., Y. Dwivedi, M. D. Williams, and N. P. Rana. 2011. A systematic review of e-government research in developing countries. *E-Governance Policies and Practices:* 3.

Bakry, S. H. 2004. Development of e-government: A STOPE view. *International Journal of Network Management* 14, no. 5: 339–350.

Belissent, J. 2011. *The Core of a Smart City Must Be Smart Governance.* Forrester Research, Cambridge, MA.

Chakrabarty, T. 2008. *Towards an Ideal E-Governance Scenario in India.* Tata Consultancy Services, Trivandrum, India.

Chan, F. K. Y., J. Y. L. Thong, V. Venkatesh, S. A. Brown, P. J. H. Hu, and K. Y. Tam. 2010. Modelling citizen satisfaction with mandatory adoption of an e-government technology. *Journal of the Association for Information Systems* 11, no. 10: 519–549.

Chatfield, A. T. 2009. Public service reform through e-government: A case study of "e-tax" in Japan. *Electronic Journal of eGovernment* 7, no. 2: 135–146.

Chatterjee, S., and A. K. Kar. 2015. Smart Cities in developing economies: A literature review and policy insights. In *International Conference on Advances in Computing, Communications and Informatics (ICACCI)*, pp. 2335–2340. IEEE.

Chen, J. V., R. J. M. Jubilado, E. P. S. Capistrano, and D. C. Yen. 2015. Factors affecting online tax filing: An application of the IS Success Model and trust theory. *Computers in Human Behavior* 43: 251–262.

Chourabi, H., T. Nam, S. Walker, et al. 2012. Understanding smart cities: An integrative framework. In *45th Hawaii International Conference on System Science (HICSS)*, pp. 2289–2297. IEEE.

Dada, D. 2006. The failure of e-government in developing countries: A literature review. *The Electronic Journal of Information Systems in Developing Countries* 26, no. 7: 1–10.

DeLone, W. H., and E. R. McLean. 1992. Information systems success: The quest for the dependent variable. *Information Systems Research* 3, no. 1: 60–95.

DeLone, W. H., and E. R. McLean. 2003. The DeLone and McLean model of information systems success: A ten-year update. *Journal of Management Information Systems* 19, no. 4: 9–30.

Ebrahim, Z., and Z. Irani. 2005. E-government adoption: Architecture and barriers. *Business Process Management Journal* 11, no. 5: 589–611.

Fenwick, W. A., and R. D. Brownstone. 2002. Electronic filing: What is it—What are its implications. *The Santa Clara Computer & High Tech Law Journal* 19: 181.

Giffinger, R., C. Fertner, H. Kramar, et al. 2007. *Smart Cities: Ranking of European Medium-Sized Cities.* Centre of Regional Science (SRF), Vienna University of Technology, Vienna, Austria. www.smart-cities. eu/download/smart_cities_final_report.pdf.

Goldkuhl, G., and A. Röstlinger. 2014. Intentions for simplicity and consequences of complexity: A diagnostic case study of an e-government portal and its back-office processes. In *The 11th Scandinavian Workshop on E-Government*, pp . 1–17.

Gupta, M. P., P. Kumar, and J. Bhattacharya. 2004. *Government Online: Opportunities and Challenges.* Tata McGraw-Hill, New Delhi, India.

Gupta, M. P., S. Kanungo, R. Kumar, et al. 2007. A study of information technology effectiveness in select government organizations in India. *Vikalpa* 32, no. 2: 7.

Hachigian, N., and J. A. Kaplan. 2002. *Roadmap for E-Government in the Developing World: 10 Questions E-Government Leaders Should Ask Themselves*. Los Angeles, CA: The Working Group on E-government in the Developing World-Pacific Council, 36.

Heeks, R., and S. Bailur. 2007. Analyzing e-government research: Perspectives, philosophies, theories, methods, and practice. *Government Information Quarterly* 24, no. 2: 243–265.

Heidemann, J., S. Muschter, and C. Rauch. 2013. How to increase public e-services usage in governments: A case study of the German federal employment agency. In *ECIS*, p. 128. AIS Electronic Library (AISeL).

Jayashree, S., and G. Marthandan. 2010. Government to e-government to e-society. *Journal of Applied Sciences* 10, no. 19: 2205–2210.

Klievink, B., and M. Janssen. 2009. Realizing joined-up government-dynamic capabilities and stage models for transformation. *Government Information Quarterly* 26, no. 2: 275–284.

Korpelainen, E. 2011. *Theories of ICT System Implementation and Adoption: A Critical Review*. Aalto University.

Layne, K., and J. Lee. 2001. Developing fully functional e-government: A four stage model. *Government Information Quarterly* 18, no. 2: 122–136.

Neirotti, P., A. De Marco, A. C. Cagliano, et al. 2014. Current trends in smart city initiatives: Some stylised facts. *Cities* 38: 25–36.

Nisar, T. 2006. E-governance in revenue collection and administration. In *The Internet Society II: Advances in Education, Commerce and Governance, Internet and Society*, pp. 265–274. WIT Press.

Ojha, A., G. P. Sahu, and M. P. Gupta. 2009. Antecedents of paperless income tax filing by young professionals in India: An exploratory study. *Transforming Government: People, Process and Policy* 3, no. 1: 65–90.

Osman, I. H., A. L. Anouze, B. Azad, et al. 2013. The elicitation of key performance indicators of e-government providers: A bottom-up approach.

Palvia, S. C. J., and S. S. Sharma. 2007. E-government and e-governance: Definitions/domain framework and status around the world. In *International Conference on E-governance*. CSI-SIGeGov.

Rowley, J. 2011. E-Government stakeholders: Who are they and what do they want? *International Journal of Information Management* 31, no. 1: 53–62.

Savoldelli, A., C. Codagnone, and G. Misuraca. 2014. Understanding the e-government paradox: Learning from literature and practice on barriers to adoption. *Government Information Quarterly* 31: S63–S71.

Shareef, M. A., V. Kumar, U. Kumar, and Y. K. Dwivedi. 2011. E-Government Adoption Model (GAM): Differing service maturity levels. *Government Information Quarterly* 28, no. 1: 17–35.

Sharma, S. 2007. Exploring best practices in public–private partnership (PPP) in e-government through select Asian case studies. *The International Information and Library Review* 39, no. 3–4: 203–210.

Sharp, J. H. 2007. Development, extension, and application: A review of the technology acceptance model. *Information Systems Education Journal* 5, no. 9.

Teo, T. S. H., and P. K. Wong. 2005. Implementing electronic filing of tax returns: Insights from the Singapore experience. *Journal of Information Technology Case and Application Research* 7, no. 2: 3–18.

Theocharis, S. A., and G. A. Tsihrintzis. 2013. Personalization as a means to improve e-services. In 2013 *International Conference on Computer, Information and Telecommunication Systems (CITS)*. IEEE.

Turner, M., B. Kitchenham, P. Brereton, et al. 2010. Does the technology acceptance model predict actual use? A systematic literature review. *Information and Software Technology* 52, no. 5: 463–479.

United Nations. 2014. United Nations e-government survey 2014: E-government for the future we want. United Nations Department of Economic and Social Affairs.

Venkatesh, V., and H. Bala. 2008. Technology acceptance model 3 and a research agenda on interventions. *Decision Sciences* 39, no. 2: 273–315.

Venkatesh, V., S. A. Brown, and H. Bala. 2013. Bridging the qualitative-quantitative divide: Guidelines for conducting mixed methods research in information systems. *MIS Quarterly* 37, no. 1: 21–54.

Venkatesh, V., and F. D. Davis. 1996. A model of the antecedents of perceived ease of use: Development and test. *Decision sciences* 27, no. 3: 451–481.

Venkatesh, V., and F. D. Davis. 2000. A theoretical extension of the technology acceptance model: Four longitudinal field studies. *Management Science* 46, no. 2: 186–204.

Venkatesh, V., M. G. Morris, G. B. Davis, et al. 2003. User acceptance of information technology: Toward a unified view. *MIS Quarterly:* 425–478.

Wang, Y. S., and Y. W. Shih. 2009. Why do people use information kiosks? A validation of the Unified Theory of Acceptance and Use of Technology. *Government Information Quarterly* 26, no. 1: 158–165.

Weerakkody, V., R. El-Haddadeh, F. Al-Sobhi, M. A. Shareef, and Y. K. Dwivedi. 2013. Examining the influence of intermediaries in facilitating e-government adoption: An empirical investigation. *International Journal of Information Management* 33, no. 5: 716–725.

Yildiz, M. 2007. E-government research: Reviewing the literature, limitations, and ways forward. *Government Information Quarterly* 24, no. 3: 646–665.

Yin, R. K. 2013. *Case Study Research: Design and Methods.* Newbury Park, CA: Sage Publications.

Zhang, H., X. Xu, and J. Xiao. 2014. Diffusion of e-government: A literature review and directions for future directions. *Government Information Quarterly* 31, no. 4: 631–636.

6

Role of Manufacturing Sector to Develop Smart Economy: A Competitiveness Study between India and China

Manoj Kumar Singh, Harish Kumar, and Manmohan Prasad Gupta

CONTENTS

6.1 Introduction...71
6.2 Industrial Policies in India 72
6.3 Manufacturing Sector: Comparison of India and China......................73
6.4 Methodology Applied 76
6.5 Conclusions..79
References 80

6.1 Introduction

There is strong competition among countries to secure investments, jobs, businesses, and talent to promote economic success. The manufacturing sector is critical for the sustainability of any country's growth model on account of its multiplier effects on employment, domestic value addition, and catering to the growing domestic market. Indian manufacturing is at a critical juncture, and the manufacturing sector is crucial for the Indian economy. The growth of the manufacturing sector supports agriculture and has a multiplier effect on the service sector, such as in trading, finance, and transportation. The manufacturing sector creates a demand for raw material and semifinished goods. Most of the Indian manufacturing firms are still very far from world-class practices (Dangayach and Deshmukh, 2003). Global competitors have kept pace with new technology and are improving manufacturing, bringing in new products and making manufacturing more proactive and responsive (Chandra Pankaj, 1998). As a result, Indian industry is facing competition from imports and from multinational companies in the domestic markets. The technology revolution is forcing markets to raise productivity and lower the product cost. India is facing big challenges from low-cost manufacturing hubs, especially China. Therefore, there are challenges to be faced, and necessary changes in policies are required to raise the competitiveness of the Indian manufacturing sector.

A major motivation for focusing on the manufacturing sector is because of strategic problems, a big challenge after liberalization and globalization. The manufacturing sector is growing at a fast rate globally; hence, the demand for technological goods is also created in the country, which is mostly fed by imports. This wipes out the foreign currency in the country. Therefore, India has to stand on its own not only to cater to the domestic demand, but also to build the technological capabilities for export and raise its share in the global market. Government must focus on policy interventions for stimulating growth of the manufacturing sector or industries. The sector needs policy interventions in order to stimulate growth of the sector.

The links between the competitiveness and challenges of the manufacturing sector are poorly understood. This creates a need for the study of the effects of policy on the competitiveness of the manufacturing sector. China was chosen for comparison for this study because the process of liberalization was started in the same decade, therefore the manufacturing sector was in focus on account of policies and other variables.

The definition of competitiveness is wide and can be interpreted in various dimensions (Boltho, 1996). Authors have defined competitiveness in various aspects, for instance on the economic environment of a country, the low cost of production in the country, the exchange rate of currency, the technological level, and so on. Fagerberg (1996), in his argument, said that several definitions of competitiveness appeared because the concept of competitiveness was invented by practitioners rather than theoreticians. In this chapter, the focus is mainly on the competitiveness of manufacturing sectors in light of the industrial policies required for a smart economy.

Now the question is how do we measure the manufacturing sector's competitiveness? The issues considered in this study are the indicator (method) and data collection with respect to the indicators. Various indicators or methods are commonly applied in previous studies. Some of those indicators are based on economic indicators such as manufacturing share in gross domestic product (GDP), GDP growth rate, and so on; each of these has its own merits and demerits.

6.2 Industrial Policies in India

Policies are the documents that refer to plans, positions, and guidelines of government, which influence decisions by government (Manitoba, 2003), and are formed in order to provide a direction to obtain an end (Thakur et al., 2012). There are various types of policies that government frames, particularly for the economy, a specific sector, or for issues such as land, labor, and so on. These policies are directed toward industrial development (Lall and Wangwea, 1998). Industrial policies are framed to give direction for economic growth through industrialization (Thakur et al., 2012). After independence, India followed the path of social pattern and self-reliance, and the first policy came in 1948 (Government of India, 1956, 1991, 2011). By 1980, industrial policies had witnessed a gradual loosening of control, and a need for importing technology and foreign capital for structural support to the manufacturing sector was felt (Nagaraj, 2003). Further, Nagaraj concluded that the industrial sector suffers from a lack of investment, and not a lack of supply, constrained by policy.

Globally, over the last two to three decades, economies have become increasingly liberalized and globalized on various aspects. Trade has become more open, and information technologies have played a vital role in easing financial transactions, making capital accounts less restricted. The trend toward less regulated markets has been observed in all regions and in most countries. Mitra and Ural (2007) have investigated the determinants in Indian manufacturing. They also suggested that trade liberalization benefits mostly the export-oriented industries located in flexible labor market institutions. The contribution of Indian trade in world trade is 1.8%, which is significantly lower than other nations. In India, the low technology sector dominates in trade liberalization, while the high technology sectors are import dependent; however, in the case of medicinal and pharmaceutical product development, India has adopted advanced technologies (Alessandrini et al., 2007).

If productivity growth declines or stagnates due to lack of competitiveness, then policies should address this issue, and if the lack of competitiveness is attributable to the "policy environment," then the government should adjust its policies (Kalirajan and Bhide, 2005). Post 1991, industrial policy brought radical changes, from inward looking to outward looking, with an open economy development strategy. The reforms were simultaneously undertaken for hardware manufacturing in terms of excise duty, tariff policy, export/import policy, technology parks, manufacturing clusters, the development of the semiconductor industry (R&D), investment, labor laws, patenting, and so on (Majumdar, 2010). The industrial policies that have raised the competitiveness of the manufacturing firms have significantly increased (Siggel and Agrawal, 2009; Siggel, 2007). Increased exports, expansion by unit cost decline, productivity growth, and an increase in its employment base were seen. Growth was achieved through important policy changes. The policy changes were seen in the liberalization of foreign trade, a reduction in industrial licensing, and opening to foreign direct investments. This has created a unique opportunity for industries in the manufacturing sector in India not only to feed the domestic market but also to increase exports.

In order to give a pictorial representation, a policy time line is drawn to compare the government policies of India and China. Reforms were introduced in both countries at the same time, but China opened up its economy to the external world as per its strategic needs, whereas India opened up in an incremental manner, very slowly. The policy time line is shown in Figures 6.1 and 6.2 for India and China, respectively.

6.3 Manufacturing Sector: Comparison of India and China

India and China have emerged as economic powerhouses. The service sector in India accounts for 56.9% of its GDP, whereas in China the industrial sector accounts for around 45.3%. The details are illustrated in Table 6.1. China acted more willingly to the world economy, reducing its trade barriers and attracting foreign direct investment (FDI) inflow, whereas in India, service-producing industries were fueled (Bosworth and Collins, 2008). The Indian industrial sector could not reach 30%, whereas in China the industrial sector accounted for half of its GDP. To some extent, the success of China's open-door policy and economic reforms increased pressures for economic reforms in India (Park, 2002).

Productivity performance in China has increased sustainably because of owner restructuring and labor reforms, and this has resulted in the increasing efficiency of enterprises, whereas in India, governments still hold substantial equity in public sectors, and labor reforms are awaited (Pandey and Dong, 2009). China is already the world's biggest exporter of computers, telecom equipment, and other high-tech electronics, and is making rapid progress in infrastructure and technology. China will soon be an export powerhouse, but China faces challenges of a poor reputation for protecting intellectual property rights, which has prevented multinationals from transferring technology to China. India, on the other hand, has an innovation market that is running at high speed as a

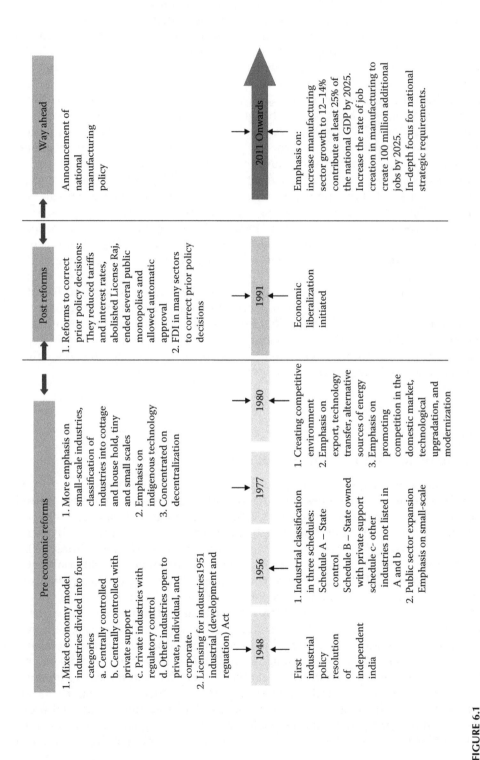

FIGURE 6.1
Policy time line of manufacturing in India. (From Khan A. R. Poverty in China in the period of globalisation: New evidence on trend and pattern, issues in development. Discussion Paper No. 22, Development Policies Department, ILO, Geneva, 1998; Annual reports 2008, 2009 and 2012, Dept. of Electronics and IT, Govt. of India, *Times of India* 5 Feb, 2014.)

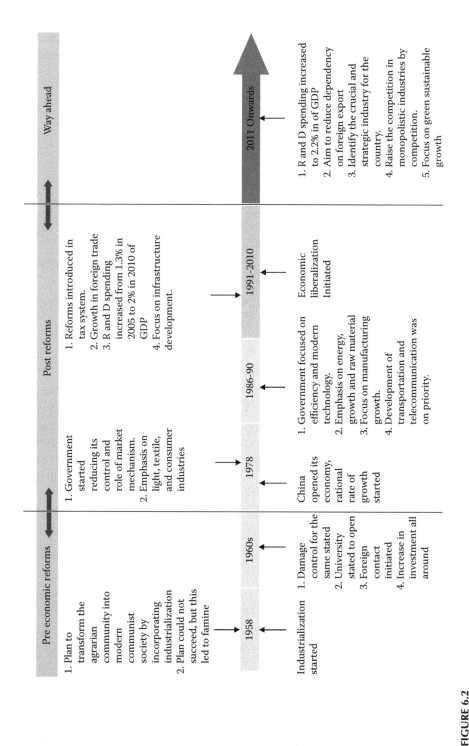

FIGURE 6.2
China's policy time line of economic reforms since independence. (From http://www.china-profile.com/history/hist_list_1.htm accessed on 20 July, 2015.)

TABLE 6.1

Share of Agriculture, Manufacturing, and Service Sectors in GDP

Country	Sectors	1980	1990	2000	2010	2012	2014
India	Agriculture	38.6	31.3	24.9	18.0	18.04	16.95
	Industry	24.2	27.6	26.9	27.6	31.93	30.05
	(Manufacturing)	16.3	17.2	15.8	14.9	17.87	17.03
	Services	27.2	41.1	48.2	54.4	50.03	52.98
China	Agriculture	30.1	27	15.9	10.1	9.52	9.16
	Industry	48.5	41.6	50.9	46.7	44.97	42.64
	(Manufacturing)	40.5	32.9	34.5	32.4	30.98	—
	Services	21.4	31.3	33.2	43.2	45.50	48.19

Source: World Bank Group. *World Development Indicators* 2012; World Bank Group. *World Development Reports* 2014 and 2015.

consequence of trends that favor domestic investment in high-value tasks. The positive trends are (Wadhwa, 2008) as follows:

1. An increase in education level, productivity, and quality of the workforce as a consequence of companies' investment in workforce education.
2. A decrease in attrition rates due to companies' internal promotion strategies (tied to the improvement in quality) that give incentives for workers to stay and add to their human capital.
3. An increase in global competitiveness due to the devaluation of the rupee.
4. Outsourcing to India due to changing business models in developed countries.
5. Recent US immigration policy, which has encouraged skilled workers to return or to stay in India.
6. The improvement in the quality and quantity of engineers. In 2004, India graduated only 125,000 bachelors in engineering; however, this number had doubled by 2007 and at present (2015) the enrolments of engineering graduates and post-graduates across India have jumped to 1,776,827, including premier institutions. Further, diploma courses increases this value to 3,095,886 enrolments.

6.4 Methodology Applied

The research methodology broadly comprised two phases. The first was an extensive literature review for extracting the indicators of manufacturing, and the second was the opinion of experts on the selected indicators. The expert team comprised seven individuals from diverse backgrounds: three from academic backgrounds, two senior government officials, and two experts from an industrial background. The factors identified from the literature were given to each expert individually. The opinion for each factor was taken from each expert separately in the first round. The result for each case was compiled. In the second round, all the experts were invited for discussion. Each factor was discussed in front of the experts and a consensus was reached on most of the factors. Two factors, electricity production and kilometers of railway lines, were dropped from the study because

TABLE 6.2

The Factors Chosen for the Study of Competitiveness of Manufacturing Sector

Factors	Description
GDP Podobnik et al. (2012); OECD, 2013	The GDP indicates a country's economic performance in a specific time period. It also calculates the relative contribution of an industry sector in the economic growth of a particular country.
GDP growth rate McCombie et al., 1994; Pelagidis, 2010	GDP growth rate indicates the changes in the economy of a country by comparing economic growth of one quarter to the last. It shows a positive rate when the economy is expanding and a negative rate when the economy is shrinking.
Manufacturing value added (% of GDP) Kogut, 1985; Jaffe et al., 1995	Manufacturing value added of an industry sector is the difference between an industry's gross output and the cost of all its inputs.
FDI Dunning, 2002; Urata and Lall, 2003; Xiaojuan, 2002	FDI is an investment in an industry sector by an investor from another country to access the markets and resources, to reduce production costs, and to build new facilities for the business.
Ease of doing business Schueth, 2011; Jayasuriya, 2011	This index has been created by the World Bank Group based on the study of laws and regulations to measure regulations directly affecting businesses. It includes different parameters such as starting a business, registering property, protecting investors, getting credits, paying taxes, trading across borders, and so on, which define the ease of doing business in a particular country.

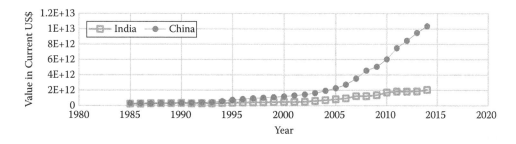

FIGURE 6.3
The GDP of India and China. (From World Bank data, 2015.)

a consensus was not reached. Finally, five factors were considered for the study. These factors are briefly described in Table 6.2, and are listed as follows:

- GDP
- GDP growth rate
- Manufacturing value added
- FDI
- Ease of doing business

Figure 6.3 shows the GDP of India and China, the data for which is collected from the World Bank. The GDP of China is more than 2.5 times that of India. This clearly indicates that China has focused on infrastructure building, better network connectivity, efficient transportation, and commercial spaces, especially for the manufacturing sector, to raise production and exports. Hence, higher GDP is recorded in the case of China (Figure 6.4).

GDP growth rate is another factor for the competitiveness of the manufacturing sector. Currently, India's economic growth rate is similar to that of China. This reflects that India can raise its GDP and match that of China if the focus is on the manufacturing sector.

The manufacturing value added in India is half that of China. This clearly shows that there is a huge gap for manufacturing value added. India announced its manufacturing policy in 2011, where the focus is on increasing the contribution of the manufacturing sector to 25% of GDP by the end of 2022. The position of the manufacturing value added is shown in Figure 6.5. At the same time, a country like India can benefit from FDI, whereas the contribution of FDI to GDP is low compared with that of China. In the case of India, FDI is mostly in the service sector, whereas for China it's in the manufacturing sector. Foreign investment and proactive manufacturing could increase business in the manufacturing sector.

Ease of doing business is also related to the competitiveness of the manufacturing sector, and at the same time FDI is also affected. The position of FDI is shown in Figure 6.6 for India and China. A country having a higher rank is more open to business and hence

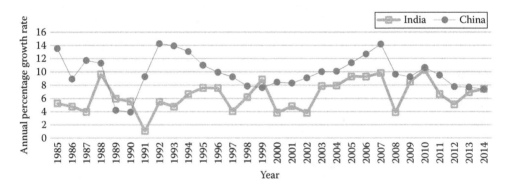

FIGURE 6.4
GDP growth rate of India and China. (From World Bank data, 2015.)

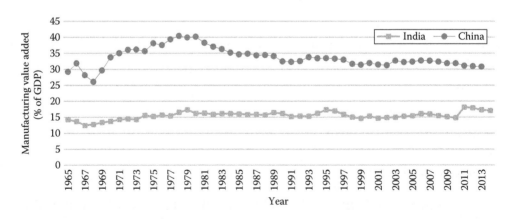

FIGURE 6.5
Comparison of manufacturing value added in terms of the percentage of GDP of India vs. China. (From World Bank data, 2015.)

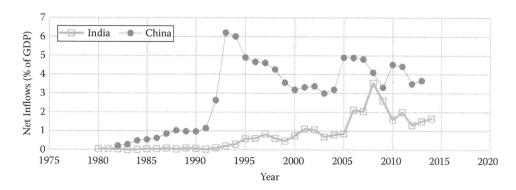

FIGURE 6.6
Comparison of FDI inflow in terms of the percentage of GDP of India vs. China. (From World Bank data, 2015.)

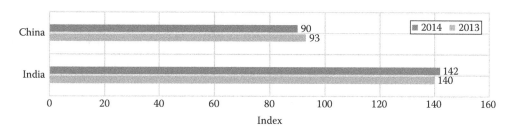

FIGURE 6.7
Comparison of FDI inflow in terms of the percentage of GDP of India vs. China. (From World Bank data, 2015.)

eases doing business. China is considered to be a more open business environment. Clear business policies could also increase the ease of doing business in a particular country. Figure 6.7 shows the rank of India and China in terms of ease of doing business. As per year 2014 data, China is at a higher rank, and is positioned at 90, while India is at 142. The position of India has deteriorated further from the previous year.

6.5 Conclusions

The notion of industrial policy triggers strong reactions, most likely because it is closely linked to the specific views of the government on the economy. It is believed that in open markets with limited government intervention, policies play an important role in the success of industries. In the case of India and China, the results demonstrate that China has outperformed in all five factors considered for study, that is, GDP, GDP growth rate, manufacturing value added (% of GDP), FDI, and ease of doing business. Simultaneously, advancement in speed and the magnitude of change over the past two decades have made China a powerhouse of manufacturing. Moreover, advanced fundamental infrastructure services such as broadband connectivity; clean, reliable, inexpensive energy; affordable housing and commercial space; efficient transportation; clear business policies; foreign investment; and proactive manufacturing may boost the overall business sentiment, and could increase industrial output and exports to develop a smart and sustainable economy for a country.

References

Alessandrini, M., Fattouh, B., and Scaramozzino, P. 2007. The changing pattern of foreign trade specialization in Indian manufacturing. *Oxford Review of Economic Policy*, 23(2), 270–291.

Boltho, A. 1996. The assessment: International competitiveness. *Oxford Review of Economic Policy*, 12(3), 1–16.

Bosworth, B., and Collins, S. M. 2008. Accounting for growth: Comparing China and India. *Journal of Economic Perspectives*, 22(1), 45–66.

Chandra Pankaj, T. S. 1998. Competitiveness of Indian manufacturing. *Vikalpa*, 23(3), 25–36.

Dangayach, G. S., and Deshmukh, S. G. 2003. Evidence of manufacturing strategies in Indian industry: A survey. *International Journal of Production Economics*, 83, 279–298.

Dunning, J. H. 2002. *Global Capitalism, FDI and Competitiveness. Vol. 2*. Cheltenham, UK: Edward Elgar.

Fagerberg, J. 1996. Technology and competitiveness. *Oxford Review of Economic Policy*, 12(3), 39–51.

Government of India. 1956. Industrial policy resolution, Ministry of Industry, April 30.

Government of India. 1991. National manufacturing policy. Ministry of Commerce and Industry, New Delhi, October 25.

Government of India. 1991. Statement on industrial policy, Ministry of Industry, New Delhi, July 24.

Jaffe, A. B., Peterson, S. R., Portney, P. R., and Stavins, R. N. 1995. Environmental regulation and the competitiveness of US manufacturing: What does the evidence tell us? *Journal of Economic Literature* 33(1), 132–163.

Jayasuriya, D. 2011. Improvements in the World Bank's ease of doing business rankings: Do they translate into greater foreign direct investment inflows? World Bank Policy Research Paper 5787.

Kalirajan, K., and Bhide, S. 2005. The post-reform performance of the manufacturing sector in India. *Asian Economic Papers* 3(2), 126–157.

Khan, A. R. 1998. Poverty in China in the period of globalisation: New evidence on trend and pattern. Issues in Development Discussion Paper No. 22. Development Policies Department, ILO, Geneva.

Kogut, B. 1985. Designing global strategies: Comparative and competitive value added chains. *Sloan Management Review*, 26, 4.

Lall, S., and Wangwea, S. 1998. Industrial policy and industrialisation in sub-Saharan Africa. *Journal of African Economies*, 70(1 Supplement), 70–107.

Majumdar, R. 2010. Did liberalization impact productivity of the Indian electronics hardware Industry? *International Journal of Economics of Business*, 17(2), 253–273.

Manitoba. 2003. A guide to policy development. Office of the Auditor General, Manitoba.

McCombie, J. S. L., Thirlwall, A. P., and Thompson, P. 1994. *Economic Growth and the Balance-of-Payments Constraint*. New York: St. Martin's Press.

Mitra, D., and Ural, B. P. 2007. Indian manufacturing: A slow sector in a rapidly growing economy. World Bank Policy Research Paper, 4233.

Nagaraj, R. 2003. Industrial policy and performance since 1980: Which way now? *Economic and Political Weekly*, 38(35), 3707–3715.

OECD. 2013. Economic outlook, Vol. 2013, Issue 1, OECD Publishing.

Pandey, M., and Dong, X. 2009. Manufacturing productivity in China and India: The role of institutional changes. *China Economic Review*, 20(4), 754–766.

Park, J. H. 2002. The two giants of Asia: Trade and development in China and India. *Journal of Developing Societies*, *18*(1), 64 –81.

Pelagidis, T. 2010. *The Greek Paradox of Falling Competitiveness and Weak Institutions in a High GDP Growth Rate Context (1995–2008)*. GreeSE Paper No 38, The Hellenic Observatory: The European Institute, Hellenic Observatory Papers on Greece and Southeast Europe.

Podobnik, B., et al. 2012. The competitiveness versus the wealth of a country. *Scientific Reports*, *2*, Article number: 678.

Schueth, S. 2011. Assembling international competitiveness: The Republic of Georgia, USAID, and the Doing Business project. *Economic Geography*, *87*(1), 51–77.

Siggel, E. 2007. Economic reforms and their impact on the manufacturing sector: Lessons from the India. Asia-Pacific Journal of Rural Development, *14*(1), 73–104.

Siggel, E., and Agrawal, P. 2009. The impact of economic reforms on indian manufacturers: evidence from a small sample survey. Working Paper Series No. E/300/2009, IEG, Retrieved September 3, 2015, http://saber.eaber.org/node/22930.

Thakur, B., Gupta, R., and Singh, R. 2012. Changing face of India's industrial policies: A look. *International Journal of Scientific and Research Publication*, *2*(12), 1–7.

Urata, S., and Lall, S., eds. 2003. *Competitiveness, FDI and Technological Activity in East Asia*. Cheltenham, UK: Edward Elgar.

Wadhwa, V. 2008. America's other immigration crises. Retrieved September 3, 2015, from The American: http://www.fosterglobal.com/policy_papers/AmericasOtherImmigrationCrisis.pdf

World Bank Group. 2012. World Development Indicators 2012. World Bank Publications.

World Bank Group. 2014. World Development Report 2014. World Bank Publications.

World Bank Group. 2015. World Development Report 2015. World Bank Publications.

Xiaojuan, J. 2002. Contributions of foreign invested enterprises in China to local economic growth, structural upgrading and competitiveness. *Social Sciences in China*, *6*, 4–14.

7

Concept of Smart Village in India:
A Proposed Ecosystem and Framework

Sheshadri Chatterjee and Arpan Kumar Kar

CONTENTS

7.1 Introduction...83
7.2 Literature Review..84
7.3 Definition of Smart Village...85
    7.3.1 Broad, General Definition...85
    7.3.2 Definition Driven by Data and Its Usage 85
    7.3.3 Definition Focusing Citizens..86
7.4 Ecosystem of a Smart Village...86
7.5 Issues and Challenges of Smart Villages in India................................86
    7.5.1 Budget Constraints 87
    7.5.2 Smart Technology 87
    7.5.3 Lack of Knowledge 87
7.6 Different Managements 88
    7.6.1 Energy Management 88
7.7 Designing a Smart Village...88
    7.7.1 Investment Scenario 88
    7.7.2 Growth Strategies 89
7.8 Governance Model of Smart Villages 89
7.9 Technique to Measure Smart Village Performance 89
7.10 Conclusion 90
References 91

7.1 Introduction

The central government of India and different state governments currently spend huge amounts of resources and put great effort into improving the infrastructure of rural areas. Improving the quality of the water supply and providing sanitation facilities for every village are a prime focus of the government. The government is desperately trying to uplift the socioeconomic scenarios of rural India in an attempt to reach out to the poorer and more economically backward section of people. There are various means through which the government is trying to achieve its goal to improve the socioeconomic status of people, such as providing subsidies of various kinds, waivers of loans, ensuring quota to marginal and economically backward people, and using several other schemes to reach rural people.

Most of these efforts by the government are fragmented, however. There is little integration, and as a result there has been little socioeconomic improvement for the rural population of India. Every village has a great number of human resources that if efficiently used can prove a huge benefit. These resources can be self-sufficient and sustainable. There are more than 700 million people in India living in rural areas, especially in villages and remote areas, and the interesting fact is that about half of them (around 350 million) are younger than 25, and could potentially be used as a skilled human resource pool of the nation if these people were properly trained. This could place India way ahead of other developing and developed countries. To achieve this success, the government should focus on (1) quality education and the training requirement of these young people; (2) improving the social infrastructure, such as improving health-care facilities, housing for all, rural roads, building schools, colleges, and so on; and (3) job creation (facilitating the establishment of new micro, small, and medium enterprises). It should also be mentioned that vocational training is as important as conventional training.

Currently, there is no integrated approach by the government to design an ideal village and formulate a policy to efficiently operate that village. The various services provided to these villages are most likely on an ad hoc basis, and there is no integrated approach. As a result, most of these projects are not finished properly, and are not maintained in a proper manner. Although there are some recent initiatives by the government, such as e-kiosks, e-payments, Internet facility to some of the villages, e-panchayats, and so on, these are not properly designed, nor integrated with the broader ecosystem of these villages. Hence, it is essential to design an ecosystem for the village with facilities such as round-the-clock electricity, good-quality drinking water, a basic health-care system, and employment opportunities, with micro and small-scale enterprises established in the villages. There is therefore a huge need today to rethink the design policy of villages, and thus the need for smart villages in India.

The main requirements for these smart villages are to have wireless connection, to have the latest technologies, and to have policies to encourage young people in these smart villages to engage in entrepreneurial activities backed by the government and other private agencies or venture capitalists, so that these smart villages can achieve self-sustainability within a shorter time frame. Therefore, the main objective of this chapter is to discuss how to achieve the overall development of these smart villages so that they can eventually become self-sufficient and sustainable.

7.2 Literature Review

Through background studies, it is observed that not many effective, substantial, and pragmatic works have so far been done on smart villages, and any work done involves smart cities. However, studying the literature on smart cities would surely help one develop the concept of smart villages, and therefore some literature review on this subject has become necessary. Modern cities will drive economic growth in terms of consumption as well as production, and in the resources domain as well (Black and Henderson, 2003; Duranton, 2007; Pumain and Moriconi-Ebrard, 1997). Here, it is to be mentioned that urbanization does not only mean the conversion of rural areas to urban areas; it also means agglomeration of the urban population (Nijkamp, 2010). Future cities should strive to become a force field as per the opinion of Dematties (1998).

The formative work by Friedman (1986) on the development of new world cities has prompted many researchers to focus on urbanization (Beaverstock et al., 1999; Knox and McCarthy, 2005; Kourtit et al., 2011; McCann, 2008; Sassen, 2006). The important role of converting developed and modern cities into "smart cities" includes competition that is metropolitan in nature and varieties among products (Abdel and Fujita, 1990; Becker and Henderson, 2003; Duranton and Puga, 2000; Glaeser et al., 1992; Quigley, 1998). Citizens of developed cities are keeping digital records for permanent preservation and for protecting privacy (Gutwirth, 2002). Here it is expected that most of the smart cities and villages will use new technologies for the first time (Technology Strategy Board; London, 2011–2013). To create new technologies that are usable by the masses requires new financial models and a supportive modern ecosystem (Sissons and Thompson, 2012). The market power of the social economy has generated a great opportunity for developing new kinds of entrepreneurial activities for local, all-round development that helps to create profit in an out of box manner (i.e., a new approach which is not traditional and is creative in nature) (Nee, 1989; Naughton, 1995; Walder, 1995; Linn, 1997). To get the best results, it is to be noted that there is a need in India for different information and communication technology (ICT) to be used, but very few papers have been published so far (Dendaal, 2003).

7.3 Definition of Smart Village

From in-depth study, it appears that there are many definitions of smart cities in different contexts, but a universal definition of smart village is not apparent. However, from studies of definitions of smart cities, we can safely come to a definition of smart village. Hence, there is a necessity for discussions on definitions of smart cities.

7.3.1 Broad, General Definition

The UK's Department of Business, Innovation, and Skills (BIS) has defined "smart cities" (Smart Cities Background Paper; London, 2013) as follows: "It does not consider 'Smart Cities' as a static outcome but on the contrary considers it as a continuous process of improvement by the help of involvement of citizens, use of hard infrastructure, use of modern technologies which would ultimately make the cities livable, resilient and capable of combating challenges." There is another definition, by British Standard Institute (BSI), of "smart cities" as (smart cities Framework; British Standard Institute, 2014): "The effective integration of physical, digital and human systems in the built environment to deliver sustainable prosperous and inclusive future for its citizens."

7.3.2 Definition Driven by Data and Its Usage

The global technology giant IBM has defined "smart cities" as "one that makes optimal use of all the interconnected information available today to better understand and control its operations and optimized the use of limited resources" (Cosgerove et al., 2011). Also, CISCO has given the definition of "smart city" as "scalable solutions that take advantage of ICT to increase efficiencies, reduce costs, and enhance quality of life" (Falconer and Mitcheli, 2012).

7.3.3 Definition Focusing Citizens

The Manchester Digital Development Agency (MDDA) has defined "smart city" as follows: "smart city means smart citizens—where the citizens have all the information they need to make informed choices about their lifestyle work and travel options." From the studies of the foregoing definitions of smart cities, we arrive at a definition of smart village as a village that provides its people or residents with a bundle of services, that is business friendly, acts as an enabler to entrepreneurs, and delivers all the required services to its residents and people in the most effective way. Services provided by smart villages include health care, retail, financial inclusion, clean water, irrigation and farming, logistics, construction, and a round-the-clock power supply, which includes renewable energy as well.

7.4 Ecosystem of a Smart Village

The definition of a smart village ecosystem can be given as an ecosystem consisting of a network of micro, small, and medium enterprises (MSME), farmers, local and central government employees, nongovernmental organizations (NGOs), private small industrial units, logistics, technologies, and ICT services. It also acts as an enabler and helps to connect the residents of the village with the external environment and certain resources, such as financial resources; natural resources; semiskilled, unskilled, and skilled human resources; and an industrial environment that interacts with each other to provide better services for a smart village. In the smart village ecosystem there are four broader focus areas. The first is digital services, which includes services such as smart transportation, various ICT services, e-books, smart education, various online services to residents of the smart villages, and better energy efficiency. The second focus area of the smart village ecosystem is the institutions or establishments that comprise village panchayats, various levels of schools, village committees, smart information centers, and so on. The third focus area is the resources that include land, energy, financial resources, human resources (unskilled, semiskilled, and skilled human resources), health-care facilities and medical resources (medicine shops, doctors, paramedical facilities, etc.), water harvesting, and so on. The fourth and final focus area of these smart villages is sustenance, which comprises renewal and clean energy, self-sustainable irrigation, attractive investment destination, land mapping, and efficient agricultural land utilization. The whole ecosystem of a smart village is shown in Figure 7.1 (Viswanadham and Vedula, 2010).

7.5 Issues and Challenges of Smart Villages in India

There is a huge requirement for smart technology to be used in these smart villages. There is a need of proper financial resources and a market to create these smart technologies. But as of now there are a lot of constraints to get the ecosystem ready for financial resources as well as for proper marketization.

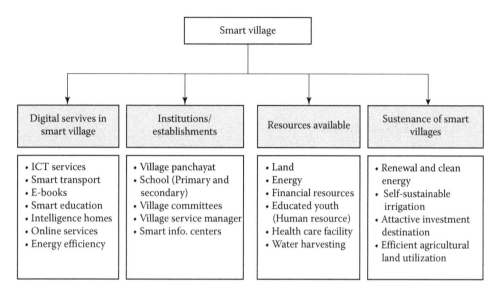

FIGURE 7.1
Ecosystem of a smart village.

7.5.1 Budget Constraints

There is a huge issue of budget constraints, which essentially has limited innovative think-ing and created obstacles for many other initiatives. The budget constraints have created many hindrances for a lot of smart initiatives that if properly nurtured could be more cost-effective and efficient (UK Government Press, 2013).

7.5.2 Smart Technology

It is considered that smart technology for these smart villages is still in the precommer-cial or in some cases the conceptual stage. And since the technology is in the pre-mature or conceptual stage, it generates uncertainties regarding return on investment as far as financial parameters are concerned. This also results in apprehension of a long payback period, and investors are unwilling to invest, which contributes to financial uncertainties for smart technology initiatives (Hirst et al., 2012).

7.5.3 Lack of Knowledge

The other challenges related to smart village initiatives in India is the lack of knowl-edge of the people using modern technology. The citizens' experience of these smart technology initiatives has largely not been good for several reasons, one of which is due to the paucity of knowledge of the common people as to how to use modern digital technologies, Internet and other modern technology, and also the fact that there are very few people, especially in rural areas of India, as with other parts of the developing world, who know how to efficiently use and apply modern digital technologies, such as "smart meters" (Bracknell Forest Homes). There are other constraints that, though not so vital, also deserve mention, such as lack of technology-related skills, constraints on integration, and limited understanding and influence over the basic available services.

Issues such as data privacy and security and political interferences also do not help to overcome the issue.

7.6 Different Managements

Many practical issues need to be ensured in the formation of smart villages, such as health hazard management, mobility in villages, water supply, sanitation, solid waste management, electricity, Internet facility, and so on. Most important is the need to manage proper use of energy, as without energy management it is very difficult to survive.

7.6.1 Energy Management

Efficient use of energy in the smart village is one of the parameters of the main focus areas of a smart village ecosystem. And for the efficient use of energy, smart energy meters could be used in these smart villages. These meters help in areas such as managing energy demand, reducing overall costs, and helping to decrease pollution, resulting in less environmental damage. To make it happen, the use of information technology is essential, and the focus needs to be on the "smart grid" (www.smartgrid.org.kr/eng). This also includes monitoring of the electrical system (Amin and Wollenberg, 2005; Amin, 2000; Kai et al., 2008). Apart from monitoring, this helps save energy and preserve data, and usage can be measured (www.google.com/powermeter/about/about.html). The system also helps to control the power source in a most efficient way, which is interactive in nature (Cai et al., 2009; Motegi et al., 2003). To be more effective, the entire energy management ecosystem needs to be fully integrated, and the involvement of different stakeholders, such as energy managers, energy suppliers, consumers, and village residents, and more importantly policy makers, is essential (Odum, 1976). Also, in this connection, it should be mentioned that the village residents should be made aware of the importance and significance of the usage of clean energy, such as renewable energy.

7.7 Designing a Smart Village

There are a few critical parameters that need to be kept in mind when designing a smart village. The two important decision methodologies that need to be focused on are (1) the scenario of investment with reference to the climate of smart villages and (2) strategies for the growth of these smart villages. In the following sections, both of these focus areas are discussed.

7.7.1 Investment Scenario

This is the scenario with reference to the investment climate of the smart village. The investment climate of a smart village will depend on many parameters, such as policy formulation, institutional and behavioral environment, legal environment, external and internal environment, which influence the risks and returns closely associated with investment.

7.7.2 Growth Strategies

The growth strategies of the village include quality services such as a reliable power supply, clean water, better sanitation facilities, and a few essential services such as health care, transportation, better infrastructure resulting in seamless connectivity, and so on, to be the core of the primary strategy for the development of these smart villages. Also, it should be mentioned that the formulation of the growth strategy of these smart villages should include sustainability; self-sufficiency; a business-friendly ecosystem, especially for the MSME sectors, for entrepreneurs to be nurtured properly; mandatory vocational training should be provided for all the residents of these smart villages who cannot afford to go to traditional schooling systems; and government employees should be properly trained to make the policies implementable at the ground level. Once the strategies are formulated and the methodologies are designed for a smart village, the logical next step is to put these strategies and methodologies into action by using an appropriate and effective governance framework.

7.8 Governance Model of Smart Villages

The president and his or her team govern the village panchayat, which is the village-level administrative head. They are elected individuals and come from a political background, but it is observed mostly that their capabilities are far below the level expected for running village administration, and hence also for the developmental activities of villages. Village governance is, as such, required to be controlled by a group including the panchayat officials. Retail business, water supply, and power and energy management should be controlled at the district level for a group of villages.

Regarding farming, primary education, and health care, local attention is needed. Here, Sarbya Siksha Mission (SSM) plays a very prominent role. Knowledge-based technologies required for growing the smartness of the villages should come from people with entrepreneurial skill and talent. Hence, it is imperative that to develop the smart village, talent is required to be imported not only from the district level but even beyond. This issue requires proper attention. The collaborative model scheme that is being discussed consists of different factors, such as industries, funding, development of new businesses, government role, local panchayat's role, and so on. The complete governance hierarchical model of a smart village is shown in Figure 7.2 (Viswanadham and Vedula, 2010).

7.9 Technique to Measure Smart Village Performance

Now that the services in smart villages are developed, they need to be assessed by measuring their performance. This includes measurement of individual services and the performance of the village as a whole. There must be standard parameters for success in reference to timeliness response and remedy of complaints, satisfaction to users, accessibility, and so on, and the performance on different parameters are compared with those

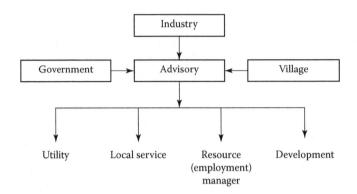

FIGURE 7.2
Governance hierarchical model of a smart village.

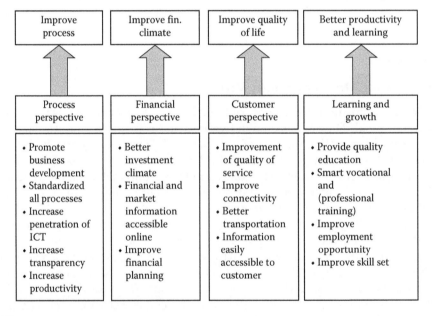

FIGURE 7.3
Performance measurement scorecard.

standards to measure the exact extent of success. A balanced scorecard approach is shown in Figure 7.3 (Kaplan, Marvin Bower). This model should be of great help.

7.10 Conclusion

Smart villages are needed for the welfare of rural people. Technologies are available to make a village smart but due to lack of appropriate strategies, lack of proper, integrated, implementable planning, lack of congenial monitoring, and above all lack of significant execution of activities, there has been failure. However, a framework comprising various factors, such as technological factors, social factors, legal and governance factors, and their measurements could be used for designing and developing smart villages in India. An ecosystem should be developed for these smart villages, focusing attention on its location as well as the investment opportunity. Here it is also suggested that in order to develop smart villages, the public–private partnership (PPP) model could be of great help. It would be compulsory for the companies taking part in the PPP model to develop these smart villages. It is expected that these concepts and recommendations can be applied in developing smart towns and semi-urban areas to develop smaller towns near the big cities of India. However, it should be kept in mind that the mere development of these smart villages may not suffice the purpose of betterment of living standards, but attention is to be focused holistically on the sustainability of these smart villages.

References

Abdel-Rahaman, M. and M. Fujita. 1990. Product variety, Marshallian externalities, and city sizes. *Journal of Regional Science*. 30, no. 2: 165–181.

Amin, M. 2000. National infrastructures as complex interactive network. In T. Samad and J. Weyrauch (Eds.). *Automation, Control, and Complexity: An Integrated Approach*, pp. 263–286. New York: Wiley.

Amin, M. and B. Wollenberg. 2005. Toward a smart grid: Power delivery for the 21st century. *IEEE Power and Energy Magazine*. 3, no. 5: 34–41.

Beaverstock, J. V., R. G. Smith, and P. J. Taylor. 1999. A roster of world cities. *Cities*. 16, no. 6: 445–448.

Becker, R. and J. V. Henderson. 2003. Intra-industry specialization and urban development. In J. M. Huriot and J. F. Thisse (Eds.). *Economics of Cities*, pp. 138–165. Cambridge: Cambridge University Press.

Black, D. and J. V. Henderson. 2003. Urban evaluation in the U.S. *Journal of Economic Geography*. 3, no. 4: 343–372.

British Standard Institute. 2014. *Smart Cities Framework: Guide to Establishing Strategies for Smart Cities and Communities PAS 181*. London: British Standard Institute.

Cai, Y. et al. 2009. An optimization model-based interactive decision support system for regional energy management systems planning and uncertainty. *Expert Systems with Applications*. 36, no. 2: 3470–3482.

Cosgerove, V. et al. 2011. Smart Cities: Introducing the IBM city operations and management solutions IBM.

Dematteis, G. 1998. The weak metropolis. In L. Mazza (Eds.). *World Cities and the Future of Metropolis*. pp. 121 –133.

Dendaal, N. O. 2003. Information and communication technology and local governance: Understanding the difference between cities in developed and emerging economies. *Computer, Environment and Urban Systems*. 27, no. 6: 585–607. Cisco IBSG © 2012.

Duranton, G. 2007. Urban evaluations: The fast, the slow, and the still. *American Economic Review*. 97, no. 1: 197–221.

Duranton, G. and D. Puga. 2000. Diversity and specialization in cities: Why, where and when does it matter? *Urban Studies*. 37, no. 3: 533–555.

Falconer, G. and S. Mitcheli. 2012. Smart City Framework: A systematic process for enabling smart connected communities. Cisco IBSG © 2012.

Friedman, J. 1986. The world city hypothesis. *Development and Change*. 17: 69–83.

Glaeser, E., H. Kallal, J. A. Scheinkman, and A. Shleifar. 1992. Growth in cities. *Journal of Political Economy*. 100, no. 6: 1126–1152.

Gutwirth, S. 2002. *Privacy and the Information Age*. Lanham, MD: Rowman and Littlefield.

Hirst, P. et al. 2012. Jessica for Smart and Sustainable Cities: Horizontal Study. Report published by European Investment Bank. no. 31.

Kai, X., L. Young- qi, Z. Zhi-zhong, and Y. ER-Keng. 2008. The vision of future smart grid. *Electric Power*. 06.

Kaplan, R. S. and Marvin Bower. Balanced score card: Insight, experience and ideas for strategy focused organizations report (The Balanced Scorecard for Public-Sector Organizations), Harvard Business School Publishing, Article Reprint No. B9911C.

Knox, P. L. and L. McCarthy. 2005. *Urbanization: An Introduction to Urban Geography*. Englewood Cliffs, NJ: Prentice Hall.

Kourtit, K., P. Nejkamp, S. Lowik, F. A. Van Vught, and P. Vulto. 2011. From Island of innovation to creative hotspots. *Regional Science Policy and Practice*. 3, no. 3: 145–161.

Linn, G. C. S. 1997. *Red Capitalism in South China*. Vancouver: University of British Columbia Press.

McCann, P. 2008. Globalization and economic geography: The world is curved not flat. *Cambridge Journal of Regions, Economy and Society*. 1, no. 3: 351–370.

Piette, M. et al. 2003. *Web Based Energy Information System for Energy Management and Demand Response in Commercial Building*. Lawrence Berkeley National Laboratory.

Naughton, B. 1995. *Growing Out of the Plan*. Cambridge: Cambridge University Press.

Nee, V. 1989. A theory of market transition: From redistribution to markets in state socialism. *American Sociological Review*. 54: 663–681.

Nijkamp, P. 2010. Megacities: Lands of hope and glory. In S. Buys, W. Tan, and D. Tunes (Eds.). *Megacities: Exploring a Sustainable Future*, pp. 100–111. Rotterdam: Old Publishers.

Odum, E. 1976. Energy eco-system development and environmental risk. *Journal of Risk and Insurance*. 43, no. 1: 1–16.

Pumain, D. and F. Moriconi-Ebrard. 1997. City size distribution and metropolisation. *Geo Journal*. 43, no. 4: 307–314.

Quigley, J. M. 1998. Urban diversity and economic growth. *Journal of Economic Perspective*. 12, no. 2: 127–138.

Sassen, S. 2006. *A Sociology of Globalization*. New York: N.W. Norton.

Sissons, A. and S. Thompson. 2012. *Market Making, a Modern Approach to Industrial Policy*. London: Big Innovation Center.

Smart Cities Background Paper. 2013. Department of Business Innovation and Skills. BIS Research Paper No. 135, International Case Studies on Smart Cities, October, London.

Technology Strategy Board, Emergency Technologies and Industries, Strategy. 2011–2013. London, UK.

UK Government Press. 2013. Guidance: Broadband delivery UK. Department for Culture, Media and Sport. 27 February. Accessed January 2015.

Viswanadham, N. and S. Vedula. 2010. *Design of Smart Villages*. Hyderabad, India: ISB.

Walder, A. 1995. China's transitional economy: Interpreting its significance. *China Quarterly*. 144: 963 –979.

www.smartgrid.org.kr-eng. Accessed Jan, 2014.

www.google.com/power meter/about/about.html. Accessed Jan 2015.

8

Smart City: An Integrated Approach Using System Dynamics

Alok Raj and Gourav Dwivedi

CONTENTS

8.1 Introduction...93
8.2 Literature Review...94
8.3 Methodology 96
    8.3.1 Causal Loop Diagram 96
    8.3.2 Stock and Flow Diagram 97
    8.3.3 Assumptions...99
8.4 Results and Analysis 99
8.5 Recommendations and Conclusions... 102
8.6 Limitations and Scope of Future Work... 102
References... 103

8.1 Introduction

Cities are drivers of growth for any country, and especially for a developing country like India. More than 50% of the world's population lives in cities, and this will increase to 66% by 2050 (World Bank, 2015). In the Indian context, 31% of the current population lives in urban areas, and contributes 63% of India's gross domestic product (GDP) (Census, 2011). This data is estimated to increase to 40% of India's population and 75% of India's GDP by 2030. India's annual population growth is 1.2% (World Bank, 2015). Due to the increase in the overall population, more people will migrate to the cities. According to one study, 25–30 people migrate from a rural area to an urban area in search of jobs and better lifestyles per day, and the urban population will reach nearly 843 million by 2050 (SM Conference, 2015). This increase in population requires comprehensive development of the city in terms of physical, social, and economic infrastructure. These terms are important pillars to improve the quality of life and the creation of jobs in the city. At the same time, these developments will negatively affect the environment in terms of pollution, and society in terms of traffic congestion due to the large number of vehicle ownership. This puts pressure on policy makers to develop a sustainable city. The smart city concept is one of the stepping stones in this direction.

The Indian government recently launched a smart city mission to develop 100 smart cities by 2024. This is the real challenge for policy makers and all the stakeholders involved in this smart transformation. Despite the attractiveness of smart cities, there is still fuzziness in the definition and dimensions of the smart city, so it is difficult to quantify the impact of the dimensions on the smart city. Nevertheless, the International Organization for

Standardization (ISO) developed an ISO 37120 in 2014 to measure city services and quality of life. In India, the Indian School of Business (ISB, 2015) also developed a smart city index to measure smartness. All these indexes will measure the smartness at a static level but due to the complexity of the smart city, it's difficult to capture the real scenario. System dynamics (SD) is one of the best tools to capture these nonlinear behavior-type scenarios (Forrester, 1997). The aim of this chapter is to analyze the impact of various dimensions on smartness and to assist policy makers in planning for smart cities.

This chapter addresses the complex structure of the smart city in an attempt to answer the following research questions:

1. How can a smart city be modeled in order to support decision makers in appropriate planning?
2. What is the structure of smart mobility with the application of an SD technique?

The remainder of the chapter is organized as follows: a literature review, followed by methodology, causal loop diagram (CLD), stock and flow diagram (CFD), assumption, results and analysis, recommendations and conclusions, limitations, and finally scope of future work.

8.2 Literature Review

The smart city concept evolved in 1998 (Van Bastelaer, 1998). During this period, the main aim was to implement information and communication technologies (ICT) in the city. Subsequently, many researchers defined the smart city in different ways. Its implementation and definitions are mainly based on a local and contextual basis. The concept and implementation strategies of the smart city vary from city to city; for example, the development of a smart city in Bihar will be different from Delhi, based on geographical location, resources, and the desires of the city residents, the level of development, and the willingness to accept transformation and reforms. There is no standard definition available in the literature of the smart city (Nam and Pardo, 2011; Neirotti et al., 2014; Caragliu et al., 2011; Hollands, 2008; Angelidou, 2015). Even "smart" is defined in different ways, such as digital or intelligent (Nam and Pardo, 2011). A smart city is an intensively technology-based city (Harrison and Donnelly, 2011; Caragliu et al., 2011), where information flows between every subsystem (Nam and Pardo, 2011), and that integrates the physical infrastructure with the human system (Harrison et al., 2010) to optimize resource usage. It is also classified as a hard and soft domain (Neirotti et al., 2014). The hard domain contains infrastructure devlopment, and the soft domain contains human involvement such as learning, social interaction, governance, and so on.

There are three fundamental components of a smart city: technological factors, human factors, and institutional factors (Nam and Pardo, 2011). Technologies such as big data and data mining are playing important roles in synchronizing the data and making better decisions (*The Economist*, 2013). An IBM corporate document states that the term *smart city* denotes an "instrumented, interconnected and intelligent city." "Instrumented" refers to the capability to capture and integrate live, real-world data through the use of sensors, meters, appliances, personal devices, and other similar sensors. "Interconnected" means the integration of this data into a computing platform that allows the communication of such information among

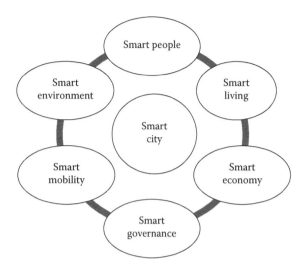

FIGURE 8.1
Smart city dimensions. (From Giffinger, R. et al. *Smart Cities-Ranking of European Medium-Sized Cities*, Vienna University of Technology, Vienna, 2007.)

the various city services. "Intelligent" refers to the inclusion of complex analytics, modeling, optimization, and visualization services to make better operational decisions (Harrison et al., 2010). A smart city should be able to optimize the use and exploitation of both tangible (e.g., transport infrastructures, energy distribution networks, and natural resources) and intangible assets (e.g., human capital, the intellectual capital of companies, and organizational capital in public administration bodies) (Neirotti et al., 2014). The dimensions of a smart city, first proposed by Giffinger et al. (2007), are shown in Figure 8.1.

A smart economy focuses on sustainable and productive jobs in the city; smart mobility describes transportation and ICT; smart people focuses on social and human capital; smart governance describes better participation between government and society; smart environment focuses on the protection of natural resources; and smart living describes the quality of life in the city. Various authors in the literature have suggested differing dimensions for measuring the performance of a smart city. A summary is given in Table 8.1.

Smart city attractiveness will increase in the future with the availability of resources. Cities consume ~75% of worldwide energy production and generate ~80% of CO_2 emissions (Lazaroiu and Roscia, 2012), so it is a real challenge to develop a sustainable smart city. Most papers deal with qualitative aspects of smart cities. Different authors have tried to define the term and its indicators. Giffinger and Gudrun (2010) have identified 6 characteristics and 18 indicators for the smart city. Lazaroiu and Roscia (2012) proposed a smart city indices using fuzzy logic and found that the smart city is mostly influenced by "sustainable, innovative and safe public transportation, fuel, GWh household and production of municipal solid waste." Authors have attempted to develop conceptual models using the SD methodology and formulated only causal feedback relationships among the various factors under different smart characteristics of a city, such as smart economy, smart people, smart governance, smart mobility, smart environment, and smart living (Das, 2013; Khansari et al., 2014; Caponio, 2014; Veldhuis et al., 2014). A quantitative model is missing in the literature, to the best of our knowledge. The SD tool is used to capture the nonlinear behavior of the system, and it gives a better analysis and result where time is an important factor and is best fitted for a policy decision.

TABLE 8.1

Smart City Dimensions

Dimensions	Source	Indicators
Smart economy	Mahizhnan (1999); Giffinger et al. (2007); Nam and Pardo (2011); Chourabi et al. (2012); Lazaroiu and Roscia (2012); Neirotti et al. (2014)	Innovative spirit, productivity, flexibility of labor market, international embeddedness, entrepreneurship, public expenditure on R&D, public expenditure on education, GDP per head of city population, unemployment rate
Smart mobility	Giffinger et al. (2007); Chourabi et al. (2012); Lazaroiu and Roscia (2012); Neirotti et al. (2014)	Local accessibility, availability of ICT infrastructure, sustainable, innovative and safe transport systems
Smart environment	Giffinger et al. (2007); Barrionuevo et al. (2012); Chourabi et al. (2012); Lazaroiu and Roscia (2012); Neirotti et al. (2014)	The ambitiousness of CO_2 emission reduction strategy, efficient use of electricity, efficient use of water, area in green space, greenhouse gas emission intensity of energy consumption, policies to contain urban sprawl, proportion of recycled waste
Smart people	Giffinger et al. (2007); Barrionuevo et al. (2012); Kourtit and Nijkamp (2012); Lazaroiu and Roscia (2012); Neirotti et al. (2014)	Percentage of population with secondary-level education, foreign language skills, participation in lifelong learning, the individual level of computer skills, patent applications per inhabitant
Smart living	Kourtit and Nijkamp (2012); Lazaroiu and Roscia (2012)	Proportion of the area for recreational sports and leisure use, number of public libraries, total book loans and other media, museum visits, theater and cinema attendance
Smart governance	Giffinger et al. (2007); Chourabi et al. (2012); Lazaroiu and Roscia (2012)	Number of universities and research centers in the city, e-government online availability, percentage of households with Internet access at home, e-government use by individuals

8.3 Methodology

The process flow diagram (PFD) of methodology is shown in Figure 8.2. The SD model is a good method to deal with the real complex problem. It is a perspective and a set of conceptual tools that enable us to understand the structure and dynamics of complex systems. Also, it deals with nonlinear behaviors of dynamics. To capture the real picture, first a mental model known as a causal and loop diagram (CLD) is drawn. It consists of variables connected by arrows denoting the causal influence among them (Forrester, 1997). There are two types of loop in a CLD: one is the positive feedback loop (self-reinforcing) and the other is the negative feedback loop (self-correcting loop). It is also known as a qualitative part of SD modeling. Stock and flow diagrams (SFD) represent the quantitative part of SD. A CLD emphasizes the feedback structure of a system. An SFD highlights the underlying physical structure of a system. Stock represents the state of the system and flow represents the rate of increase or decrease of the stock (Sterman 2000).

8.3.1 Causal Loop Diagram

In this chapter, the authors use the smart city attractiveness index as a measure of the smartness of a city. A smart city's council defines the smart city index, which is impacted

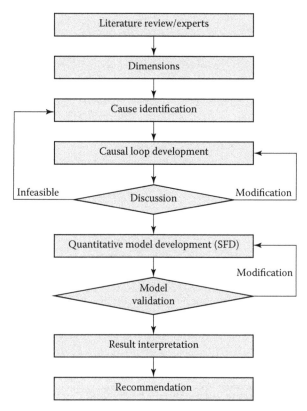

FIGURE 8.2
Methodology of flow diagram.

by all six dimensions. Neirotti et al. (2014) and Lazaroiu and Roscia (2012) indicate that mobility and energy are at the highest priority in a smart city index. Due to the complexity and large variables involved in the smart city index, only smart mobility is considered in our final quantitative simulation model for detailed analysis. A CLD of smart mobility is given in Figure 8.3. As per the literature, smart mobility influences the smartness of the city and mobility depends on local accessibility and ICT infrastructure. Local accessibility depends on transportation. Due to higher smart city attractiveness, population inflow will increase in the city, which will increase the population density. The government will need to invest to enhance the infrastructure of the city based on the gap between targets and existing infrastructure. After some delay, public transport will increase, which will increase local accessibility. At the same time, buses will also increase congestion in the city, and will reduce local accessibility. There are nine total balancing loops and one reinforcing loop that explain the interrelationships of the variables.

8.3.2 Stock and Flow Diagram

Based on a CLD, we prepared a quantitative model for the simulation part, which is shown as an SFD in Figure 8.4. This model measures the variability on timescale due to the cause and effect relationships of variables. CLDs represent a complete mental model for understanding the relationship. An SFD is a mathematical simulation model where the stock and flow of the system captures the dynamic nature of the system. In our SFD

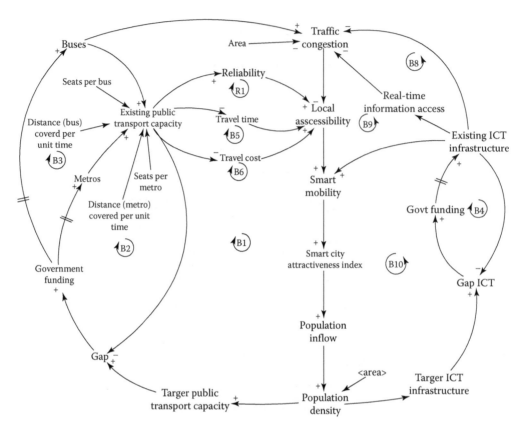

FIGURE 8.3
Close loop diagram.

model, there are four stocks: public bus capacity, metro capacity, population, and ICT infrastructure. To make a smart city, a government needs to invest in relevant infrastructures, such as public transportation and ICT infrastructure. This investment will lead to the enhancement of both public transport, in the form of new metros and buses, and the ICT infrastructure, after the implementation time delays. Here, only two transportation modes, buses and metros, have been taken for the analysis, as buses contribute to nearly half of public transport, and metros are preferred as a smart choice of transportation. New public transport capacity will increase public transport reliability, and will reduce travel time and cost. The increase in public transport capacity will also positively impact local accessibility. On the other hand, more buses will lead to more traffic congestion, negatively impacting local accessibility. The degree of local accessibility and ICT infrastructure defines our smart city attractiveness index. The population will increase by two different modes: one is through normal population, and the other is due to smart city attractiveness. Since the requirement for public transport and ICT infrastructure will increase due to the increase in population, the government will infuse money to make a sustained smart city, based on the gap between the target and existing capacities. Vensim Software is used to run the model. Initial values, based on Lucknow city data, are used for the calculation given in Table 8.2.

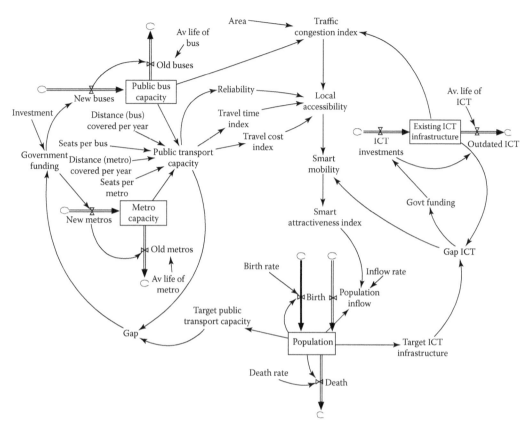

FIGURE 8.4
Stock and flow diagram.

8.3.3 Assumptions

1. Only one dimension, smart mobility, has been taken for the study.
2. Energy perspective on greenhouse gas emission is not considered directly, as only buses and metros have been considered in public transportation.
3. Private funding is not considered separately.
4. Private vehicle, vehicle ownership, and GDP factors are not included in the model.
5. The city area is constant over the period of analysis.

8.4 Results and Analysis

The results for the main variables are shown in Figures 8.5 through 8.8. Public transport capacity (Figure 8.5) increases after some initial delay. There is a dip in the curve around year 15 because initially increased capacity will run out around this time.

The slope of the curve diminishes after this, as the gap between target and existing capacities will lessen. The increase in public transport capacity will bring about higher

TABLE 8.2

Details of Variables

Variables	Values	Source
Birth rate	0.184/year	http://www.censusindia.gov.in/vital_statistics/AHSBulletins/files2012/Uttar%20Pradesh_Bulletin%202011-12.pdf
Death rate	0.065/year	http://www.censusindia.gov.in/vital_statistics/AHSBulletins/files2012/Uttar%20Pradesh_Bulletin%202011-12.pdf
Initial population	45,89,838	Lucknow District Population Census 2011, Uttar Pradesh literacy sex ratio and density. Census 2011. Retrieved 4 August 2014.
Number of buses	300	https://en.wikipedia.org/wiki/Lucknow_Mahanagar_Parivahan_Sewa
Seats in buses	40	https://www.upsrtconline.co.in
Distance covered by bus	100/day	http://tcpomud.gov.in
Area of the city	2528 km²	Lucknow District Population Census 2011, Uttar Pradesh literacy sex ratio and density. Census 2011. Retrieved 4 August 2014.
Travel time	25 (km/h)	https://www.upsrtconline.co.in
Travel cost	0–5 (15), 5–10 (15), 10–15 (15), 15–20 (20), 20–30 (25)	https://www.upsrtconline.co.in
Target investment on transport annually	2100	http://india.Smartcitiescouncil.com/
Initial investment in ICT annually	350	http://india.Smartcitiescouncil.com/
Government funding target	35,000 crore annually	http://india.Smartcitiescouncil.com/
Initial value 5000 crore	500	http://india.Smartcitiescouncil.com/
Reliability (B/D)/10,000	0.21	Central Institute of Road Transport (10–11)

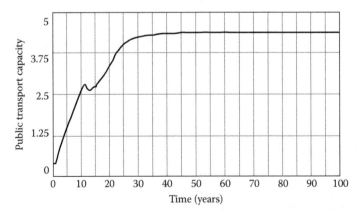

FIGURE 8.5
Time vs. public transport.

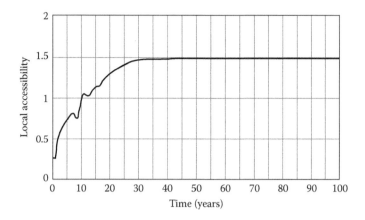

FIGURE 8.6
Time vs. local accessibility.

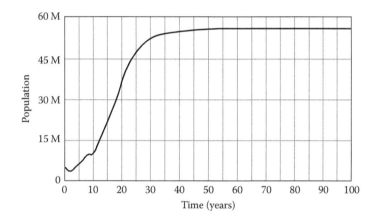

FIGURE 8.7
Time vs. population.

local accessibility (Figure 8.6), resulting in an increase in the smart city attractiveness index (Figure 8.8). This will result in a higher population inflow and a rapid growth in the population (Figure 8.7). This higher growth causes a dip in the local accessibility curve (Figure 8.6) around year 8. The second dip is due to lessening transportation capacity. The same explanation is used for the ups and down in the smart city attractiveness index (Figure 8.8). Public transport capacity increases initially, and will be constant after 30 years, since the government is investing funding initially in building the smart city.

In regard to the analysis of transportation, the area of the city is assumed to be a constant parameter over the analysis period. With this assumption, it is appropriate to say that the population will be constant after the stabilization period. After the stabilization period, if more buses are introduced into the city, this will increase traffic congestion, which will nullify any effect on smart mobility and attractiveness. A population increase due to the net birth rate and inflow is balanced by the same amount of decrease due to the outflow of people from the specified city area to another part, which may be a suburb or other high-smartness index city. The role of any SD model is mainly to see the pattern and

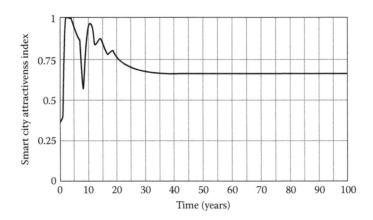

FIGURE 8.8
Time vs. smart city attractiveness index.

behavior due to different policy decisions (Forrester, 1997). These results suffice for our purpose at this stage.

8.5 Recommendations and Conclusions

A smart city is fundamentally regarded as a good-performing city in all its characteristics, and the development is based on self-influence and citizen participation. Smart city attractiveness depends on various factors, primarily economy, mobility, environment, people, living, and governance. The selected dimension for study, smart mobility, will increase with government investment, but this will also cause population growth in the city. The population will stagnate after 30 years, which, considering the area of the city to be constant and the smart city attractiveness index to be decreasing, means that the government should expand the area of the city or create innovative policies. The role of any SD model is mainly to see the pattern and behavior due to different policy decisions (Sterman, 2000). This is not a predictive tool for exact analysis but rather an assisting tool for understanding how the pattern changes with different input in the form of sensitivity analysis and making appropriate decisions. In this way, we may conclude that we are successfully demonstrating how the SD model is helpful in smart city planning using one major dimension. This study shows that SD, with its integrative nature, is well suited to undertake such modeling challenges.

8.6 Limitations and Scope of Future Work

The development of smart cities involves specific modeling features, including interdependency and causal relationships among the numerous parameters. Lack of adequate data, reservations of stakeholders in explaining the causal relationships, and other prominent aspects regarding people, governance, environment, and living conditions, limits any SD model, and may also be said to be the major limitation of our model. To present the holistic view of smart city development planning, all six dimensions mentioned in the literature review part must be included in future modeling, along with the involvement of stakeholders for appropriate quantification of causal relationships.

References

Angelidou, M. 2015. Smart cities: A conjuncture of four forces. *Cities* 47 (September): 95–106.

Barrionuevo, J. M., P. Berrone, and J. E. Ricart. 2012. Smart cities, sustainable progress. *IESE Insight* 14, 50–57.

Caponio, G. 2014. Energy strategic planning of a smart city by dynamic simulation. http://www.researchgate.net/profile/Giancarlo_Caponio/publication/270159237_Energy_Strategic_Planning_of_a_Smart_City_by_Dynamic_Simulation/links/54a161ef0cf267bdb902b8d7.pdf.

Caragliu, A., C. D. Bo, and P. Nijkamp. 2011. Smart cities in Europe. *Journal of Urban Technology* 18, no. 2 (April 1): 65–82.

Census. 2011. Indian population. Retrieved December 25, 2015, from http://censusindia.gov.in/

Chourabi, H., T. Nam, S. Walker, J. R. Gil-Garcia, S. Mellouli, K. Nahon, et al. 2012. Understanding smart cities: An integrative framework. In *System Science (HICSS), 2012 45th Hawaii International Conference on* (pp. 2289–2297), January. IEEE.

Das, D. K. 2013. Using system dynamics principles for conceptual modelling of smart city development in South Africa. *Interim: Interdisciplinary Journal* 12, no. 3: 42–59.

Forrester, J. W. 1997. Industrial dynamics. *Journal of the Operational Research Society* 48, no. 10: 1037–1041.

Giffinger, R., C. Fertner, H. Kramar, R. Kalasek, N. Pichler-Milanovic, and E. Meijers. 2007. *Smart Cities-Ranking of European Medium-Sized Cities*. Vienna: Vienna University of Technology.

Giffinger, R., and H. Gudrun. 2010. Smart cities ranking: An effective instrument for the positioning of the cities? http://upcommons.upc.edu/handle/2099/8550.

Harrison, C., and I. A. Donnelly. 2011. A theory of smart cities. In *Proceedings of the 55th Annual Meeting of the ISSS-2011*, Hull, UK. Vol. 55.

Harrison, C., B. Eckman, R. Hamilton, P. Hartswick, J. Kalagnanam, J. Paraszczak, and P. Williams. 2010. Foundations for smarter cities. *IBM Journal of Research and Development* 54, no. 4: 1–16.

Hollands, R. G. 2008. Will the real smart city please stand up? *City* 12, no. 3: 303–320.

ISB. 2015. http://www.isb.edu/smartcitylabs.

Khansari, N., A. Mostashari, and M. Mansouri. 2014. Impacting sustainable behavior and planning in smart city. *International Journal of Sustainable Land Use and Urban Planning (IJSLUP)* 1, no. 2.

Kourtit, K., and P. Nijkamp. 2012. Smart cities in the innovation age. *Innovation: The European Journal of Social Science Research* 25, no. 2: 93–95.

Lazaroiu, G. C., and M. Roscia. 2012. Definition methodology for the smart cities model. *Energy* 47, no. 1: 326–332.

Mahizhnan, A. (1999). Smart cities: The singapore case. *Cities* 16, no. 1: 13–18.

Nam, T., and T. A. Pardo. 2011. Conceptualizing smart city with dimensions of technology, people, and institutions. In *Proceedings of the 12th Annual International Digital Government Research Conference: Digital Government Innovation in Challenging Times*, 282–291. Dg.o'11. New York: ACM.

Neirotti, P., A. De Marco, A. C. Cagliano, G. Mangano, and F. Scorrano. 2014. Current trends in smart city initiatives: Some stylised facts. *Cities* 38: 25–36.

SM Conference. 2015. Smarter solutions for a better tomorrow. https://eu-smartcities.eu/sites/all/files/events/uploads/Smart%20Cities%20India%202015%20Brochure_0.pdf.

Sterman, J. D. 2000. *Business Dynamics: Systems Thinking and Modeling for a Complex World*. Vol. 19. Boston, MA: Irwin/McGraw-Hill.

The Economist. 2013. Mining the urban data: Cities will become smarter, but in different ways than many people expected (21 Nov 2012).

Van Bastelaer, B. 1998. Digital cities and transferability of results. In *The Proceedings of the 4th EDC Conference on Digital Cities*, Salzburg, October 29–30.

Veldhuis, G. A., P. G. M. van Scheepstal, and N. Vink. 2014. Development of a generic Smart City model using MARVEL. In Davidsen, P. Rouwette, EAJA, *32nd International Conference of the System Dynamics Society, 20–24 July 2014*, 124–125. Delft, The Netherlands: The System Dynamics Society.

World Bank. 2015. http://data.worldbank.org/indicator/SP.POP.GROW.

9

Smart City Technologies: An Oversell Product of Global Technology Companies or the Ultimate Solution to the Challenges Persisting in Urban India

Alok Tiwari

CONTENTS

9.1 Introduction.. 105
9.2 Concept of Smart City 106
9.3 Big Data in a Smart City.. 106
9.4 Internet of Things and Smart City 108
9.5 What Makes a Smart City Successful?... 108
9.6 How Relevant Are Smart Cities in the Indian Urban Context? 109
    9.6.1 Will Copying Ideas from Developed Countries Work? 109
    9.6.2 How Much Easier Will Land Acquisition Be for Smart Cities?...... 110
    9.6.3 Who Is Going to Control the Smart City? 110
    9.6.4 Smart City Must Not Be Just an IT Solution 110
    9.6.5 End Users as an Obstacle to Energy Efficiencies and Sustainability 110
    9.6.6 An Oversimplified Idea 111
    9.6.7 Legitimacy of Smart City.. 111
    9.6.8 Safeguarding Slum Dwellers 111
    9.6.9 Where Will the Natural (Organic) Growth Be? 111
9.7 Conclusion 111
References... 112

9.1 Introduction

More than half of the world's population is now living in cities (UN-HABITAT 2013), while according to the latest population projections, three countries alone, namely India, China, and Nigeria, will be the home of 37% of urban dwellers at a global level (United Nations 2014). The McKinsey Global Institute has predicted that by 2030, the urban population in India will reach 590 million. To accommodate the demands of such huge numbers of people, 1.2 trillion USD will be required to invest in a mass rapid transport system, affordable housing, employment generation, construction of roads and sewers, health and education, and many other amenities and infrastructure (Sankhe et al. 2010).

Obviously, planning and management of such a huge number of urban dwellers in India will not be an easy job; many more cities will be needed to address the rapid urbanization and population growth while urban policy makers and planners will be in exigent need for a dynamic, efficient, capable, and competent tool to do so.

In the past two or more decades, however, urban scientists and thinkers have been observing a transitory urban boom, passing through a period of time where information and communication technologies (ICTs) have been profoundly transforming the character, construct, and commands of city planning, functioning, management, infrastructure, and almost every component of day-to-day life.

Arguably, ICT-infused solutions to city planning, management, and other operations are widely acknowledged as smart city technologies in general.

9.2 Concept of Smart City

Scholars are not in agreement on defining a city that is "smart" in the real sense. The traces of the term *smart city* can be excavated from several momentous theories on urbanism, such as "wired cities" (Dutton et al. 1987), "technocities" (Downey and McGuigan 1999), "connected cities" (Healey 2000), "network cities" (Townsend 2001), "intelligent cities" (Komninos 2002), "cyber cities" (Graham and Marvin 2004), "creative cities" (Florida 2005), "sentient cities" (Crang and Graham 2007), "knowledge-based cities" (Carrillo 2006), "cognitive cities" (Tusnovics 2007), "digital cities" (Komninos 2008), "wireless cities" (Sukumar and Christian 2008), and many more. All these concepts delineate a new type of urbanism that takes advantage of knowledge, information, communication, and the digital revolution to plan and manage cities in a sustainable fashion and, most importantly, to take informed decisions aimed at better services and productivity over an urban space. All of the previously mentioned characterizations might be considered as the first wave of the smart city upsurge.

The second wave of smart cities was purportedly initiated by global technological companies (GTCs) as a catalyst of productive capital to overcome the economic recession in recent years with utopian goals (Swilling 2013; Paroutis et al. 2014). GTCs brought smart cities back into the limelight, promising the ideal city through the profuse use of ICTs in urban planning and management tasks aimed mainly at improved resource efficiency and enhanced quality of life for city residents (IBM 2009; Accenture 2011).

Though contested, a smart city could be defined as an intelligent or "hi-tech" city, built upon the skeleton of ICTs and with an objective to solve immense urban challenges, including traffic congestion, environmental pollution, and security. A variety of sensors, applications, and Internet of things (IOT)-like items guarantee the success of a smart city. The smart city concept gestures toward an ideal model that utilizes human, technological, and collective assets in city operations (Angelidou 2014). Additionally, Hazer (2014) maintained that a smart city will scrutinize city operations through big data, and utilize outcomes for real-time urban management.

The GTCs assert that big data and IOT are their infallible instruments by which they visualize how quality of life and resource efficacy in an urban fabric could be achieved in a sustainable manner; hence, it is obvious to evaluate these two subjects.

9.3 Big Data in a Smart City

The fact is that humanity is currently encountering a data deluge as digital data becomes pervasive (*The Economist* 2010). Big data is a concept that has received serious consideration in business, academia, and government to portray types of data that are difficult to manage using traditional computing praxes. It can be understood as "any data that cannot fit into an Excel spreadsheet" (Betty 2013). Big data promoters have described it as data that are too big in terms of volume, variety, velocity, and veracity (Zikopoulos et al. 2015). This section further examines the importance of big data, crowdsourcing for big data, and the role that big data is playing in the inception of smart cities.

Dijcks (2011) argued that managers can accomplish their assignments in a more systematic and intelligent way to achieve productivity and service delivery if big data is refined and examined with customary organizational data; this exercise can also give enterprises a strong competitive and innovative position.

In another report, the McKinsey Global Institute (MCI 2011) has identified strategic merits of big data including producing transparency, experimentation to explore versatile desires aimed at performance improvements, organizing talented individuals for specific tasks, shifting from manual decision making to automated action, and developing innovative products, services, and business models.

As an emergent archetype, big data produces a variety of challenges for managers. A large portion of big data is unstructured and depends on the intellect of information technology (IT) managers for how they deal with its roaring power; in fact, they should reposition themselves to set their priorities to the analysis and assembly of vital data, formulate strategy to use this meaningful data with existing information and intelligence, experiment in storage and computing techniques to make it outstanding, and assess the awareness and resources in the enterprise to manage such big data through nascent technology and tools and a plan to appreciate upward corporate demand (Gupta 2013).

Initially, big data was limited to the business arena, although recognition of informed management decision making has transformed the zeal for the concept of big data. The vibrant attributes of big data made it inevitable for the development sector as it is digitally created, passively produced, spontaneously collected, spatially trackable, and continuously analyzed (United Nations 2012). Burns (2015) argues that big data is a new tradition that establishes a distinct epistemology and that is fundamental to social relations in the realm of digital humanitarianism.

Big data opponents argue that it eludes historical traces that can prove prominent in knowing the root causes of today's problems (Barnes 2013), while others consider big data as a disruptive innovation (Kitchin 2014b).

Scientists claim that smart cities will need a variety of data to manage themselves; the huge amount of data required for the purpose brings big data into context to make real-time judicious decisions (Kramer 2013; Perboli et al. 2014). Townsend (2013) maintained that insights from big data will maximize sustainability and efficiency, the main challenge persisting in the urban fabric. In fact, the dominance of big data in smart city operation compelled Swilling (2015) to regard such types of urbanism as "algorithmic urbanism."

A recent report by the World Bank (2015) highlights the importance of data in sustaining urbanization in South Asian countries, including India, and commends the investment in data to confirm efficiency in urban management practices to bring about livability and prosperity. Big data offers solutions to serve smart city aspirations in countless ways, such as scrutinizing their intelligence and reduced or efficient uses of energy (Marsal-Llacuna et al. 2015; Karmers et al. 2014).

Big data–sustained smart cities are often criticized because of their entrepreneurial focus combined with excessive stress on an urban governance system built on technology and the impending jeopardy of mass surveillance (Greenfield 2013; Hollands 2008; Kitchin 2014a).

9.4 Internet of Things and Smart City

According to Atzori et al. (2010), IOT is the futuristic gears for interactive digital data communication of continuous uses, armed with transceivers and microcontrollers that essentially work over Internet protocols. Also known as the future of Internet, IOT has been anticipated to be an integral part of smart cities (Zanella et al. 2014) and attempts to look for automated applications in the very field of urban spaces in the home and in industry, geriatric care, medical assistance, smart grids, traffic management, and energy management, among others (Bellavista et al. 2013). Marr (2015) indicated that IOT will be the apparatuses "that will speak to each other"; however, IOT prototypes are frequently embraced as business models that are strongly exploited to make the environs really "smart"; as an example, the Glasgow city government in Scotland has allocated millions of euros to IOT to make the city smarter, safer, and more sustainable.

Research and development into IOT is still in progress in the pursuit of more sophisticated applications for smart cities. IOT can be labeled as "sensing" gadgets that are wearable (by individuals), movable (installed in vehicles, smartphones, and personal data assistance devices), or static (fixed in houses, power grids, green and open spaces, streets, traffic lights, and other places), and connected to the Internet to generate big data for sustainable smart city operations, mostly in real time.

9.5 What Makes a Smart City Successful?

ICT through big data and IOT is doubtlessly a crucial facilitator for smart city success; nevertheless, there are other enablers. The success of smart cities also depends on a series of actors and sectors. Giffinger et al. (2007) identified six dimensions or axes of the smart city: smart environment, smart people, smart economy, smart mobility, smart living, and smart governance. Similarly, a report on smart cities in the European Union points out that vision, people, and processes (Figure 9.1) are three strategic factors that make a city really smart (Manville et al. 2014).

First, smart vision focuses on the inclusion and participation of each and every individual and place to evade any future disparity between rich and poor people and areas.

Second, smart people includes the city leaders (champions) who set a vision and work to create a participatory environment to empower, encourage, and engage businesses, public sectors, and citizens to contribute.

Third, smart processes offer present and future learning and collaboration through open data platforms with central control and local coordination to manage ideas, innovations, projects, stakeholders, and beneficiaries. The United Nations (2015) also echoes similar sentiments about the smart city in their Goal 11, with an objective to make cities inclusive, safe, resilient, and sustainable.

Therefore, smart cities are not just about ICT, big data, IOT, and the like; rather, they are more than these entities.

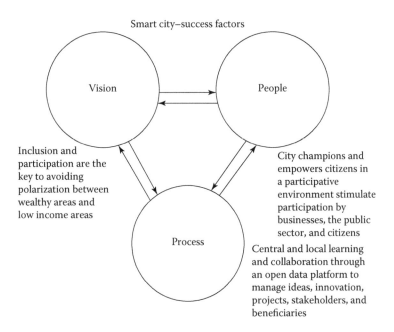

Smart city–success factors

FIGURE 9.1
Success factors in a smart city.

9.6 How Relevant Are Smart Cities in the Indian Urban Context?

A few points are exceedingly pertinent to consider regarding smart cities in an Indian context. First, scholarship on the smart city discourse predominantly revolves around the technology from which the term is perceived, and is defined differently by different sectors and actors (UN-HABITAT 2015). Second, the role of ICT has long been acknowledged as a tool to sustain better efficiency in a city system (Johnston and Taylor 1995). Third, India definitely needs an efficient system to build, plan, and manage its unwarranted future urban growth, for which smart city offers ICT-based tools. Finally, India's 100 smart city initiatives appears as a major comeback for the smart city business model of urban development (Tiwari 2014; Bunnell 2015) that undermines social justice (Datta 2015).

Smart cities in India are still in the phase of incubation, although the implementation of such mega-scale projects is quite debatable.

Some crucial points of debate are described in the following sections.

9.6.1 Will Copying Ideas from Developed Countries Work?

Cities in India are fundamentally different from the smart cities of Europe, South Korea, or the Middle East in their geographies, culture, customs, lifestyles, traditions, conditions, and realities. Smart people with a higher sense of ownership and active engagement (TNN 2014) are needed who are willing to adopt smart urbanism (Luque-Ayala and Marvin 2015), a serious notion of urbanism that is action based, integrative, solution oriented, and concrete, not just verbal.

On the one hand, global marketers of smart city solutions will attempt to sell their products to local municipalities while the applicability of these solutions in the local scenario is still not tested. On the other hand, the participation of the people who live in slums (17%) and others who are not tech savvy is doubtful.

9.6.2 How Much Easier Will Land Acquisition Be for Smart Cities?

Being pro-agricultural in any land acquisition remains contested in Indian politics, and is true in the case of Dholera, India's first smart city, which is planned to be twice the size of Mumbai and has been criticized because of threats to dispossess small-scale subsistence and landless farmers. The Special Investment Region Act (March 2009) gives greater powers to acquire land for building smart cities and is argued to be surpassing India's Land Acquisition Act, leading to conflicts in central–state relations (Datta 2014).

9.6.3 Who Is Going to Control the Smart City?

We have to be very cautious about speculative panaceas such as the smart city, because the ICT upkeep for their implementation will be primarily carried out by GTCs and whether they can guarantee the privacy of an individual's data and information is dubious. So, the striking question is who will control the smart city, and for what reason? Additionally, the profit motive of the smart city business model diminishes the value of these urban utopias.

9.6.4 Smart City Must Not Be Just an IT Solution

A recent smart city policy initiative taken by the Union Government of India has opened an endless dispute on its shape, size, nature, financing, and on the environment in which it will operate. At first glance, this policy initiative seems extra ambitious while basic infrastructure in most of the existing cities is not in order, including sanitation, water supply, electricity, sewer systems, storm water drainage, and traffic management.

It has been argued by Greg Clark that

> "Smart cities could not be seen just as an IT solution rather it offers an opportunity to align Good Governance, investments, institutions and time." (Kow 2014)

Similarly, Burdett (2014) contended that in some cases, making a smart city is not merely about technology, it is about solving more fundamental challenges than can be done through IT.

9.6.5 End Users as an Obstacle to Energy Efficiencies and Sustainability

While the smart city stresses energy and material efficiencies and sustainability through the use of advanced technologies, a higher percentage of energy use remains in the hands of end users and their behavior (Puri 2014).

There are further barriers to achieving resource and energy efficiencies for environmental improvements via the smart city route. The UK Environmental Industries Commission report reveals the smart city potential for cleaning urban environments (reducing levels of particulate emissions, decreasing carbon emissions, stopping water loss from leaking pipes, and improving recycling) is not yet proved because of certain barriers (EIC 2014).

9.6.6 An Oversimplified Idea

GTCs have advertised the smart city as a simple and ultimate solution, which has enthralled leaders and policy makers despite urban problems being much more complicated in nature, thus attracting certain preconditions to manage the change before moving toward a sustainable solution. Kajaria (2014) condemned the smart city concept because of its oversimplified technological vision that believes that technology is the answer to each and every urban challenge without a fundamental change in the lifestyle of urban people.

9.6.7 Legitimacy of Smart City

A major transgression of smart city policy is its legitimacy, as it is not really clear whether smart cities will have any specific constitutional mandate such as special economic zones, which are already contested or will be executed by strengthening the existing powers of urban local bodies, similar to the 74th Constitutional Amendment Act, 1992 (Sethi 2014).

9.6.8 Safeguarding Slum Dwellers

In India, a huge number of urbanites still live in slums, and these informal settlers will number 104 million by 2017 (Dash 2013). No smart city policy will be fruitful if it excludes slum dwellers.

9.6.9 Where Will the Natural (Organic) Growth Be?

Urban planners are panicking about whether the providers of smart city solutions are really aware of the organic growth of a city. It will be quite demanding for a service provider from a different milieu to appreciate the key aspects of urbanism in a specific city and to grasp how the city really grows and what is required to transform it.

Admittedly, India is standing on the verge of the latest ICT-driven urbanism, acknowledged as smart city; at this juncture, a lot of things are going to happen in the far future, although policy makers have to be thoughtful and not rush into large-scale execution of such projects. Moreover, hesitation about the smart city model must be resolved before the next step.

9.7 Conclusion

The projected growth of the urban population and urbanization in India calls for sustainable and efficient solutions for city operations. Smart cities possess great potential to solve urban challenges through the entrenched use of ICT, big data, and IOT. The triumphs of Indian smart cities are uncertain because of profit-motivated GTCs that oversell the idea, despite the other societal, legal, and procedural obstacles. An overemphasis on business models hinders the possible application of smart city for social equity. Additionally, it seems that the preconditions of smart city implementation are somewhat overlooked. It is recommended to not be in a rush for such an ambitious project before all doubts are properly investigated and resolved. Finally, we have to understand that smart cities are just a means (tool) to an end (sustainable urbanization and livable cities).

References

Accenture. 2011. Building and managing an intelligent city. http://www.accenture.com/SiteCollectionDocuments/PDF/Accenture-Building-Managing-Intelligent-City.pdf (accessed January 1, 2016).

Angelidou, M. 2014. Smart city policies: A spatial approach, *Cities*, 41:3–11.

Atzori, L., Iera, A., and Morabito, G. 2010. The internet of things: A survey, *Computer Networks*, 54-15:2787–2805.

Barnes, T.J. 2013. Big data, little history, *Dialogues in Human Geography*, 3-3:297–302.

Bellavista, P., Cardone, G., Corradi, A., and Foschini, L. 2013. Convergence of MANET and WSN in IoT urban scenarios, *Sensors Journal, IEEE*, 13-10:3558–3567.

Betty, M. 2013. Big data, smart cities and city planning, *Dialogues in Human Geography*, 3-3:274–279.

Bunnell, T. 2015. Smart city returns, *Dialogues in Human Geography*, 5-1:45–48.

Burdett, R. 2014. Urban planner: "Smart cities" are problematic. http://www.dw.de/urban-planner-smart-cities-are-problematic/a-18057258 (accessed January 2, 2015).

Burns, R. 2015. Rethinking big data in digital humanitarianism: Practices, epistemologies, and social relations, *GeoJournal*, 80:477–490.

Carrillo, F.J. ed. 2006. *Knowledge Cities: Approaches, Experiences and Perspectives*. Burlington, MA: Routledge.

Crang, M., and Graham, S. 2007. Sentient cities ambient intelligence and the politics of urban space, *Information, Communication and Society*, 10-6:789–817.

Dash, D.K. 2013. By 2017, India's slum population will rise to 104 million. http://timesofindia.indiatimes.com/india/By-2017-Indias-slum-population-will-rise-to-104-million/articleshow/21927474.cms (accessed December 31, 2015).

Datta, A. 2014. India's smart city craze: Big, green and doomed from the start? *The Guardian*. http://www.theguardian.com/cities/2014/apr/17/india-smart-city-dholera-flood-farmers-investors (accessed January 2016).

Datta, A. 2015. New urban utopias of postcolonial India "Entrepreneurial urbanization" in Dholera smart city, Gujarat, *Dialogues in Human Geography*, 5-1:3–22.

Dijcks, J.P. 2011. Read up on the overall big data solution, Oracle Blog. https://blogs.oracle.com/data-warehousing/entry/read_up_on_the_overall (accessed October 17, 2015).

Downey, J. and McGuigan, J. 1999. *Technocities*. London: Sage.

Dutton, W.H., Kraemer, K.L., and Blumler, J.G. 1987. *Wired Cities: Shaping the Future of Communications*. Indianopolis, IN: Macmillan.

The Economist. 2010. The Data Deluge. http://www.economist.com/node/15579717 (accessed October 14, 2015).

EIC. 2014. Getting the green light: Will smart technology clean up city environments? The Environmental Industries Commission. http://www.eic-uk.co.uk/Documents/Files/Smart%20Cities%20Report%20-%20Interactive.pdf (accessed January 2, 2016).

Florida, R. 2005. *Cities and the Creative Class*. New York: Routledge.

Giffinger, R., Fertner, C., Kramar, H., Kalasek, R., Pichler-Milanović, N., and Meijers, E. 2007. *Smart Cities: Ranking of European Medium-Sized Cities*. Vienna, Austria: Centre of Regional Science (SRF), Vienna University of Technology. http://www.smart-cities.eu/download/smart_cities_final_report.pdf (accessed December 29, 2015).

Graham, S., and Marvin, S. 2004. *Planning Cyber-Cities? Integrating Telecommunications into Urban Planning*. The Cybercities Reader. London: Routledge, 341–347.

Greenfield, A. 2013. *Against the Smart City*. Kindle Edition. New York.

Gupta, S. 2013. Sundar Ram: Big data needs big decisions, IT. http://www.itnext.in/articles/16735/sundar-ram-big-data-needs-big-decisions (accessed October 22, 2015).

Hajer, M. 2014. On being smart about cities. Seven considerations for a new urban planning & design. In M. Hajer (Ed.), *Smart about Cities: Visualising the Challenge for 21st Century Urbanism*, 11–43. Rotterdam: Nai010 Publishers and The Hague: PBL.

Healey, P. 2000. Connected cities. *Town and Country Planning Association*, 69-2:55–57.

Hollands, R. 2008. Will the real smart city please stand up? Intelligent, progressive or entrepreneurial? *City*, 12: 303–320.

IBM. 2009. A vision of smarter cities. http://www-03.ibm.com/press/attachments/IBV_Smarter_Cities_-_Final.pdf (accessed December 29, 2015).

Johnston, R.J., and Taylor, P.J. 1995. Geographic information systems and geography. In J. Pickles (Ed.), *Ground Truth: The Social Implications of Geographic Information Systems*, 51–67. New York: Guilford Press.

Kajaria, P. 2014. *Are India's "Smart Cities" A Smart Move?, The Diplomat*, October 2, 2014. http://the-diplomat.com/2014/10/are-indias-smart-cities-a-smart-move/ (accessed December 29, 2015).

Karmer, D. 2013. Smart cities will need big data, *Physics Today*, 66-9: 19.

Kitchin, R. 2014a. Big data, new epistemologies and paradigm shifts, *Big Data & Society*, April–June: 1–12.

Kitchin, R. 2014b. The real-time city? Big data and smart urbanism, *GeoJournal*, 79: 1–14.

Komninos, N. 2002. *Intelligent Cities*. London: Spon.

Komninos, N. 2008. *Intelligent Cities and Globalisation of Innovation Networks*. London: Routledge.

Kow, J.K. 2014. "In Search of India's Smart Cities" in the World Bank Blog on End Poverty in South Asia. http://blogs.worldbank.org/endpovertyinsouthasia/search-india-s-smart-cities (accessed January 2, 2016).

Luque-Ayala, A., and Marvin, S. 2015. Developing a critical understanding of smart urbanism? *Urban Stud*, 52-12:2105–2116.

Manville, C., Cochrane, G., Cave, J., Millard, J., Pederson, J.K., Thaarup, R.K., Liebe, A., Wissner, M., Massink, R., and Kotterink, B. 2014. *Mapping Smart Cities in the EU*. Luxembourg: Publications Office.

Marr, B. 2015. How big data and the Internet of things create smarter cities, Forbes/Tech. http://www.forbes.com/sites/bernardmarr/2015/05/19/how-big-data-and-the-internet-of-things-create-smarter-cities/ (accessed January 3, 2016).

Marsal-Llacuna, M., Colomer-Llinàs, J., and Meléndez-Frigola, J. 2015. Lessons in urban monitoring taken from sustainable and livable cities to better address the Smart Cities initiative, *Technological Forecasting and Social Change*, 90: 611–622.

MCI. 2011. Big data: The next frontier for innovation, competition, and productivity, The McKinsey Global Institute. http://www.mckinsey.com/insights/business_technology/big_data_the_next_frontier_for_innovation (accessed October 28, 2015).

Paroutis, S., Bennett, M., and Heracleous, L. 2014. A strategic view on smart city technology: The case of IBM Smarter Cities during a recession. *Technological Forecasting and Social Change*, 89: 262–272.

Perboli, G., Marcoc, A.D., Perfettia, F. and Maroned, M. 2014. A new taxonomy of smart city projects, *Transportation Research Procedia*, 3-2014:470–478.

Puri, A. 2014. *What are Smart Cities, The Hindu*, August 15, 2014. http://www.thehindu.com/features/homes-and-gardens/green-living/what-are-smart-cities/article6321332.ece (accessed January 2, 2016).

Sankhe, S., Vittal, I., Dobbs, R., Mohan, A., Gulati, A., Ablett, J., Gupta, S., et al. 2010. *India's Urban Awakening: Building Inclusive Cities, Sustaining Economic Growth*. Mumbai, India: McKinsey Global Institute -MGI.

Sethi, M. 2014. India needs to be clever about smart cities, East Asia Forum, October 2, 2014. http://www.eastasiaforum.org/2014/10/02/india-needs-to-be-clever-about-smart-cities/(accessed December 30, 2015).

Sukumar, G., and Christian, F.S. 2008. "The wireless city," 2008, *International Journal of Electronic Government Research-IJEGR*, 4-4:54–68.

Swilling, M. 2013. *City-Level Decoupling: Urban Resource Flows and the Governance of Infrastructure Transitions*. Paris: UNEP.

Swilling, M. 2015. Towards sustainable urban infrastructures for the urban Anthropocene. In Allen, A., Lampis, A., and Swilling, M. (Eds), *Untamed Urbanisms*, London: Routledge.

Tiwari, A. 2014. Urban sciences, big data and India's smart initiative. *Global Journal of Multidisciplinary Studies*, 3(12).

TNN-Times News Network. 2014. "Smart city needs smart populace," TNN, September 20, 2014. http://timesofindia.indiatimes.com/city/hyderabad/Smart-city-needs-smart-populace/articleshow/42949863.cms (accessed December 25, 2016).

Townsend, A. M. 2001. The Internet and the rise of the new network cities, 1969–1999. *Environment and Planning B*, 28-1:39–58.

Townsend, A. M. 2013. *Smart Cities: Big Data, Civic Hackers, and the Quest for a New Utopia*. New York: W.W. Norton.

Tusnovics, D. A. 2007. Cognitive cities: Interdisciplinary approach reconsidering the process of (re)inventing urban habitat. REAL CORP 007 Proceedings, Tagungsband Vienna, May 20–23.

UN-HABITAT. 2013. *State of the World's Cities 2012/2013: Prosperity of Cities*. London: Routledge.

UN-HABITAT. 2015. Issue Paper on Smart Cities: UN-HABITAT, New York, non-edited version 2.0. http://unhabitat.org/wp-content/uploads/2015/04/Habitat-III-Issue-Paper-21_Smart-Cities-2.0.pdf (accessed December 28, 2015).

United Nations. 2012. Big Data for Development: Challenges & Opportunities, UN Global Pulse. http://www.unglobalpulse.org/sites/default/files/BigDataforDevelopment-UNGlobalPulse June2012.pdf (accessed October 22, 2015).

United Nations. 2014. World Urbanization Prospects: The 2014 Revision (Vol. 352), Department of Economic and Social Affairs, United Nations, United Nations Publications.

United Nations. 2015. Sustainable Development Goals: 17 Goals to transform our World, United Nations. http://www.un.org/sustainabledevelopment/cities/ (accessed December 29, 2015).

Zanella, A., Bui, N., Castellani, A., Vangelista, L., and Zorzi, M. 2014. Internet of things for smart cities. *Internet of Things Journal, IEEE*, 1-1:22–32.

Zikopoulos, P., deRoos, D., Bienko, C., Buglio, R., and Andrews, M. 2015. *Big Data beyond the Hype a Guide to Conversations for Today's Data Center*. New York: McGraw-Hill Education, p. 8.

10

A Cloud-Based Mobile Application for Cashless Payments to Enhance Transportation Mobility in India

Arunava Ghosh

CONTENTS

10.1 Introduction 115
10.2 Literature Review 116
    10.2.1 Existing Models 117
    10.2.2 Rise in Mobile Phone Internet Users in India 117
10.3 Proposed Cloud-Based Model 118
10.4 Merits 122
10.5 Limitations 123
10.6 Conclusion and Future Scope 123
References 124

10.1 Introduction

Mobile phones and tablets are an essential part of communication in day-to-day life (Epps 2005). There has been an increase in the number of mobile subscriptions across India (Trimi and Sheng 2008). A mobile phone is now an important part of life and has many features other than receiving and making calls (Ghosh et al. 2014). The ease of mobile use has made life more comfortable. The *Economic Times*, in February 2015, rated India as the second largest smartphone market globally and expected the growth of smartphones to be over 650 million in the next 4 years, as predicted in a study by Cisco, a networking solutions giant (*Economic Times* 2015). Technologies such as cloud computing help to reduce the cost of building infrastructure (Zhang et al. 2010). Cloud computing has spread across nations and boundaries (Rochwerger et al. 2009). Facilities in the cloud can be hired on a pay per use basis (Ghosh et al. 2012). Cloud storage helps to improve remote access to data using an Internet connection.

This chapter proposes a mobile application (app) to improve transportation mobility in smart cities in India. A smart city is one in which the urban system structures are made clear and responsive using technology and design (Kenworthy 2006). Safe and efficient sustainable mobility is the pillar of a smart city. Smartphones help in accessing the Internet. The use of Internet-based mobile phone apps provides scope for improving urban planning and detecting and overcoming inefficiencies in the present urban systems (Steenbruggen et al. 2015). Data collected from these mobile phone apps can be used to enable geographic or social science planning in cities. There are smart city e-services mobile apps that provide services for changing and developing the local economy and tourism and improving transportation mobility, health care, education, and security services (Escher Group 2016).

Over the past few years, many smart city projects have come up with solutions to the challenges that cities are facing (Veeckman and Graaf 2014). Various challenges such as traffic issues in busy cities and environmental pollution demand better and more efficient methods to manage urban life. Therefore, governments are investing in information and communication technology to provide the necessary information. Horizon 2020, a European Union funding program, is promoting the development of smart cities throughout Europe (Veeckman and Graaf 2015). The US government has invested over $160 million in federal research and has collaborated with 25 new technology corporations to reduce traffic congestion issues and crime rates and manage climate change (House and Secretary 2015). Microsoft is building the Smart Destination, a mobile app that retrieves, transforms, and filters data from social media feeds to guide tourists to city attractions in real time. The Belgian city Ghent in western Europe uses a Google-owned navigation app through which users can report accidents and traffic jams. The data collected via this app help the local government with traffic management and emergency response dispatch (Bradshaw 2016). Uber, an urban transport app, connects cabs through a mobile app platform. One click on the app and a cab will pick you up from your current location. Blind Square, popularly used in Europe, helps blind people to know their surroundings by collecting information from Foursquare. The app helps users to get around town more easily. Smart parking, a mobile app used in Barcelona, uses a network of sensors to display parking availability information throughout the city (China Academy of Information and Communications Technology 2016).

According to Make in India, the Government of India allocated 1.2 billion USD to the smart cities budget for 2014–2015. India has signed partnerships with Germany, Spain, the United States, and Singapore for developing smart cities. The Clean India mobile app encourages safer and cleaner surroundings for citizens. Users take photos via this mobile app to report streets that need cleaning. Indian Railways has introduced a mobile app and short message service (SMS) that enable passengers to register complaints about unclean compartments and request an emergency response dispatch if needed.

This chapter proposes a cloud-based mobile payment model for a developing country such as India. The model can be used to pay transportation fares on the go and avoids the need to carry loose coins to pay the exact fare. This model is compatible with all smartphones and is easy to use.

The chapter is structured as follows: The first section discusses the existing models of cashless payments during travel and the growth of the Internet-enabled mobile wireless subscriber base in India. The second section discusses the proposed cloud-based model that can be used for the payment of fares. The third section discusses the key benefits of the model. The fourth section discusses the limitations of the model. The last section proposes the conclusion and future scope of the model.

10.2 Literature Review

The cashless transaction is an established concept. In commercial cashless transactions, a person uses his or her card to interact with transaction terminals to perform cashless transactions. Each terminal processes the data and, at the end of the transaction, updates the data stored in the card (Hogan 1996).

10.2.1 Existing Models

1. In London, Oyster cards have been introduced to ease traveling without cash (Blythe 2004). Oyster is a plastic card with an embedded chip that can hold pay-as-you-go credit. At the bus station, you need to place your card over the electronic card reader at the terminal. An amount equivalent to the fare is deducted from your card's balance. If the balance on the card is less than the required fare, the fare is credited. The card must be recharged after it crosses a specified credit value.

2. In Mumbai (India), Bombay Electric Supply and Transport buses have introduced a cashless travel facility. This will release passengers from the burden of tendering the exact change toward the fare. The commuter has to first opt for an identity card from a bus pass sale counter. While traveling, the commuter has to produce this card for purchasing tickets to his or her destination. An amount equivalent to the ticket fare is deducted immediately, and a ticket is generated with the balance amount printed.

3. We already use our mobile phones for electronic payment of bills (Kim et al. 2010). Also, mobile phones are used to transfer money from one account to another. M-PESA is a mobile phone–based service for sending money, offered by Safaricom, Kenya's largest mobile service provider (Morawczynski and Pickens 2009).

4. In India, Airtel Money services are offered by Airtel M-Commerce Services Limited (Jenkins 2008). Airtel Money can be used for mobile phone top up, DTH recharge, movie ticket bookings, and electricity and gas payments.

5. PayTM and PayUMoney: New taxi providers are using these facilities such as Uber, where you don't even need to pay directly from your card, thus preventing the chance of credit card fraud. You can recharge and pay from your mobile wallet on the go. This mobile wallet can also be used to pay for other purchases that you make online through e-commerce sites. The transaction costs of using online mobile wallets are low.

The use of mobile phones for the payment of fares as we travel is a new prospect that solves the problem of carrying the exact change for the fare. Most people don't favor the use of smart cards for travel as they create the additional burden of ensuring that the card doesn't get misplaced and that a proper balance is maintained. The existing models are used to perform payment operations for specific purposes, but the proposed model can be used for the payment of fares for all public transport vehicles including cabs, buses, and metros throughout the country.

10.2.2 Rise in Mobile Phone Internet Users in India

The number of subscribers to mobile services in India is increasing daily (Abraham 2006). Based on a report published by the Telecom Regulatory Authority of India in May 2015, the upward growth in mobile subscribers continues. Based on this report, in May 2015, a total of 2.44 million new mobile subscribers were added. Most of the new mobile subscriber additions were from rural areas. The total number of Internet subscribers had increased

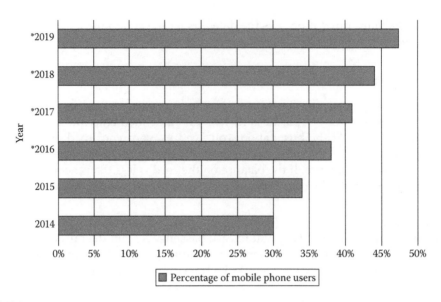

FIGURE 10.1
The rise in the percentage of mobile phone Internet users in India with respect to previous years. (From Statista, Mobile phone Internet user penetration in India from 2015 to 2021. https://www.statista.com/statistics/309019/india-mobile-phone-internet-user-penetration/. 2015; accessed December 11, 2015.)

from 251.59 million at the end of March 2014 to 259.14 million at the end of June 2014, representing a quarterly growth of 3% of which 18.55 million subscribers were wired Internet subscribers and 240.60 million were wireless Internet subscribers.

Figure 10.1 clearly shows that every year there has been a significant rise in the percentage of mobile phone Internet users in India, with respect to the previous year. The predicted rise in the percentage of mobile phone Internet users is shown for the years 2016–2019.

10.3 Proposed Cloud-Based Model

This chapter proposes a cloud-based model for mobile phones. A flow diagram of the model is presented in Figure 10.2. The cloud-based model diagram is presented in Figure 10.3. Figure 10.4 shows the use case diagram of the passenger and the mobile phone app. Figure 10.5 shows the use case diagram of the conductor and the e-validator (electronic ticket-issuing machine [ETIM]). Figure 10.6 shows the mobile app interface.

The model used for the payment of a fare needs two actors: the conductor/staff and the passenger. Our assumptions regarding the bus conductor/staff and the passengers are as follows:

1. Passengers have Internet-enabled smartphones or tablets connected to the Internet and also have an account registered with the mobile phone app that will be used to pay the fare. The passenger database is maintained by the transport authorities in the cloud.

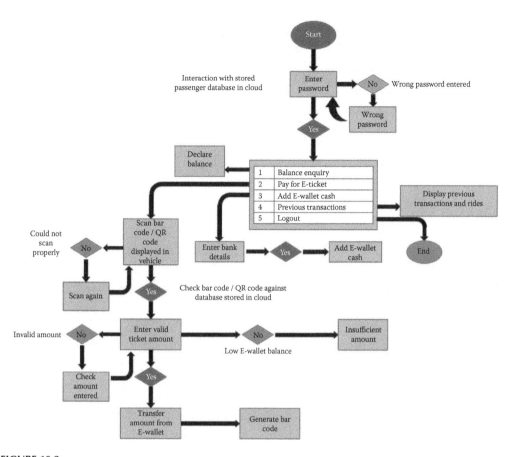

FIGURE 10.2
Flow diagram showing the interaction of the passenger with the mobile phone application.

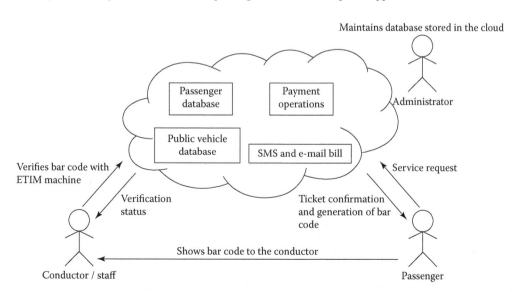

FIGURE 10.3
Mobile phone–based cashless travel model in the cloud.

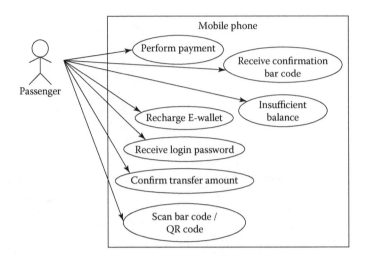

FIGURE 10.4
Use case diagram showing the interaction between the passenger and the mobile phone application.

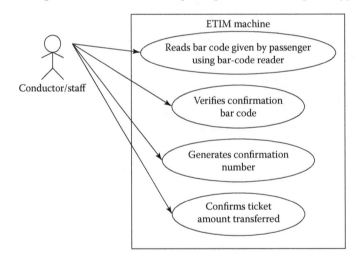

FIGURE 10.5
Use case diagram showing the interaction between the conductor/staff and the e-validator, also known as ETIM.

2. The conductor or public transport vehicle staff has the ETIM that will be used to generate the fare transaction confirmation number for the passenger after successful verification of the bar code generated after online payment of the fare by the passenger via his or her mobile phone app.

All operations, such as signing into the mobile app, performing fare payment, checking the remaining balance, and getting details of previous transactions corresponding to a passenger, are performed in the cloud.

One has to register in the mobile app from any mobile phone. The login username and password generated can be used for signing in to any mobile phone or tablet having the app. So, in case a passenger loses his or her mobile phone, he or she can use the username and password generated earlier for signing into his or her new mobile phone after installing the app.

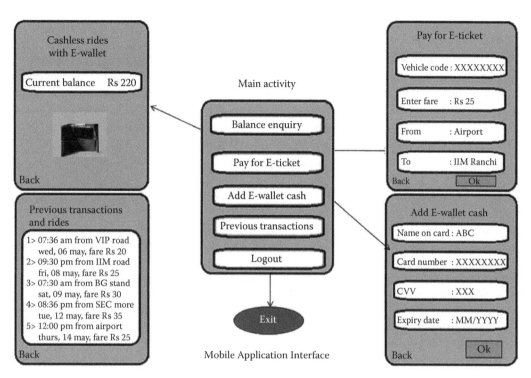

FIGURE 10.6
Various activities of the mobile phone application used for the online payment of fares.

From the flow diagram in Figure 10.2, it can be seen that the mobile phone app for online payment of fares has the following functionalities:

1. Assuming that the passenger is registered on the app, he or she signs into the app using his or her username and password. If the login details are correct, the passenger is taken to the main menu containing the options balance enquiry, pay for e-ticket, add e-wallet cash, previous transactions, and log out. If the login details are incorrect, the mobile activity displays *wrong password* and redirects the user back to the login activity.

2. Balance enquiry: This option shows the current balance in the e-wallet maintained on the cloud and connected to the mobile phone app.

3. Pay for e-ticket: Each form of public transport, such as public buses, has a unique bar code/quick response (QR) code issued by the transport authorities. Passengers traveling via public transport need to scan in the bar code/QR code (displayed in the bus or other public transport) to the mobile phone app with the mobile phone camera. If the code is not scanned properly, a message is issued requesting the user to scan again and redirecting him or her back to the scan bar code/QR code displayed in vehicle activity. If the scanned code is correct, the user is asked to enter the valid ticket amount. If the amount entered is invalid (example: if fares are in denominations of Rs 15 or Rs 25 and the passenger enters Rs 17), then a message is issued requesting the user to check the amount entered. If the amount entered is valid, the amount equivalent to the fare is deducted from the user's e-wallet and

a confirmation bar code is generated that he or she has to submit to the conductor or bus staff with the ETIM.

4. Add e-wallet cash: Selecting this option from the main menu will ask for the user's bank details. After entering the bank details, the e-wallet is recharged. Also, users can connect their bank accounts with the e-wallet, allowing autorecharge at the end of each week.

5. Previous transactions: Selecting this option will display the fares paid for the current week along with their transaction identification (ID).

6. Log out: Sign out of the app when not using the app.

Figure 10.3 explains the model in the cloud. The cloud contains the passenger details in the database and the payment operations that can be performed. It also stores the unique bar codes/QR codes issued by the transport authorities for all public vehicles in the database. The administrator maintains the cloud. The passenger sends a request for fare payment to the cloud via the mobile phone app. After a successful transaction, the confirmation bar code is displayed to the passenger. The passenger shows the confirmation bar code to the conductor/staff. The conductor verifies the confirmation bar code with the e-validator machine (ETIM). The e-validator machine verifies the passenger database and the payment operations performed in the cloud. After successful verification, the ETIM confirms the transaction.

The use case diagram in Figure 10.4 shows that the passenger can interact with the mobile phone app to receive a login password after successful registration on the app, perform payment, check balance in the e-wallet, recharge the e-wallet, scan the bar code/QR code, or receive the confirmation bar code after a successful fare transaction.

The use case diagram in Figure 10.5 shows that the conductor/staff can interact with the e-validator machine (or ETIM) by using the bar-code reader to read and verify the bar code displayed by the passenger, confirm the fare paid, and then generate the confirmation number.

Figure 10.6 illustrates the various activities of the mobile phone app to be designed for the online payment of fares. These activities can be coded and designed for the Android platform.

10.4 Merits

While using smart cards for the purpose of paying fares, there can be various issues such as payment of fare on a crowded bus as this will create difficulties in swiping so many smart cards. Another disadvantage is that the card can be used only for a particular closed system, such as metro prepaid cards that can be used only on metro systems in India. Outside the system, the person can't utilize the prepaid cards. Also, in the case of the identity cards used on Bombay Electric Supply and Transport buses, one has to go to a recharge station to increase the balance. In case of a low e-wallet balance on the mobile phone app-based model, the account can be recharged online and also during the journey itself. The passenger details submitted at the time of online registration are stored in the cloud and maintained by the cloud admin. During the months when the traveling frequency of passengers is high, there is a demand for a faster service. Cloud computing, as a utility, involves renting on demand (Armbrust et al. 2010), so additional servers can be rented when the network traffic is too high. This mobile phone–based app model can also be used on any public transport throughout the country, which has been issued a unique bar code/QR code by the transport authorities. Also, here the balance is deducted from the e-wallet and not directly from the bank, so bank transaction costs are not applicable (Akinci et al. 2004). The e-wallet can be recharged once and can be used for multiple rides if the balance doesn't fall below a threshold point prescribed by the transport authorities. Since it is a mobile phone–based app, there is no chance of loss such as in the case of Bombay Electric Supply and Transport, where one can lose one's identity card. In case the identity card is lost, the balance on the card is not transferred to a new card. But in the case of a mobile phone–based app, the same username and password can be used on any mobile phone that has the app installed. Since the balance in this case is stored in the cloud, it would be available irrespective of the mobile phone being used. Also, the mobile phone–based app is easy to use as the traveler has only to scan the QR code/bar code displayed and enter the fare that he or she wants to pay. Thus, based on the technology acceptance model theory, usefulness and ease of use of the mobile phone–based app are achieved.

10.5 Limitations

When recharging the e-wallet balance online, chances are that the bank server might be down. In case of slow Internet speeds, this model might not work. Especially in rural areas, Internet subscriptions may have no coverage. Connectivity is achieved by making long-distance calls to nearby cities. This results in slow and unreliable access (Rao 2004). Analysis of e-governance also describes the general resistance of people to change. People don't wish to change, and skill shortages and low information technology literacy add to this. The high cost of Internet use is another hindrance (Backus 2001). These are the reasons for the failure of e-governance in India.

Another limitation is username and password theft (Chou et al. 2004). If we lose our mobile phones or if someone gains knowledge about the username and password, that person might get access to our e-wallet balance. This is the same disadvantage as in the present card system. If the card falls into the wrong hands, unauthorized access might occur. A challenge also lies in preventing forgery (Vatanen 2001). This chapter does not incorporate the financial implications of implementing this model.

10.6 Conclusion and Future Scope

This chapter introduced a mobile cashless payment model for India. The increasing use of mobile phones and the additional facilities that can be provided by them has been explored. A cloud-based mobile phone app for the payment of fares has been introduced.

On metros and buses, instead of the card or mobile phone app, one could carry only its bar-code image print. Displaying the bar-code image print to the bar-code reader would automatically read one's unique ID and connect to the cloud to access the user's e-wallet account to transact the fare. Then, one has to enter the fare amount he or she has to pay into the ETIM. The payment gets processed after that. So, in the case of no mobile Internet or mobile phone, the bar-code image will work. One can check the balance on the account's e-wallet online or by calling customer care and giving the unique ID number, thus knowing the e-wallet balance when one doesn't wish to use the app to check the balance. This is also valid for nonsmartphones. Thus, senior citizens, children, and physically challenged people accessing public transport facilities would benefit as carrying a bar-code image print would be easier for them. But if the bar-code image print gets lost, it could be misused. Also, the carrying of the bar-code image print will have the same disadvantages as those found in systems that accept payments via smart cards.

Interactive voice response (IVR) systems or SMS modes of paying fares through mobile phones can also be introduced for those who don't wish to use the mobile phone app. Also, IVR-based models or SMS modes can function on nonsmartphones. IVR-based models in the cloud are very rare (Ghosh et al. 2014). Most people in India use low-cost technology such as low-end mobile phones. Many people are semiliterate or illiterate and would have difficulty in using the user interfaces (Medhi et al. 2011). Therefore, voice-based user interfaces can be more effective than text-based user interfaces (Medhi et al. 2006).

Also, a uniform transport rate chart can be loaded for a particular city, which can be accessed online anytime. Therefore, the chances of illegal charging of excess fares from passengers will be prevented.

References

Abraham, Reuben. 2006. Mobile phones and economic development: Evidence from the fishing industry in India. In *Information and Communication Technologies and Development, 2006. ICTD'06. International Conference on*, pp. 48–56. IEEE. doi:10.1109/ICTD.2006.301837.

Akinci, Serkan, Safak Aksoy, and Eda Atilgan. 2004. Adoption of internet banking among sophisticated consumer segments in an advanced developing country. *International Journal of Bank Marketing* 22.3: 212–232. http://www.emeraldinsight.com/doi/pdf/10.1108/02652320410530322.

Armbrust, Michael, Armando Fox, Rean Griffith, Anthony D. Joseph, Randy Katz, Andy Konwinski, Gunho Lee et al. 2010. A view of cloud computing. *Communications of the ACM* 53.4: 50–58.

Backus, Michiel. 2001. E-governance in developing countries. IICD Research Brief 1.3. http://www.academia.edu/download/6979277/report3.doc.

Blythe, Philip T. 2004. Improving public transport ticketing through smart cards. *Proceedings of the Institution of Civil Engineers, Municipal Engineer* 157.1: 47–54. http://citeseerx.ist.psu.edu/viewdoc/download?doi=10.1.1.112.7895&rep=rep1&type=pdf.

Bradshaw, Tim. 2016. Mobiles could be the secret to "smart" cities. *Financial Times*, Accessed on April 10, 2016. http://www.ft.com/cms/s/2/c3a7f4c4-bae8-11e5-b151-8e15c9a029fb.html# axzz 42xhTDUJ1.

China Academy of Information and Communications Technology, EU-China Policy Dialogues Support Facility II. 2016. *Comparative Study of Smart Cities in Europe and China 2014*. Current Chinese Economic Report Series. Berlin, Heidelberg: Springer.

Chou, Neil, Robert Ledesma, Yuka Teraguchi, and John C. Mitchell. 2004. Client-side defense against web-based identity theft. In *NDSS*. http://www.isoc.org/isoc/conferences/ndss/04/proceedings/Papers/Chou.pdf.

Economic Times. 2015. India to have 651 million smartphones, 18.7 million tablets by 2019. *Economic Times*, February 3, 2015. http://www.academia.edu/download/6979277/report3.doc. Accessed on April 10, 2016.

Epps, Randy. 2005. Cellular telephone based payment apparatus and method for use in purchase of good and services. U.S. Patent Application 11/140,443, filed May 27. https://www.google.com/patents/US20060080232.

Escher Group. 2016. Five ICT essentials for smart cities. Accessed on April 10, 2016. https://www.eschergroup.com/files/8914/4491/8222/Smart_City_Planning.pdf.

Ghosh, Amitava, Abhishek Chakraborty, Sourav Saha, and Ambuj Mahanti. 2012. Cloud computing in Indian higher education. *IIM Kozhikode Society and Management Review* 1.2: 85–95. http://ksm.sagepub.com/content/1/2/85.short.

Ghosh, Amitava, Sourya Joyee De, and Ambuj Mahanti. 2014. A mobile banking model in the cloud for financial inclusion in India. In *Proceedings of the 32nd ACM International Conference on The Design of Communication CD-ROM*, p. 3. ACM. http://dl.acm.org/citation.cfm?id=2666218.

Hogan, Edward J. 1996. System and method for conducting cashless transactions. U.S. Patent 5,557,516, issued on September 17. https://www.google.com/patents/US5557516.

Jenkins, Beth. 2008. *Developing Mobile Money Ecosystems*. Washington, DC: International Finance Corporation and Harvard Kennedy School.

Kenworthy, Jeffrey R. 2006. The eco-city: Ten key transport and planning dimensions for sustainable city development. *Environment and Urbanization* 18.1: 67–85. http://eau.sagepub.com/content/18/1/67.short.

Kim, Changsu, Mirsobit Mirusmonov, and In Lee. 2010. An empirical examination of factors influencing the intention to use mobile payment. *Computers in Human Behavior* 26.3: 310–322. http://www.sciencedirect.com/science/article/pii/S074756320900168X.

Medhi, Indrani, Somani Patnaik, Emma Brunskill, S. N. Gautama, William Thies, and Kentaro Toyama. 2011. Designing mobile interfaces for novice and low-literacy users. *ACM Transactions on Computer-Human Interaction (TOCHI)* 18.1: 2. http://dl.acm.org/citation.cfm?id=1959024.

Medhi, Indrani, Aman Sagar, and Kentaro Toyama. 2006. Text-Free user interfaces for illiterate and semi-literate users. In *Information and Communication Technologies and Development. ICTD'06. International Conference on*, pp. 72–82. IEEE. http://ieeexplore.ieee.org/xpls/abs_all.jsp?arnumber=4085517.

Morawczynski, Olga, and Mark Pickens. 2009. Poor people using mobile financial services: Observations on customer usage and impact from M-PESA. Washington, DC: World Bank.

Rochwerger, Benny, David Breitgand, and Eliezer Levy. 2009. The reservoir model and architecture for open federated cloud computing. *IBM Journal of Research and Development* 53.4: 4–1. http://ieeexplore.ieee.org/xpls/abs_all.jsp?arnumber=5429058.

Statista. 2015. Mobile phone Internet user penetration in India from 2015 to 2021. https://www.statista.com/statistics/309019/india-mobile-phone-internet-user-penetration/. Accessed December 11, 2015.

Steenbruggen, John, Emmanouil Tranos, and Peter Nijkamp. 2015. Data from mobile phone operators: A tool for smarter cities? *Telecommunications Policy* 39.3: 335–346. http://www.sciencedirect.com/science/article/pii/S0308596114000603.

Subba Rao, Siriginidi. 2004. Role of ICTs in India's rural community information systems. *Info* 6.4: 261–269. http://www.emeraldinsight.com/doi/abs/10.1108/14636690410555663.

Trimi, Silvana, and Hong Sheng. 2008. Emerging trends in M-government. *Communications of the ACM* 51.5: 53–58. http://dl.acm.org/citation.cfm?id=1342338.

Vatanen, Harri Tapani. 2001. Mobile telephone system and method for carrying out financial transactions using a mobile telephone system. U.S. Patent 6,169,890, issued January 2. https://www.google.com/patents/US6169890.

Veeckman, Carina, and Shenja van der Graaf. 2014. The city as living laboratory: A playground for the innovative development of smart city applications. In *Engineering, Technology and Innovation (ICE), 2014 International ICE Conference on*, pp. 1–10. IEEE. http://ieeexplore.ieee.org/xpls/abs_all.jsp?arnumber=6871621.

Veeckman, Carina, and Shenja van der Graaf. 2015. The city as living laboratory: Empowering citizens with the citadel toolkit. *Technology Innovation Management Review* 5.3. http://timreview.ca/article/877

The White House and Office of the Press Secretary. 2015. FACT SHEET: Administration announces new "Smart Cities" initiative to help communities tackle local challenges and improve city services. The White House. https://www.whitehouse.gov/the-press-office/2015/09/14/fact-sheet-administration-announces-new-smart-cities-initiative-help.

Zhang, Qi, Lu Cheng, and Raouf Boutaba. 2010. Cloud computing: State-of-the-art and research challenges. *Journal of Internet Services and Applications* 1.1: 7–18. http://link.springer.com/article/10.1007/s13174-010-0007-6.

11

Financial Viability of Energy Conservation Using Natural Light in an Institutional Building in India

Pooja Sharma and Dibakar Rakshit

CONTENTS

11.1 Introduction...127
11.2 Methodology 129
11.3 Results and Discussions 129
    11.3.1 Optimizing Daylight Level 129
        11.3.1.1 Orientation 129
        11.3.1.2 Visual Light Transmittance of the Window Glazing.........131
        11.3.1.3 Window-to-Wall Ratio..133
        11.3.1.4 Window-to-Wall Ratio Combined with VLT 134
    11.3.2 Suggested Passive Techniques for Daylight Optimization...........135
        11.3.2.1 Light Shelves..135
        11.3.2.2 Light Pipe with Multiple Reflectors.............................139
    11.3.3 Reducing Lighting Power Density of Artificial Lighting 141
    11.3.4 Techno-Economic Evaluation..141
        11.3.4.1 Initial Capital Cost 142
        11.3.4.2 Benefit-to-Cost Ratio...144
    11.3.5 CO_2 Emissions Reduction 145
11.4 Conclusions...146
References 146

11.1 Introduction

In accordance with the *Buildings Energy Data Book* (2011) (Pacific Northwest National Laboratory 2012), the lighting consumption of a commercial building in 2010 was estimated to be approximately 20.2%. It is therefore imperative to develop techniques that depreciate lighting energy consumption to develop energy-efficient buildings. The sun is the major source of energy on Earth. Light from the sun can cause the most significant reduction in the lighting energy consumption of a building. Natural light is the most economical source of illuminance in a building. Utilizing natural light leads to a reduction in the usage of artificial lighting, thereby saving energy. The U.S. Green Building Council estimates that a 50%–80% reduction in lighting energy load can be achieved from a well-designed daylight-lit building (USGBC 1996). Lighting solutions have direct repercussions on occupant performance, comfort, health, and satisfaction. They are also prime effectors of annual building energy consumption. The importance of the availability of daylight in indoor environmental conditions has been spotlighted by innumerable works and reviews, especially in recent years.

Turner et al. (2014) presented a new methodology for characterizing the energy performance of buildings suitable for city-scale, top-down energy modeling. They observed that building properties have the greatest impact on simulated energy performance as identified via a review of sensitivity analysis studies. Khansari et al. (2014) used a complex, large-scale, interconnected, open, and sociotechnical (CLIOS) model, a conceptual soft systems model to explore the impact of smart city technologies on the behavioral change of households with regard to energy consumption.

There are many studies analyzing the concepts of energy consumption in buildings. These studies mainly explain energy conservation through the reduction of space conditioning load or lighting load. Tagliabue et al. (2012) studied three different window opening configurations for an office building in Italy. Their analysis was based on the optimization of natural lighting, visual comfort, electricity consumption, cooling/heating demand and consumption, orientation, and location. It was observed that, considering the visual comfort parameters, the north window-lit and the skylight-lit offices presented better conditions of luminance, illuminance, and daylight factor, without specific problems of glare compared with the southern aspect. Kralikova et al. (2015) presented new trends and progressive strategies to reduce the energy consumption of lighting systems for a building in Slovakia. They observed that, in new constructions, the installation of energy-efficient lighting cost more compared with less efficient lighting, but that the consumption of energy was lower, more economical, and environment friendly. They also observed that lighting controls, daylight utilization, adequate spacing, and use of light-colored walls and ceilings were used as energy-saving techniques.

Studies by Bulow (2008) pertaining to daylight availability and electricity use for lighting in offices demonstrated that it is possible to reduce energy use by 50% with different proposals for occupancy and lighting control. In the context of daylight studies of South Asian countries for building energy conservation, Chel (2014) analyzed skylight illuminance inside a dome-shaped adobe house under the composite climate of New Delhi (India). He observed that daylight is cool light compared with artificial light, which leads to additional heat gain due to the inefficiency of artificial lighting. Ghoshal and Neogi (2014) evaluated different types of glazing for Indian climatic zones in terms of visual light transmittance (VLT) and thermal conductivity, and found that electrochromic evacuated glazing was advantageous in reducing energy consumption and controlling solar gain.

Manzan and Padovan (2014) presented an optimization approach to designing a fixed external shading device for an energy-efficient office to protect it against external thermal load. They took into account energy demands for heating, cooling, and lighting appliances, along with the interaction with an internal movable venetian blind for providing shade from sunlight. A study undertaken by Gul and Patidar (2015) analyzed the relationship between the electrical energy requirement pattern and the user activity and occupancy pattern for a nonresidential building. Bellia et al. (2014) studied the winter and summer daylight characteristics of office spaces and concluded that the spectral distributions and correlated color temperature of the light reaching the eye of a person seated at a desk in these offices were similar. This similarity exists irrespective of the different sky conditions and seasons and of the rooms' different characteristics. Appelfeld and Svendsen (2013) evaluated the dynamic performance of a prototype shading and daylight-redirecting system. Keeping an account of visual comfort, the study concluded that 20% of lighting energy can be saved by using daylight.

This literature survey considers that daylight utilization is another remarkable factor that can be utilized for reducing building energy consumption and contributing toward the establishment of smart cities. However, a detailed analysis reflecting passive techniques for increasing luminous flux level, VLT, window-to-wall ratio (WWR), and controlled usage of artificial lighting for a building on the Indian subcontinent has not been dealt with. This chapter will attempt to discuss these aspects and provide insight to make decisions regarding their utilization in building energy conservation. Natural light enters a workspace through glazed areas. Thus, the primary approach to enhance lighting energy performance is to increase the amount of daylight in a building.

Finally, this chapter will set forth the optimum techniques that should be adopted to increase the amount of daylight entering a building while also considering the financial effect of adopting these techniques and, finally, the impact on carbon dioxide (CO_2) emissions. The chapter elucidates the building orientation, VLT of glazing, WWR, and the combination of these factors.

11.2 Methodology

In the present analysis, an east–west-oriented academic block of an institutional building in New Delhi (N 28.58°, E 77.2°) with six floors has been studied for its illuminance peculiarities. The analysis was carried out on September 22 (the day of the equinox). The building is modeled and simulated using Virtual Environment software from Integrated Environmental Solutions (Figures 11.1 and 11.2).

Weather data were obtained from the Office of Energy Efficiency and Renewable Energy. Performance analysis was carried out for the present case and for a set of proposed cases. The values of the various parameters considered for simulation analysis are presented in Table 11.1.

The analysis evaluates the factors that affect the amount of natural light entering the regularly occupied spaces thereby creating a better quality environment in the space. Utilizing maximum natural light also abolishes the need for artificial methods of lighting and reduces the final energy consumption, which ultimately leads to a reduction in CO_2 emissions.

11.3 Results and Discussions

11.3.1 Optimizing Daylight Level

Daylight level is one of the important parameters that determine the level of human comfort and the indoor environment quality of a space. To optimize luminous flux, the following approaches are undertaken for daylight characteristics analysis:

11.3.1.1 Orientation

Based on analysis, first and foremost, the optimal orientation of the building is suggested according to the building operating duration and how much impact it will create on building performance in terms of luminous flux. The optimized orientation is also determined

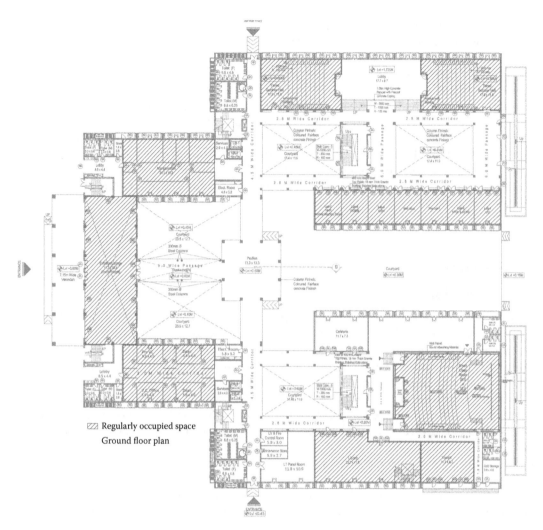

FIGURE 11.1
Building floor plans.

by the amount of glazed area in each direction. The building is located in the Northern Hemisphere and ideally operates between 9 a.m. and 4 p.m. In this condition, the sun moves due south from east to west (Figure 11.3). Thus, the façade that has maximum glazing should be exposed to the sun during the operating duration.

It can be observed in Figure 11.4 that the building has a maximum window area on the western façade, which amounts to 50% of the total building area, whereas the the southern façade, which faces the sun during the major operational hours, has only 1.4% of the total window percentage of the building.

Hence, it is desirable to orient the building in a north–south orientation in order to have the maximum window area on the southern façade, that is, 50%. Therefore, the building is rotated by 90° to achieve maximum daylight and the rest of the analysis is carried out after orienting the building in a north–south direction. The proposed orientation window percentage graph is presented in Figure 11.5.

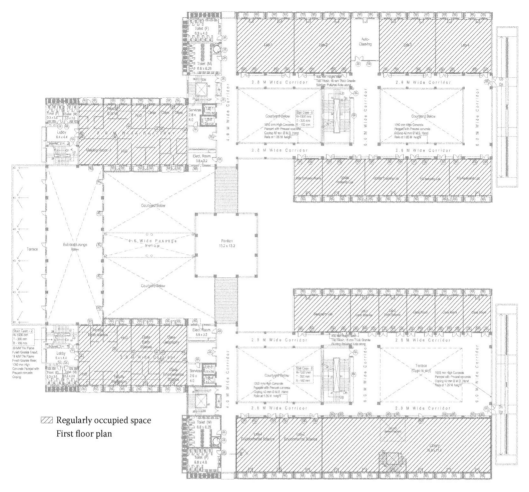

FIGURE 11.1 (CONTINUED)

Thus, changing the orientation of the building maximizes the amount of daylight entering the spaces as it increases the surface area for light transmittance. This is one of the primary feasible options as no cost is involved in changing the orientation of the building.

11.3.1.2 Visual Light Transmittance of the Window Glazing

VLT is the fraction of visible light transmitted through the glazing. The analysis proceeds after optimizing the building orientation to north–south. The building has glass of uniform properties throughout the building. Since the chapter focuses on maximizing daylight, the VLT of the glass is the most important property to be optimized. The chapter follows the threshold values of luminous flux as recommended in the National Building Code (NBC), Part 8, Section 1, table 4 (Bureau of Indian Standards 2005) for each type of space. It is worth mentioning that the NBC doesn't quantify the minimum percentage of area that should be above the threshold value, so a space is considered compliant according to the USGBC's Leadership in Energy and Environmental Design (LEED) version 4 daylighting standards (USGBC 2013). According to LEED, a space is

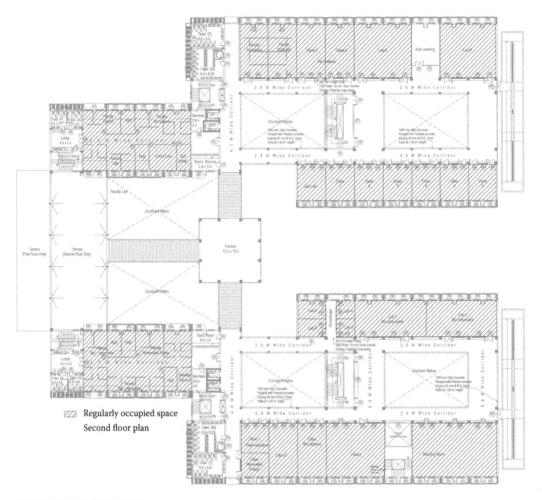

FIGURE 11.1 (CONTINUED)

considered compliant with standards if it receives the threshold value of luminous flux in at least 75% of the space.

In the present case, glass of VLT 45% is used throughout the building for glazing purposes. The building is simulated to estimate the lighting pattern and luminous flux in all regularly occupied spaces. According to the simulations, the worst case of poor luminous flux received within the building is in the pharmaceutical classroom situated on the second floor of the building (Figure 11.1). Therefore, the basis of all further analysis is this worst-case scenario, receiving a threshold value of luminous flux of 200 lux in only 9% of the total room area.

The optimization of VLT to increase the amount of daylight is another primary approach as it doesn't alter the architectural definition of the building. A study of the effect of increasing VLT on luminous flux was done for the present WWR of 20%. Figure 11.6 illustrates this effect.

It is noted that as the VLT increases, the flux increases in the space because the amount of daylight entering the space increases. The increase in VLT is competitive enough to increase the luminous flux in a regularly occupied space. The average illumination in the worst case

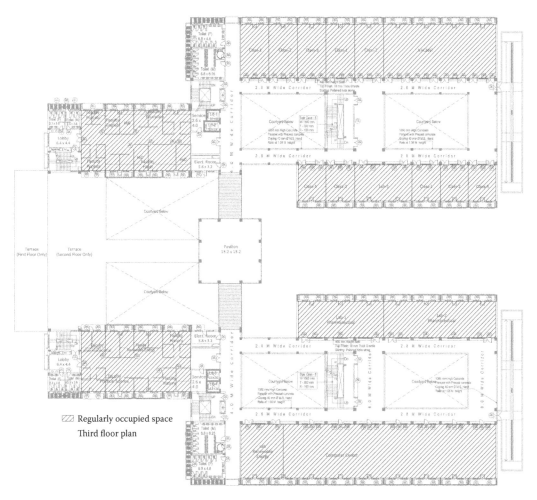

FIGURE 11.1 (CONTINUED)

of the pharmaceutical classroom is also increased to a maximum of 255.63 lux, providing a threshold value of 200 lux at 90% VLT in 28.2% of the room area. But the percentage floor area above the threshold value of illumination is still less than 200 lux, as can be seen in Table 11.2. Thus, for this specific case, a more suitable alternative is again sought.

11.3.1.3 Window-to-Wall Ratio

It was observed in the previous section that, even after a significant increase in average illumination, an increase in VLT is unable to suffice the required increase in luminous flux above the threshold value of 200 lux for a minimum 75% area. Thus, another measure to satisfy the objective is to increase the glazed surface area on the façade. Keeping the VLT of glass constant as proposed in the present case, that is 45%, the change in flux due to an increase in WWR is studied (Figure 11.7). The maximum WWR is limited to 60%.

It can be seen from the graph in Figure 11.7 that the average luminous flux increases with an increase in WWR as more surface area is available for the transmittance of daylight. Considering the worst case under study, an increase in WWR to 60% increases the

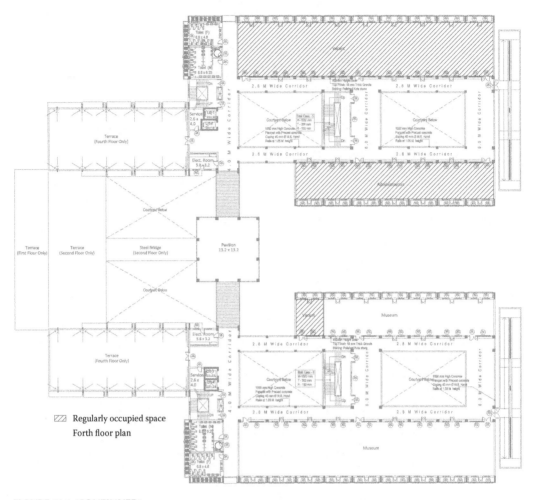

FIGURE 11.1 (CONTINUED)

percentage of floor area above the threshold value of 200 lux to 76.8% from an initial value of 9%, as represented in Table 11.3, by achieving an average luminous flux of 424.05 lux.

11.3.1.4 Window-to-Wall Ratio Combined with VLT

Increasing the glazed area to the maximum limit possible helps in achieving the desired luminous flux through daylighting, but on the other hand also decreases the financial viability as it increases the cost to almost 3.5 times the initial cost. It is also observed from Figure 11.6 that using a glass of higher transmittance also increases the luminous flux but, for the worst case in the given analysis, an increase in VLT to the maximum limit available still doesn't satisfy the luminous flux requirement. For this, the proposed set of VLT and WWR combinations are simulated in conjunction for the worst case. The combination of VLT and WWR finally leads to the desired luminous flux of 200 lux in a minimum of 75% of the room area (Table 11.4).

The values highlighted in Table 11.4 depict that, for the combination of VLT and WWR, the desired luminous flux in the worst-case scenario is achieved. A comparison

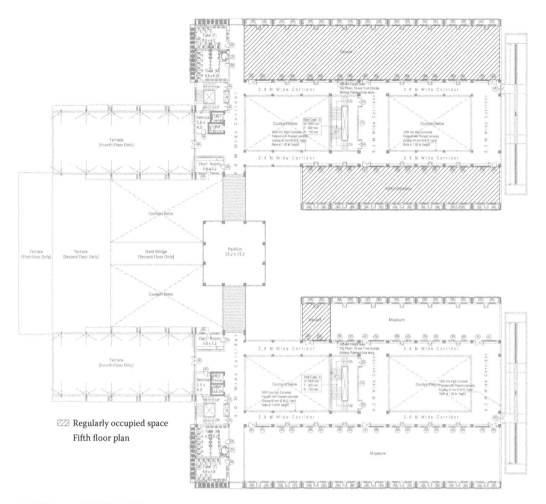

FIGURE 11.1 (CONTINUED)

of all the feasible solutions, in terms of percentage area above threshold, is expressed in Figure 11.8.

11.3.2 Suggested Passive Techniques for Daylight Optimization

Apart from the techniques mentioned previously, some techniques have been explored that always enhance the luminous flux achieved due to daylighting. This chapter highlights the physics involved in the usage of these techniques.

11.3.2.1 Light Shelves

Light shelves are horizontal reflective surfaces used as a passive technique to enhance daylighting from windows into regularly occupied spaces and simultaneously to provide shading to control glare problems.

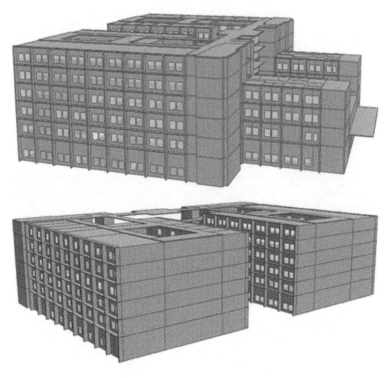

FIGURE 11.2
Building isometric view depicting the modeled building in the simulation program.

TABLE 11.1

Value of Various Parameters Considered for Simulation Analysis

Serial no.	Parameter	Value
Material property		
1.	Roof (150 mm RCC 40 mm PUF)	U-value = 0.493 W/m²°C
2.	Wall (300 mm AAC block)	U-value = 0.474 W/m²°C
3.	Glass (present case)	U-value = 5.7 W/m²°C; transmittance—45%
Reflectance		
1.	Roof	Inner 70%; outer 10%
2.	Wall	Inner 50%; outer 10%
3.	Ground	20%

Note: RCC, reinforced cement concrete; PUF, polyurethane foam; AAC, autoclaved aerated concrete.

Light shelves direct daylight to the extreme ends of regularly occupied spaces and improve the luminous flux. They protect the window from direct radiant energy and thus also help in the reduction of the cooling load. The light shelf extends beyond the shadow created by the overhang and reflects daylight upward to illuminate the room ceiling. This reflected light contains reflective illumination from the ceiling that reduces the need for artificial illumination (Figure 11.9).

It has already been found that light shelves on south-facing façades of buildings increase remarkably daylighting quality; improve inner space illumination through the

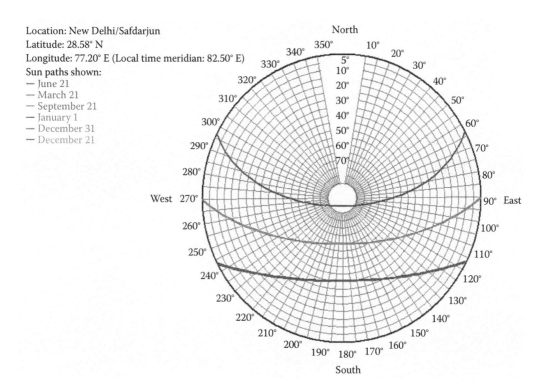

FIGURE 11.3
Movement of the sun in the Northern Hemisphere. (Adapted from IES VE, Sun Cast Tool.)

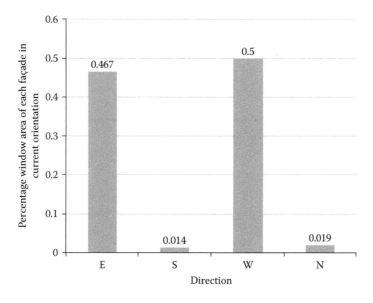

FIGURE 11.4
Percentage window area on each façade in the current orientation.

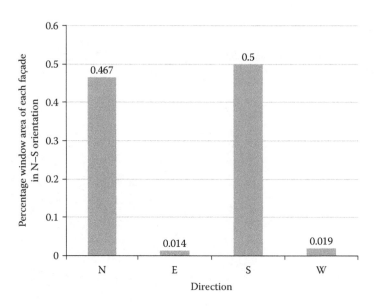

FIGURE 11.5
Percentage window area on each façade in a north–south orientation.

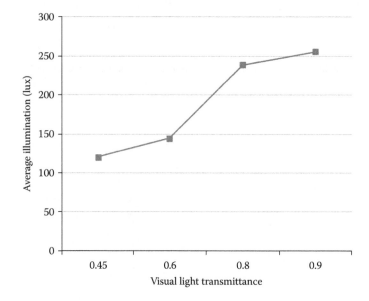

FIGURE 11.6
Variation in average illumination with VLT at 18% WWR.

TABLE 11.2

Results of Simulation Showing Percentage Room Area above
Threshold Value of Luminous Flux with WWR 18%

VLT	45%	60%	85%	90%
Percentage area above threshold	9.0%	15.4%	26.9%	28.2%
Average illumination (lux)	120.54	144.66	238.78	255.63

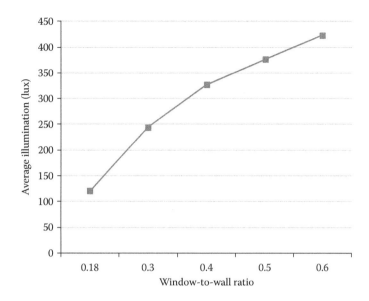

FIGURE 11.7
Variation in average illumination with WWR at 45% VLT.

TABLE 11.3

Results of Simulation Showing Percentage Room Area above Threshold Value of Luminous Flux with WWR 18%

WWR	18%	30%	40%	50%	60%
Percentage area above threshold	9.0%	37.8%	51.9%	63.5%	76.3%
Average illumination (lux)	120.54	245.08	327.23	376.22	424.05

TABLE 11.4

Results of Simulation Showing Percentage Room Area above Threshold at Varying VLT and WWR

	VLT 45%	VLT 60%	VLT 85%	VLT 90%
WWR 18%	9.0%	15.4%	26.9%	28.2%
WWR 30%	37.8%	47.4%	69.2%	72.4%
WWR 40%	51.9%	63.5%	96.8%	99.4%
WWR 50%	63.5%	78.8%	100.0%	100.0%
WWR 60%	76.3%	96.8%	100.0%	100.0%

improvement of light distribution, which can lead to glare reduction; increase the degree of health and physical comfort; and increase light penetration in inner functional spaces (Malin 2007).

11.3.2.2 Light Pipe with Multiple Reflectors

A light pipe is a device that facilitates the transmission of daylight into the interior areas of a building that have insufficient luminous flux. It works without any electrical energy consumption and thus can be considered a source of renewable energy.

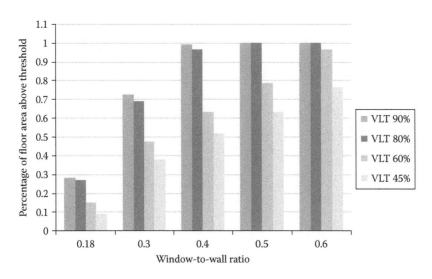

FIGURE 11.8
Comparative analysis of proposed feasible solutions.

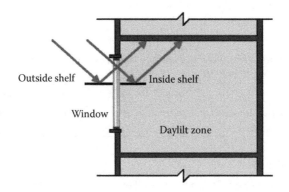

FIGURE 11.9
Working principle of the light shelf.

The working principle of a light pipe involves refraction and reflection (Figure 11.10).

A light pipe involves daylight being brought into the space by the reflection inside the pipe, and the light ray supply thus becomes the lighting function inside the building. The light is guided through the pipe by two phenomena:

1. The total internal refraction of the light pipe
2. The reflection of the mirror

In a composite type of climate under clear sky conditions, the transmittance of the light pipe was observed to be 40%–45%. This was during midday hours (12 pm–2 pm). Around 25% of transmittance was during evening and morning hours. For a partly overcast sky, transmittance was found to be in the range of 30%–40% (Patil and Kaushik 2015). The light pipe transmits both beam and diffuse illuminance, causing an uneven distribution of illuminance on the working plane.

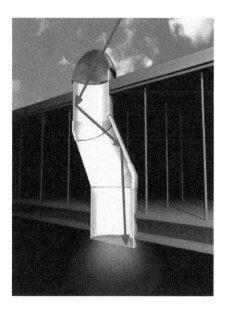

FIGURE 11.10
Working principle of the light pipe.

11.3.3 Reducing Lighting Power Density of Artificial Lighting

Lighting power density (LPD) is a simple evaluation that signifies whether a space can achieve energy savings. LPD is defined as watts of lighting per square meter of room floor area (W/m^2). The analysis focuses on the financial benefits and enhanced energy performance of using daylight instead of artificial light. If, in some cases, there are no options to optimize the luminous flux by any of the previously discussed techniques but enhanced energy performance is still the target, then the most dynamic approach is to reduce the LPD.

All energy-efficient buildings in India provide LPD as per Energy Conservation Building Code (ECBC) guidelines (Bureau of Energy Efficiency, ECBC user guide 2007). They do not exceed the limiting values proposed by the ECBC. In the present building, all spaces follow the same standard. The energy consumption of all regularly occupied spaces turns out to be 215,625.55 kWh/year. A set of reduced LPD values for each space type is also proposed in accordance with the ANSI/ASHRAE/IESNA standard 90.1–2007 requirement, which reduces the energy consumption of regularly occupied spaces to 110,748.16 kWh/year. The existing and proposed LPD values are enumerated in Table 11.5.

The most important effect of LPD reduction is the reduction of the environmental and economic impact associated with excessive energy use.

11.3.4 Techno-Economic Evaluation

When we consider energy conservation, we must also consider the barriers that obstruct the implementation of energy conservation measures. Along with performance analysis, it is also essential to evaluate the financial viability of optimization measures.

TABLE 11.5

Existing and Proposed Case Lighting Power Densities

Type of Space	Existing ECBC-based LPD (W/m²)	Proposed LPD (W/m²)
Cabins/vacant	11.8	3.49
Classrooms	15.1	3.26
Services	7.5	7.5
Cafeteria	9.7	9.7
Laboratories	15.1	3.95
Library	12.9	12.9
Seminar hall	14	14
Fitness center	4.3	4.3
Museum	10.8	10.8
Lounge	12.9	3.55
Common room	11.8	3.94

In this chapter, the optimization measures are evaluated in terms of

1. Initial capital cost
2. Benefit-to-cost ratio (BCR)

The most effective tool to easily understand the financial viability in this situation is the BCR. Calculating the benefit to cost for new or improved energy technologies is a simple economic function. When comparing projects, the BCR provides an indication of the investment risk involved in the project.

11.3.4.1 Initial Capital Cost

Initial capital cost is the direct capital cost accrued at the time of purchasing. In this chapter, the direct optimization measures have been compared to evaluate each and find out the most suitable solution, as can be seen in Figure 11.7.

It can be seen from the physics discussed previously and according to the simulation outputs that increasing WWR has a substantial effect on increases in luminous flux as compared with VLT. But, according to Figure 11.11, the cost incurred decreases with increased VLT whereas, in the case of WWR, it increases substantially.

Thus, Figure 11.10 provides a cost comparison of all possible solutions obtained from the simulation (tabulated in Table 11.4). The cost of glass has been sourced from Saint Gobain.

Moving on to passive techniques (Section 4.2), the cost of implementing these techniques is expressed in rupees per meter squared (Figure 11.12).

It can be seen that the highest cost is incurred in the case of the light pipe, which costs approximately Rs. 37,800/m². Also, the cost of the light shelf is much higher, costing approximately Rs. 9450/m² compared with the cost of optimizing WWR, which is approximately Rs. 550/m².

It can be seen that increasing WWR escalates the cost of improving the indoor environmental conditions to Rs. 4,061,728 from an initial amount of Rs. 1,205,627, which financially is not a feasible and practical option (Figure 11.13). Also, lower VLT glass is high-performance glass, as seen in terms of thermal loads; hence, it is expensive.

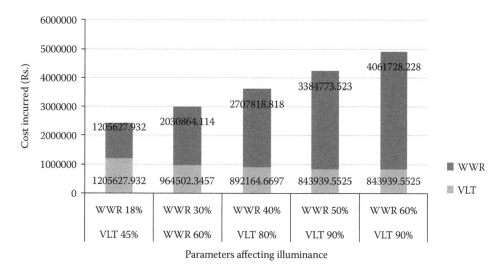

FIGURE 11.11
Cost analysis of increasing WWR and VLT.

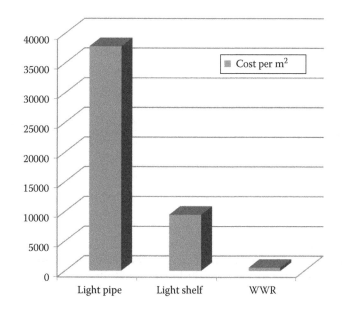

FIGURE 11.12
Cost comparison of light shelf, WWR, and light pipe.

An increase in VLT also does not cause any increase in the cost of optimization; however, as can be seen from the results discussed previously, increasing VLT in this case does not suffice the requirement.

Increasing the glazed area (WWR) to the maximum limit possible helps in achieving the desired luminous flux through daylighting but, on the other hand, it also increases the cost of optimization as observed in Figure 11.13.

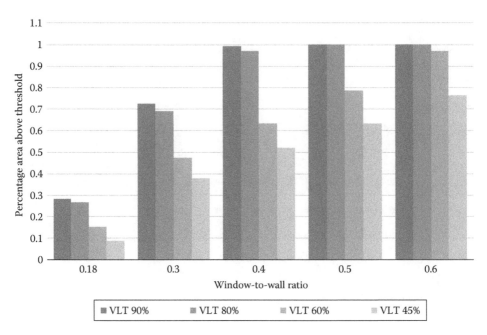

FIGURE 11.13
Cost comparison of proposed feasible VLT and WWR solutions.

Thus, it is essential to figure out the most technically and economically feasible solution, which could be a combination of identifying the most feasible options along with satisfying the objective to achieve a desired luminous flux through daylighting, and also financially viable for the user.

11.3.4.2 Benefit-to-Cost Ratio

The BCR is the ratio of the net present value of benefits to the net present value of costs. It is an effective tool for decision making. It is most useful because it provides a starting point from which to begin the evaluation of a project.

The BCR is also useful because it allows comparisons to be made between investments or projects. These comparisons are made easier because all investments are evaluated using the same method. It can be calculated using the following equation (Brent 2007):

$$\mathrm{BCR} = \frac{\dfrac{B_t}{(1+r)^t}}{\dfrac{C_t}{(1+r)^t}} \tag{11.1}$$

where:
- B_t is the benefit in time t
- C_t is the cost in time t
- r is the discount rate
- t is the year in which future benefits are realized

TABLE 11.6

Values of Various Parameters Considered for Benefit Cost Analysis

Parameter	Unit	Value
90% VLT Glass with 18% WWR		
Initial investment	INR	843,939.55
Electricity cost saved at the end of 5 years	INR	7,297,140.87
45% VLT glass with 18% WWR		
Initial investment	INR	1,205,627.93
Electricity cost saved at the end of 5 years	INR	7,297,140.87
45% VLT glass with 60% WWR		
Initial investment	INR	4,061,728.23
Electricity cost saved at the end of 5 years	INR	7,297,140.87

If the BCR exceeds 1, then the project might be a good candidate for acceptance. Table 11.6 defines the values of various parameters used to determine the BCR for all suggested techniques.

It is assumed that the benefits accrue at the end of 5 years at a discount rate of 10%. It should also be noted that the cost of a light shelf and a light pipe is available only as the cost per meter squared as this cost is finalized after the design and placing of the installation. Hence, the BCR allows a comparison only among direct techniques.

Using Equation 11.1, the BCR is calculated as follows:

1. BCR for 90% VLT glass with 18% WWR = 0.12
2. BCR for 45% VLT glass with 18% WWR = 0.17
3. BCR for 45% VLT glass with 60% WWR = 0.56

The best possible solution may be the most efficient, but it is not necessarily financially possible or have the best BCR. Therefore, we need to identify a solution that, apart from being energy efficient, is also financially viable.

11.3.5 CO_2 Emissions Reduction

The latest World Bank data show that CO_2 emissions in India increased from 1.6 to 1.7 metric tons per capita from 2010 to 2011. India is the third highest country in terms of absolute emissions, but 127th in terms of per capita output with 1.7 metric tons per capita. India contributes 6.41% to total global CO_2 emissions, which emphasizes the need to reduce CO_2 emissions from various sources.

Apart from energy savings and lighting load reduction, the most important impact of using natural light is the reduction of CO_2 emissions in the environment. In the present case, the use of natural light in 100% of regularly occupied spaces reduces the overall CO_2 emissions from artificial lighting consumption of these spaces by 100%. Also, if artificial lighting with reduced LPD is employed, CO_2 emissions are cut by 55.6%.

11.4 Conclusions

This chapter has presented the results of energy conservation in an institutional build-ing using daylighting instead of artificial lighting to achieve the desired luminous flux. Several solutions for the worst-case scenario have been presented. The most important finding is that all of the solutions have a positive impact on the luminous flux require-ments of the space. The passive techniques proposed have a significant positive effect on daylighting, avoiding the direct penetration of sunlight into the room.

Lighting is a factor that provides a significant opportunity to reduce operating costs, improve occupant performance, and reduce greenhouse gases that contribute to global warming. The aspect of the daylighting technique to be considered for enhancing lumi-nous flux is its cost-effectiveness. As observed in Section 4.4, increasing VLT as a measure, which has a minimum initial investment, also has the least BCR, whereas maximizing WWR with a high-performance glass, which has low VLT, has a high initial investment cost but a greater BCR.

From these results, and considering the worst case, it is observed that substantial lumi-nous flux through natural light only can be achieved by increasing the WWR in combina-tion with VLT or by using passive techniques such as light pipes and light shelves. VLT alone also increases the luminous flux but, for the case under analysis here, the desired results could not be achieved.

A reduction in the LPD of artificial lighting systems is also proposed, and reduces the total lighting load of all regularly occupied spaces to 110,748.16 kWh/year from 251,625.55 kWh/year.

Achieving the required luminous flux through daylighting helps in attaining approxi-mately 100% energy savings in the gross wattage consumption of the regularly occupied spaces and also reduces CO_2 emissions by 55.8%. Hence, using natural light not only improves the indoor air quality but also favors the improvement of outdoor environmen-tal conditions.

Multifactor optimization is denoted as a very efficient technique since it takes into con-sideration all the parameters involved and can lead to the selection of an optimal solution to be implemented for the project.

The present analysis identifies the critical/worst case that shows the worst luminous flux, and hence determines the best feasible solutions. For further analysis, the impact of the optimization of the parameters for daylighting on cooling load can be explored, which could yield the most viable elucidation to optimize both cooling load and luminous flux simultaneously.

References

Appefled, D., Svendsen, S. 2013. Performance of a daylight-redirecting glass-shading system. *Energy and Buildings* 64: 309–316.

Bellia, L., Pedace, A., Barbato, G. 2014. Winter and summer analysis of daylight characteristics in offices. *Building and Environment* 81.4: 150–161.

Brent, R.J. 2008. *Applied Cost-Benefit Analysis*, 2nd edn. Cheltenham: Edward Elgar Publishing.

Bulow, H. 2008. *Daylight in Glazed Office Buildings. A Comparative Study of Daylight Availability, Luminance and Illuminance Distribution for an Office Room with Three Different Glass Areas.* Lund: Department of Architecture and Built Environment, Division of Energy and Building Design, Lund University, Faculty of Engineering.

Bureau of Energy Efficiency. 2007. *Energy Conservation Building Code User Guide.* New Delhi: Bureau of Energy Efficiency.

Bureau of Indian Standards. 2005. *National Building Code of India*, 2nd Revision. New Delhi: Bureau of Indian Standards.

Chel, A. 2014. Performance of skylight illuminance inside a dome shaped adobe house under composite climate at New Delhi (India): A typical zero energy passive house. *Alexandria Engineering Journal* 53.2: 385–397.

Ghoshal, S., Neogi, S. 2014. Advance glazing system: Energy efficiency approach for buildings: A review. *Energy Procedia* 51.1: 352–358.

Gul, M.S., Patidar, S. 2015. Understanding the energy consumption and occupancy of a multi-purpose academic building. *Energy and Buildings* 87: 155–165.

Khansari, N., Mostashari, A., Mansouri, M. 2014. Conceptual modeling of the impact of smart cities on household energy consumption. *Procedia Computer Science* 28: 81–86.

Kralikova, R., Andrejiova, M., Wessely, E. 2015. Energy saving techniques and strategies for illumination in industry. *Procedia Engineering* 100: 187–195.

Malin, N. 2007. Light Louver Offers Low-Profile Alternative to Light Shelves. Retrieved from https://www2.buildinggreen.com/article/lightlouver-offers-low-profile-alternative-light-shelves.

Manzan, M., Padovan, R. 2014. Multi-criteria energy and daylighting optimization for an office with fixed and moveable shading devices. *Advances in Building Research* 9.2: 238–252.

NREL (National Renewable Energy Laboratory). 2015. Field test best practices. NREL Buildings Research. U.S. Department of Energy. https://buildingsfieldtest.nrel.gov/.

Pacific Northwest National Laboratory, ed. 2012. *Buildings Energy Data Book 2011: Chapter 3, page no. 2.* Washington, DC: U.S. DOE Energy Efficiency and Renewable Energy.

Patil, K.N., Kaushik, S.C. 2015. Performance study of a light pipe daylight system in composite climate of India. Advances in Power Generation from Renewable Energy Sources Conference, Rajasthan Technical University, Kota June 15–16. APGRESS.

Tagliabue, L.C., Buzzetti, M., Arosio, B. 2012. Energy saving through the sun: Analysis of visual comfort and energy consumption in office space. *Energy Procedia* 30: 693–703.

Turner, J.N., Kinnane, O., Basu, B. 2014. Demand-side characterization of the smart city for energy modelling. *Energy and Buildings* 62: 160–169.

U.S. Green Building Council. 1996. Indoor quality update. October, Vol. 9, No. 10. Washington, DC: U.S. Green Building Council.

U.S. Green Building Council, 2013. *LEED v4 for Building Design and Construction*. Washington, DC: U.S. Green Building Council.

12

Management of Multidimensional Risk for Digital Services in Smart Cities

Syed Ziaul Mustafa and Arpan Kumar Kar

CONTENTS

12.1 Introduction..150
    12.1.1 Overview of Smart Cities..150
    12.1.2 Definitions of Smart Cities 150
        12.1.2.1 Smart City Dimensions 150
        12.1.2.2 Smart People 151
        12.1.2.3 Smart Economy 151
        12.1.2.4 Smart Mobility...152
        12.1.2.5 Smart Environment 152
        12.1.2.6 Smart Living 152
    12.1.3 Smart Governance 152
        12.1.3.1 Smart City Governance 153
    12.1.4 Public Utilities and Information-Based Services 153
12.2 What Are Digital Services?...153
    12.2.1 Service versus Digital Service...153
    12.2.2 What Are the Different Categorizations/Classifications of Digital
        Services? 154
        12.2.2.1 Categorization of Digital Services in Published Literature 155
12.3 What Is Risk? 157
    12.3.1 Perceived Risk 157
    12.3.2 Dimensions of Perceived Risk..157
12.4 Multifaceted Risk Mapping for Different Categories of Digital Services.................160
    12.4.1 Multifaceted Risk Mapping for Technology-Assisted Consumer Contact....160
    12.4.2 Multifaceted Risk Mapping for Technology-Facilitated Consumer Contact....161
    12.4.3 Multifaceted Risk Mapping for Technology-Mediated Consumer Contact....161
    12.4.4 Multifaceted Risk Mapping for Technology-Generated Consumer Contact....161
    12.4.5 Multifaceted Risk Mapping for Technology-Free Consumer Contact 162
12.5 Conclusion 162
12.6 Future Research 163
References 163

12.1 Introduction

Smart cities are creative, sustainable, and livable cities that are part of urban management and development. Experts from various domains, such as consultants, corporations, marketing specialists, and city officials, are involved in framing how smart cities will be conceptualized, understood, and planned.

Smart cites can be divided into two major categories, one that focuses on technological aspects and a second that focuses on the object of analysis. A smart city can be defined as an assemblage of technologies such as information and communication technologies (ICT) infrastructure, smart cards for public transport, and e-governance aimed at increasing competitiveness and administrative efficiency as well as social inclusion.

Since 2011, contributions to smart cities have been critically scrutinized from different viewpoints such as science and technology, political economy, government mentality studies, and ideological critique. In general, smart cities create a relationship between technology and society. There are lots of discussions in the literature regarding the impact of ICT in cities.

12.1.1 Overview of Smart Cities

With the increased concentration of people in the urban agglomeration, there have been calls to design new strategies in order to improve and maintain a livable, accessible, sustainable, and economically viable environment for citizens. Recent digital technologies enable cities and policy makers to sense the relationship between urban development and ICT. Most of the marketing and theoretical concepts have been introduced, such as cyber cities (Graham and Marvin, 1999), techno cities (Downey and McGuigan, 1999), wired cities (Dutton et al., 1987), knowledge-based cities (Carrillo, 2006), Wiki cities (Calabrese et al., 2007), real-time cities (Townsend, 2000), networked cities (Castells, 1996), digital cities (Komninos, 2006), and sentient cities (Shepard, 2011).

The revolution in digital services has enabled cities and policy makers to link ICTs and urban development. In response, various theoretical and marketing conceptualizations have been introduced. The concept of smart cities has gained the widest recognition among the urban researcher and the practitioner, despite many variances. Various definitions of smart cities are found in the literature, since the term *smart city* is a fuzzy concept and is not consistent in the literature.

12.1.2 Definitions of Smart Cities

The concept of smart cities originated from various definitions such as information city, intelligent city, digital city, knowledge city, and ubiquitous city. According to a paper on smart cities by Angelidou (2015), the smart city is defined as follows:

Smart cities represent a conceptual urban development model on the basis of the utilization of human, collective, and technological capital for the development of urban agglomerations (Angelidou, 2015).

12.1.2.1 Smart City Dimensions

The smart city concept has evolved from "information city," and later evolved to an idea of an ICT-centered smart city. The major dimensions of the smart city are smart people, smart mobility, smart economy, smart living, smart environment, and smart governance (Kumar, 2015).

12.1.2.2 Smart People

Smart people should have attributes as shown in Figure 12.1. The Human Development Index is considered the most important aspect. The next most important attribute is the graduate enrolment ratio, followed by the level of qualification. Smart people should have the zeal for lifelong learning as well as social and ethnic plurality. Open-mindedness is also a quality of smart people, as is the flexibility to adapt to changes in the environment as well as being creative enough to contribute to the educational world. Smart people possess a democratic nature and participate in public life.

12.1.2.3 Smart Economy

A smart economy is driven by innovation and supported by universities. The economy of the city is such that it creates an economic image globally and will also have a trademark. Productivity and a flexible labor market should be provided by the city administrative authority. The economy should have international branding as well as generate high diversity.

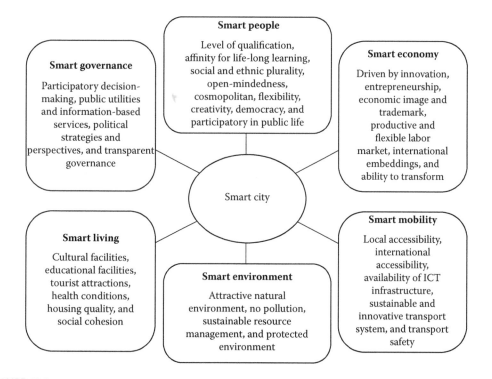

FIGURE 12.1
Dimensions of the smart city. (Adapted from Kumar, T. M. Vinod., *E-Governance for Smart Cities*, Springer, Singapore, 2015.)

12.1.2.4 Smart Mobility

Smart mobility means that the city should have national and international accessibility. Use of ICT ensures that technology has been used widely during the design of national highways and bridges. Metros, monorails, and an intelligent transport system will be used by daily commuters. The urban design should be such that it gives importance to "last-mile" connectivity. The transport system should be sustainable and innovative, and should also address the safety of daily and occasional commuters within and outside the city.

12.1.2.5 Smart Environment

A smart environment refers to an attractive, natural environment with no pollution. Importance has been given to the carbon footprint and the natural resources available. There should be greenery in almost every part of the city, which should have a waste management system as well as natural resource management. The city should also have a system to protect the existing greenery of the city from any external factor.

12.1.2.6 Smart Living

Smart living is characterized by diverse cultural facilities available to all kinds of religions, whether they belong to major or minor communities. World-class education facilities will be provided by establishing world-class colleges and universities. Smart living should also include tourist attractions as well as a world-class hospital with all the latest technology-enabled devices and equipment to ensure that residents have healthy lives. Good quality housing as well as social cohesion will be provided to the citizens of the city.

12.1.3 Smart Governance

Smart governance is an advanced form of e-governance. It is about making the right policy choices and the implementation of same. The "knowledge society" is given a set of elements for smart governance, which are open sharing of information and its use, transparent decision making, collaboration of stakeholders and their participation, improvement in government services, and operation through the use of intelligent technologies as shown in Figure 12.2.

> **Smart governance**
>
> Participatory decision-making, public utilities and information-based services, political strategies and perspectives, and transparent governance

FIGURE 12.2
Smart governance. (From Kumar, T. M. Vinod., *E-Governance for Smart Cities*, Springer, Singapore, 2015.)

12.1.3.1 Smart City Governance

A smart city should develop a governance model that brings together various stakeholders to provide growth and adaptability of smart services. Public–private partnership and citizen participation is an important element of smart city governance (Lee et al., 2013).

Smart governance is about the investment in emergent technologies along with innovative strategies to creatively achieve a more agile and resilient government structure.

12.1.4 Public Utilities and Information-Based Services

In order to provide better services to the citizens of a country, the government should provide government services online as e-services/digital services.

Nowadays, public services need a connection between the technology provider and the public manager in order to ensure better service to the citizens of the city and meet the current needs and demands of the citizens. This framework describes ease of use as one of the main parameters for a smart city (Belanche-Gracia et al.).

12.2 What Are Digital Services?

There are various definitions of digital services or e-services in the literature. The more generic definition is "Services or resources accessed and/or provided via digital transaction" (Buchanan and McMenemy, 2012; Williams et al., 2008).

12.2.1 Service versus Digital Service

Services delivered digitally are more restrictive than normal services as they need to connect to and use the infrastructure of the Internet protocol (IP)-based Internet. In digital services, humans cannot participate without the use of computer technology, which represents the main difference from normal services. For digital services, all services are not necessarily digital. For example, for amazon.com or flipkart.com, the website represents the digital service but the delivery of the product can be a physical product such as books, although in many ways this differs from a physical book store. The interaction between the fast-changing services. amazon.com has a wide range of e-books in digital form. Generally, utility services such as water service or gas service, in which a physical product is involved, are referred to as services where a delivery person delivers the physical product. In the case of digital services, a physical product may or may not be involved.

The second difference between normal and digital services is tangibility. Tangibility is the ability to perceive a thing or physical product with the sense of touch. A product is said to be tangible when it is hard in the sense of touch. Another difference is the idea of ownership of intangible assets such as songs or software, where the physical possession of the product is difficult. Now, ownership rights and digital rights for pictures can be included. Legal protection has shifted, such as a business process not being patented as it is just the intellectual property of the owner. Intellectual property protection is usually important for digital services but, on the other hand, it is important to be able to reproduce it easily in order to provide services and support scalability. It also helps to distinguish between competitors. There has been a complex interaction between products and services

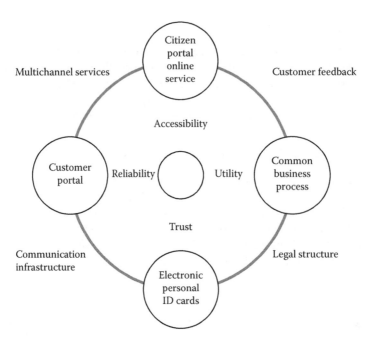

FIGURE 12.3
Factors needed for better transparency and participation. (Adapted from Kumar, T. M. Vinod., *E-Governance for Smart Cities*, Springer, Singapore, 2015.)

by including more legal protection. Nondigital services are mainly based on a personal relationship between parties where, as in the case of digital services, the service provider may never know the service consumer (Weightman and McDonagh, 2003).

Digital service providers provide services to digital service users. In some contexts, both are called the digital service provider as well as the consumer. Some of the differences between organizations with the same artifact can determine the success and failure of the organization in the marketplace. This is because integration and implementation of the same application becomes the advantageous factor for one organization over another. As an example, Figure 12.3 illustrates different factors for better transparency and participation, which leads to better adoption of digital services.

12.2.2 What Are the Different Categorizations/Classifications of Digital Services?

Electronic services (e-services) are accessed via the Internet with the use of interactive software. An e-service is generally referred to as an information asset that is made available through the Internet. E-services play an important role in business-to-consumer transactions as they provide an on-demand solution to customers, strengthening the relation between the seller and the consumer. They also create transactional efficiencies and improve customer satisfaction. The most sought-after examples of e-services are online purchasing, banking, and financial portfolio management.

During a literature survey of the different types of digital services and their classification, it has been found that digital services can be categorized and classified in many ways. In this chapter, however, we have taken three classifications as an example and, based on that, we have chosen one of these because of its interactive characteristics.

12.2.2.1 Categorization of Digital Services in Published Literature

William et al. (2008) has explained the categorization of services into three levels, namely, level 1, level 2, and level 3, and Kwon et al. (2013) has discussed the classification of digital services on a more granular level, that is, at level 4. The detailed categorization of services is shown in Table 12.1. Level 1 of the classified digital services is services that are generic in nature, such as communication services, information services, entertainment services, and business services. The next level is level 2, at which the services given in level 1 are further divided into different segments of services. For example, messaging and call services are part of communication services, traffic and local information services are part of information services, and so on. The next level, level 3 services, are part of level 2 services such as short message service (SMS), multimedia messaging service (MMS), instant messaging (IM), group mobile subscribers (GMS), and e-mail. These are part of messaging services, which in turn are part of communication services, voice over IP (VoIP) call, video call, group call, and so on, and part of call services that in turn are a part of the same communication services. Services are further categorized as level 4 services, which gives us more depth about the communication services mentioned in level 1.

With the advancement of ICT, there are many ways in which the customer can interact with the service provider to influence the customer's perception with the service experience. In this categorization of digital services, the service consumer and service provider interact with the use of technology. The five possible ways that the service consumer and the service provider interact are classified as the different types of digital service. The customer in contact with the physical proximity interacting with a human service provider is represented as the service consumer, whereas the physical proximity providing service to the service consumer is referred to as the service provider. The categorization of digital services adapted from Froehle and Roth (2004) is presented in the next section. The classification of digital services is initially based on how the service consumer contacts the service provider, whether "face-to-face" or "face-to-screen." Face-to-face consumer contact is further classified into three types, namely, technology-free consumer contact,

TABLE 12.1

Categorization of Digital Services in Published Literature

Level 1	Level 2	Level 3	Level 4
Communication	Messaging	SMS, MMS, IM, group MS, e-mail	Facebook.com chat, Google e-mail
	Call	VoIP call, Video call, Group call	Cisco VoIP product
Information	Traffic service	Map, navigation	Google maps,
	Local information service	Local events, local weather, news, notices	*New York Times*, Wikipedia.com
Entertainment	Data service	File transfer, multimedia streaming	YouTube.com, Apple.com/iTunes
	Game	Real-time game	Candy crush saga, Worldofwarcraft.com
Business	Shopping	Shopping	Amazon.com, Ebay.com
	Advertisement	Advertisement	Craigslist.org
	Coupon	Coupon	Cookbook village
	Banking	Banking	SBI Internet banking

Source: Adapted from Williams, K. et al., *European Journal of Information Systems*, 17.5, 505–517, 2008; Kwon, H.-C., et al. Methods of updating into service category table in device and device for same. US patent application, 2013.

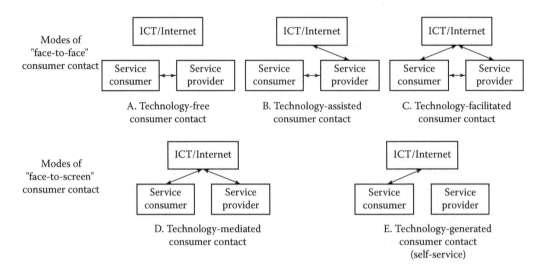

FIGURE 12.4
Conceptual archetypes of customer contact in relation to technology. (Adapted from Froehle, Craig M., and Aleda V. Roth, *Journal of Operations Management*, 22.1, 1–21, 2004.)

technology-assisted consumer contact, and technology-facilitated consumer contact. Face-to-screen contact is further classified into technology-mediated consumer contact and technology-generated consumer contact (Figure 12.4).

12.2.2.1.1 Technology-Free Consumer Contact

In this archetype, the consumer interacts with the provider without using technology, which is also seen in traditional shopping. The consumer contact is face-to-face with the provider, and technology does not play any role between the provider and the consumer. Examples of this include customer contact with a psychiatrist, patient contact with a doctor, a general clerk transacting the sale of merchandise with the cash drawer, and a retail bank teller exchanging a customer's coins for paper currency.

12.2.2.1.2 Technology-Assisted Consumer Contact

In this type of contact, consumer contact with the provider is in such a way that the service provider uses technology whereas the service consumer does not have access to technology. The medium of communication between the service provider and the consumer is face-to-face. An example of this includes airline check-in, where the service representative (service provider) uses technology to interact with the system but has face-to-face contact with the passenger (service consumer).

12.2.2.1.3 Technology-Facilitated Consumer Contact

This archetype represents the interaction between the service provider and the consumer as well as the technology. In this type, both the service consumer and the service provider use technology to interact. Here, technology enhances the face-to-face interaction between the two. An example includes a financial consultant using PowerPoint in a meeting with a client, or an insurance sales representative trying to sell his or her services to a consumer.

12.2.2.1.4 Technology-Mediated Consumer Contact

In this category of digital service, the service provider and the service consumer do not interact face-to-face but rather face-to-screen. In order for the service provider and the consumer to communicate, ICT/the Internet is used as a medium of interaction such as a telephone call or instant online messaging with a customer service representative in the back-office call center.

12.2.2.1.5 Technology-Generated Consumer Contact

The last category of digital service is technology-generated consumer contact in which the consumer does not need to contact the service provider but directly interacts with the screen, with the help of the Internet or ICT. This is the most technologically intensive solution as the service provider is entirely replaced by the technology itself. For example, self-service kiosks, bank ATMs, automated carwashes, and website-based services offer a service that does not need any assistance. We have noticed that, when technology is more digitalized, there is an increase in customer use of the screen display, such as the screen of an ATM machine or mobile device used to communicate with the service provider (Froehle and Roth, 2004).

12.3 What Is Risk?

According to the *McGraw-Hill Dictionary of Engineering*, risk is defined as the potential realization of undesirable consequences from hazards arising from a possible event.

Risk is perceived mostly by the consumer during purchasing of a product or service, so perceived risk is not only associated with what is acquired but also how and where it is acquired. Risk is generally perceived as higher during home shopping, such as ordering by telephone. Cox and Rich (1964) have found that the general reason for not shopping by telephone is the fear of not getting what is ordered.

12.3.1 Perceived Risk

Perceived risk is generally thought of as the uncertainty felt with respect to the negative consequences of using a product or service. In 1960, Bauer introduced the concept of risk and defined it as "a combination of uncertainty plus seriousness of outcome involved," whereas Peter and Ryan (1976) defined it as "the expectation of losses associated with the purchase and acts as an inhibitor to purchase behavior."

12.3.2 Dimensions of Perceived Risk

In 1960, Bauer introduced the concept of risk and defined it as a combination of uncertainty plus seriousness of outcome involved. Chapman and Ward (1999) define risk as the probability of a downside risk event multiplied by its impact. Perceived risk has also been defined by many other authors (Peter and Tarpey, 1975; Peter and Ryan, 1976; Vincent and Zikmund, 1976; Bearden and Mason, 1978; Dowling, 1985) as two dimensions, that is, importance and probability of loss.

The different facets of perceived risk have been listed in this section. In 1967, Cunningham identified two major categories of perceived risk: performance and psychological. Later, performance was broken into three types: economic, temporal, and effort; and psychological into two types: psychological and social. Cunningham (1967) further classified perceived risk into six dimensions: performance, financial, opportunity/time, safety, social, and psychological loss. He posited that all risk dimensions stem from performance risk. The literature supports that these facets of risks are used to understand consumer perception toward the product and services. Taking the automobile industry as an example, the physical (safety) risk can be minimized but the financial risk will increase. Bellman et al. (1999) has given more importance to the time dimension of risk as it was found that harried consumers with less time are more likely to purchase from the Internet in order to save valuable time. It has therefore become evident that consumers are time sensitive and do not want to waste time during the purchasing of products or services. This gives an opportunity for the digital service provider to reduce the time risk during Internet shopping. The consumer is also very sensitive to the privacy and security of the product or services that he or she owns through the Internet. The reason behind this is the fear of theft of the product or of having private information misused by the company (Featherman et al., 2003).

1. *Performance risk*: The possibility that the product or services are not delivering the desired benefits as advertised and designed.
2. *Financial risk:* The price associated with the purchase of the product or services and the subsequent maintenance costs associated with it.
3. *Opportunity/time risk:* The lost time associated with a bad purchase decision such as researching, making the purchase, or learning how to use the product or services.
4. *Psychological risk:* The risk that using the product or services will decrease the self-image of the consumer.
5. *Social risk:* The risk that use of the product or service will lead to embarrassment on social media.
6. *Privacy risk:* The risk associated with the loss of personal information without the consumer's permission.
7. *Physical/safety risk:* The risk associated with the safety of consumers while using the product or services.
8. *Overall risk:* The risk measured when all criteria are evaluated together (Luo et al., 2010).

Various studies have been reported in the literature since the introduction of the concept of perceived risk by Bauer in 1960. Table 12.2 shows some of the research that has been done on the multiple dimensions of perceived risk by multiple authors, spanning through the time till date. Luo et al. (2010) have reiterated the same definition of perceived risk as given by Bauer, and further classified it into the eight facets of perceived risk mentioned in this section.

These risks empirically test the effect of the aforementioned facets of perceived risk. Different authors have defined the concept of perceived risk from different perspectives. Some authors have defined it from the consumers' perspective and some have defined it by keeping in mind organizations such as information technology firms, the manufacturing industry, hospitals, and so on. Table 12.3 shows the different definitions of perceived risk from the perspective of the consumer and organization.

TABLE 12.2

Information Risk Dimension and its Studies in Published Literature

Perceived Risk Dimension	Studies Done
Performance risk	Cunningham (1967); Jacoby and Kaplan (1972); Lutz and Reilly (1973); Peter and Tarpey (1975); Peter and Ryan (1976); Locander and Hermann (1979); Brooker (1984); Singh (1986); Bromiley (1991); Grewal et al. (1994); Nidumolu (1995); Wood and Scheer (1996); Mitchell (1999); Agarwal and Teas (2001); Cases (2002); Pavlou (2003); Lim (2003); Forsythe and Shi (2003); Agarwal and Teas (2004); Biswas et al. (2006); Mills et al. (2006); Fung et al. (2008)
Financial/economic risk	Cunningham (1967); Jacoby and Kaplan (1972); Peter and Tarpey (1975); Peter and Ryan (1976); Brooker (1984); Grewal et al. (1994); Wood and Scheer (1996); Mitchell (1999); Agarwal and Teas (2001); Cases (2002); Pavlou (2003); Forsythe and Shi (2003); Lim (2003); Agarwal and Teas (2004); Youn (2005); Biswas et al. (2006)
Opportunity/time risk	Cunningham (1967); Roselius (1971); Peter and Tarpey (1975); Peter and Ryan (1976); Brooker (1984); Mitchell (1999); Cases (2002); Forsythe and Shi (2003); Lim (2003); Youn (2005)
Psychological risk	Cunningham (1967); Jacoby and Kaplan (1972); Peter and Tarpey (1975); Peter and Ryan (1976); Brooker (1984); Mitchell (1992); Mitchell (1999); Cases (2002); Forsythe and Shi (2003); Lim (2003); Youn (2005)
Social risk	Cunningham (1967); Jacoby and Kaplan (1972); Lutz and Reilly (1973); Peter and Tarpey (1975); Peter and Ryan (1976); Locander and Hermann (1979); Brooker (1984); Mitchell (1999); Cases (2002); Lim (2003); Youn (2005); Youn (2005)
Privacy risk	Lim (2003); Cases (2002); Pavlou (2003); Youn (2005); Pan and Zinkhan (2006); Dinev and Hart (2006); Featherman et al. (2010)
Safety/physical risk	Jacoby and Kaplan (1972); Peter and Tarpey (1975); Brooker (1984); Peter and Ryan (1976); Cases (2002); Lim (2003)
Overall risk	Allen and Jagtiani (2000); Kaiser et al. (2002); Heinrich (2005); Campbell (2005); Cao et al. (2011)

TABLE 12.3

Definitions of Risk from Consumer and Organization Perspectives

Consumer Perspective	Organization Perspective
Bauer introduced the concept of perceived risk and defined it as a combination of uncertainty plus seriousness of outcome involved (Bauer, 1960; Luo et al., 2010).	Decision theorist defines "risk" as a situation where a decision maker has prior knowledge of both the consequences of the alternatives and their probability of occurrence (Dowling, 1986).
Perceived risk is a two-dimensional construct comprising the uncertainty involved in a purchase decision and the consequences of taking an unfavorable action (Bettman, 1973; Cunningham, 1967; Schiffman, 1972)	Waring and Glendon (1998) define risk as the "probability or likelihood that (for a pure risk) a specified hazard will result in a specified undesired event or (for a speculative risk) a specified event or course of action will result in a specified gain or enhancement and/or specified loss or detriment."
Perceived risk refers to the nature and amount of risk perceived by a consumer in contemplating a particular purchase decision (Cox and Rich, 1964).	Horton et al. (2000) says that risk is based on the possibility of harm or loss used to express uncertainty about events and outcomes that could have an undesirable effect on an organization and its goals.
Featherman and Pavlou (2003) define perceived risk as "the potential for loss in the pursuit of a desired outcome of using an e-service."	

12.4 Multifaceted Risk Mapping for Different Categories of Digital Services

Multifaceted risk mapping for different types of digital services is shown in Figure 12.5. Each type of information-related risk, such as performance risk, has been mapped to all of the different types of digital services including technology-assisted consumer contact, technology-facilitated consumer contact, technology-mediated consumer contact, technology-generated consumer contact, and technology-free consumer contact. The mapping shows how performance risk is associated with the different digital services.

12.4.1 Multifaceted Risk Mapping for Technology-Assisted Consumer Contact

In technology-assisted consumer contact, the service provider has access to the technology whereas the service consumer does not have access to the technology during the interaction with the service provider. The contact between the two is therefore face-to-face. The different types of perceived risk associated with technology-assisted consumer contact are shown in Table 12.4.

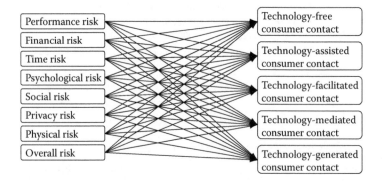

FIGURE 12.5
Multifaceted risk mapping with different categorization of digital services.

TABLE 12.4

Multifaceted Risk Mapping of Technology-Assisted Consumer Contact

	Technology-Assisted Consumer Contact
Performance risk	Travel agent failure to provide ticket or receptionist unable to book hotel room
Financial risk	Loss of ticket price for traveler, loss due to nonbooking of room
Time risk	Time spent with the travel agent or time spent with the receptionist
Psychological risk	Trust of travel agency, trust of the hotel
Social risk	Reputation of travel agency; reputation and brand image of the hotel
Privacy risk	Personal information or credit card information of the traveler
Physical risk	Travel to the wrong destination or taking a different hotel room
Overall risk	Harassment of traveler

12.4.2 Multifaceted Risk Mapping for Technology-Facilitated Consumer Contact

In technology-facilitated consumer contact, both the service provider and the service consumer have access to the technology and the interaction between them is face-to-face. The different types of perceived risk associated with technology-facilitated consumer contact are shown in Table 12.5.

12.4.3 Multifaceted Risk Mapping for Technology-Mediated Consumer Contact

In technology-mediated consumer contact, both the service provider and the service consumer have access to the technology and the interaction between them is face-to-screen, as shown in Figure 12.5. The different types of perceived risk associated with technology-mediated consumer contact are shown in Table 12.6.

12.4.4 Multifaceted Risk Mapping for Technology-Generated Consumer Contact

In technology-generated consumer contact, the service consumer has access to the technology but there is minimal use of the service provider and the interaction between them is face-to-screen. The different types of perceived risk associated with technology-generated consumer contact are shown in Table 12.7.

TABLE 12.5

Multifaceted Risk Mapping of Technology-Facilitated Consumer Contact

	Technology-Facilitated Consumer Contact
Performance risk	Insurance agent unable to provide the right policy or financial consultant unable to convince a client
Financial risk	Value of insurance at stake or consultancy fees at risk
Time risk	Time spent by both the agent and customer or time spent both by the consultant and client
Psychological risk	Trust in the insurance agent or client trust of the consultant
Social risk	Reputation of the insurance agency or consultancy
Privacy risk	Personal information of the customer or client
Physical risk	Wrong insurance policy provided or improper advice by the consultant
Overall risk	Bad impression of the insurance agency or of the consultant

TABLE 12.6

Multifaceted Risk Mapping of Technology-Mediated Consumer Contact

	Technology-Mediated Consumer Contact
Performance risk	Customer representative unable to take the customer's order, or professional advice given by a consulting company via video conferencing fails
Financial risk	Amount lost due to calling the customer representative or money lost during the setup of a video conference
Time risk	Time spent during a phone call or conference call
Psychological risk	Calling the customer representative again or setting up a conference call again
Social risk	Loss of morale of the company or lack of professional advice
Privacy risk	Personal information of the customer or confidential information of the company
Physical risk	Unable to receive the customer's call or establish a location for the next setup
Overall risk	Loss of company reputation or reputation of a consultancy

TABLE 12.7

Multifaceted Risk Mapping of Technology-Generated Consumer Contact

	Technology-Generated Consumer Contact
Performance risk	ATM unable to dispense cash or self-service kiosk unable to get electricity bill details
Financial risk	Amount stuck in the ATM or amount spent at the kiosk
Time risk	Time spent at the ATM or at the kiosk
Psychological risk	Going again to the ATM for cash or standing in a queue
Social risk	Loss of trust in the ATM or the kiosk
Privacy risk	Customer personal information or personal billing information
Physical risk	Installation and maintenance of the ATM or kiosk
Overall risk	Loss of the bank's reputation or loss of faith in the self-service kiosk

TABLE 12.8

Multifaceted Risk Mapping of Technology-Free Consumer Contact

	Technology-Free Consumer Contact
Performance risk	Doctor in consultation with a patient failing to diagnose the patient; seller providing a defective product
Financial risk	Consultation fees of the patient; money received for the product
Time risk	Time spent by the patient during diagnosis; time taken to purchase the product
Psychological risk	Patient trust in the doctor; trust in the product for future purchase
Social risk	Reputation of the doctor with the patient; self-image of the customer in using the product
Privacy risk	Use of patient's personal information; use of personal information of the customer
Physical risk	Consumption of the wrong medicine; use of a defective product
Overall risk	Severe damage to the patient's health; underutilization of the product

12.4.5 Multifaceted Risk Mapping for Technology-Free Consumer Contact

In technology-free consumer contact, neither the service consumer nor the service provider has access to the technology and there is minimal use of ICT/the Internet so the interaction between them is face-to-face. The different types of perceived risk associated with technology-free consumer contact are shown in Table 12.8.

12.5 Conclusion

During the evaluation of risks, it was observed that risk was first introduced by Bauer in 1960 as the risk perceived by the customer. Risk is basically introduced as perceived risk. Later, this risk became several dimensions of risk such as performance risk, financial risk, opportunity/time risk, psychological risk, social risk, privacy risk, safety/physical risk, and overall risk. These risks are mapped to the different types of digital services that are being offered by the public and private organizations of a smart city. The digital services of smart cities are basically divided into two types: face-to-face and face-to-screen. Face-to-face services are further divided into three types: technology-free consumer contact, technology-assisted consumer contact, and technology-facilitated consumer contact. Face-to-screen digital services are further classified into two types: technology-mediated consumer contact and technology-generated consumer contact. All digital services have been mapped to the multiple dimensions of risk mentioned in this chapter to show how the relationship with the digital services of a smart city has an impact on the perceived risk.

12.6 Future Research

The scope of this chapter was limited to multidimensional risk mapping of different types of digital services, as shown in Figure 12.5. Future research can be undertaken by considering other aspects of risk such as inherent risk, handled risk, personal risk, source risk, project risk, market risk, credit risk, health risk, delivery risk, service risk, and risk related to the customer supplier within the service categories as evaluated by the Government of India.

References

Agarwal, Sanjeev, and R. Kenneth Teas. 2001. Perceived value: Mediating role of perceived risk. *Journal of Marketing Theory and Practice* 9.4: 1–14.

Agarwal, Sanjeev, and R. Kenneth Teas. 2004. Cross-national applicability of a perceived risk-value model. *Journal of Product and Brand Management* 13.4: 242–256.

Allen, Linda, and Julapa Jagtiani. 2000. The risk effects of combining banking, securities, and insurance activities. *Journal of Economics and Business* 52.6: 485–497.

Angelidou, Margarita. 2015. Smart cities: A conjuncture of four forces. *Cities* 47: 95–106.

Bauer, Raymond A. 1960. Consumer behavior as risk taking. In *Dynamic Marketing for a Changing World*, 398. Chicago, IL: American Marketing Association.

Bearden, William O., and J. Barry Mason. 1978. Consumer-perceived risk and attitudes toward generically prescribed drugs. *Journal of Applied Psychology* 63.6: 741.

Bellman, Steven, Gerald L. Lohse, and Eric J. Johnson. 1999. Predictors of online buying behavior. *Communications of the ACM* 42.12: 32–38.

Bettman, James R. 1973. Perceived risk and its components: A model and empirical test. *Journal of Marketing Research* 10.2: 184 –190.

Biswas, Dipayan, Abhijit Biswas, and Neel Das. 2006. The differential effects of celebrity and expert endorsements on consumer risk perceptions. The role of consumer knowledge, perceived congruency, and product technology orientation. *Journal of Advertising* 35.2: 17–31.

Bromiley, Philip. 1991. Testing a causal model of corporate risk taking and performance. *Academy of Management Journal* 34.1: 37–59.

Brooker, George. 1984. An assessment of an expanded measure of perceived risk. *NA-Advances in Consumer Research* 11: 439–446.

Buchanan, Steven, and David McMenemy. 2012. Digital service analysis and design: The role of process modelling. *International Journal of Information Management* 32.3: 251–256.

Calabrese, Francesco, Kristian Kloeckl, and Carlo Ratti. 2007. WikiCity: Connecting the tangible and the virtual realm of a city. *GeoInformatics* 10.8: 42 –45.

Campbell, Scott. 2005. Determining overall risk. *Journal of Risk Research* 8.4: 569–581.

Cao, Qiming, Qiming Yu, and Des W. Connell. 2011. Health risk characterisation for environmental pollutants with a new concept of overall risk probability. *Journal of Hazardous Materials* 187.1: 480–487.

Carrillo, Francisco Javier, ed. 2006. *Knowledge Cities: Approaches, Experiences and Perspectives*. New York: Routledge.

Castells, Manuel. 1996. *The Network Society*. Vol. 469. Oxford: Blackwell.

Cases, Anne-Sophie. 2002. Perceived risk and risk-reduction strategies in Internet shopping. *The International Review of Retail, Distribution and Consumer Research* 12.4: 375–394.

Chapman, Chris, and Stephen Ward. 2003. *Project Risk Management: Processes, Techniques and Insights*. Chichester: Wiley.

Cox, Donald F., and Stuart U. Rich. 1964. Perceived risk and consumer decision-making: The case of telephone shopping. *Journal of Marketing Research* 1.4: 32–39.

Cunningham, Scott M. 1967. The major dimensions of perceived risk. In *Risk Taking and Information Handling in Consumer Behavior*, edited by D. F. Cox, 82-111. Boston, MA: Harvard University Press.

Dinev, Tamara, and Paul Hart. 2006. An extended privacy calculus model for e-commerce transactions. *Information Systems Research* 17.1: 61–80.

Dowling, Grahame R. 1985. The effectiveness of advertising explicit warranties. *Journal of Public Policy and Marketing* 4: 142–152.

Dowling, Grahame R. 1986. Perceived risk: The concept and its measurement. *Psychology and Marketing* 3.3: 193–210.

Downey, John, and Jim McGuigan, eds. 1999. *Technocities: The Culture and Political Economy of the Digital Revolution*. London: Sage.

Dutton, William H., Kenneth L. Kraemer, and Jay G. Blumler. 1987. *Wired Cities: Shaping the Future of Communications*. London: Macmillan.

Featherman, Mauricio S., Anthony D. Miyazaki, and David E. Sprott. 2010. Reducing online privacy risk to facilitate e-service adoption: The influence of perceived ease of use and corporate credibility. *Journal of Services Marketing* 24.3: 219–229.

Featherman, Mauricio S., and Paul A. Pavlou. 2003. Predicting e-services adoption: A perceived risk facets perspective. *International Journal of Human-Computer Studies* 59.4: 451–474.

Forsythe, Sandra M., and Bo Shi. 2003. Consumer patronage and risk perceptions in Internet shopping. *Journal of Business Research* 56.11: 867–875.

Froehle, Craig M., and Aleda V. Roth. 2004. New measurement scales for evaluating perceptions of the technology-mediated customer service experience. *Journal of Operations Management* 22.1: 1–21.

Fung, William, David A. Hsieh, Narayan Y. Naik, and Tarun Ramadorai. 2008. Hedge funds: Performance, risk, and capital formation. *The Journal of Finance* 63.4: 1777–1803.

Graham, Stephen, and Simon Marvin. 1999. Planning cybercities: Integrating telecommunications into urban planning. *Town Planning Review* 70.1: 89.

Grewal, Dhruv, Jerry Gotlieb, and Howard Marmorstein. 1994. The moderating effects of message framing and source credibility on the price-perceived risk relationship. *Journal of Consumer Research* 21.1: 145–153.

Heinrich, Nicolas. 2005. Overall risk in a system. US Patent US20050114186.

Horton, Thomas R., Charles H. LeGrand, William H. Murray, William J. Ozier, and Dianne B. Parker. 2000. Managing information security risks. The Institute of Internal Auditors.

Jacoby, Jacob, and Leon B. Kaplan. 1972. The components of perceived risk. In *SV-Proceedings of the Third Annual Conference of the Association for Consumer Research*.

Kaiser, Janez, Bogomir Horvat, and Zdravko Kačič. 2002. Overall risk criterion estimation of hidden Markov model parameters. *Speech Communication* 38.3: 383–398.

Komninos, Nicos. 2006. The architecture of intelligent cities: Integrating human, collective and artificial intelligence to enhance knowledge and innovation. In *Intelligent Environments, 2006. IE 06. 2nd IET International Conference on Intelligent Environments*, Vol. 1, 13–20. Athens: Institution of Engineering and Technology.

Kumar, T. M. Vinod. 2015. E-governance for smart cities. In *E-governance for Smart Cities*, 1–43. Singapore: Springer.

Kwon, Hyuk-Choon, Seung-hoon Park, Ho-Dong Kim, Hae-Young Jun, and Soo-Yeon Jung. 2013. Methods of updating into service category table in device and device for same. US patent application.

Lee, Jung Hoon, Marguerite Gong Hancock, and Mei-Chih Hu. 2013. Towards an effective framework for building smart cities: Lessons from Seoul and San Francisco. *Technological Forecasting and Social Change* 89: 80–99.

Lim, Nena. 2003. Consumers' perceived risk: Sources versus consequences. *Electronic Commerce Research and Applications* 2.3: 216–228.

Locander, William B., and Peter W. Hermann. 1979. The effect of self-confidence and anxiety on information seeking in consumer risk reduction. *Journal of Marketing Research* 16.2: 268–274.

Luo, Xin, Han Li, Jie Zhang, and J. P. Shim. 2010. Examining multi-dimensional trust and multi-faceted risk in initial acceptance of emerging technologies: An empirical study of mobile banking services. *Decision Support Systems* 49.2: 222–234.

Lutz, Richard J., and Patrick J. Reilly. 1973. An exploration of the effects of perceived social and performance risk on consumer information acquisition. *NA-Advances in Consumer Research* 01: 393–405.

Mills, Evan, Steve Kromer, Gary Weiss, and Paul A. Mathew. 2006. From volatility to value: Analysing and managing financial and performance risk in energy savings projects. *Energy Policy* 34.2: 188–199.

Mitchell, Vincent-Wayne. 1999. Consumer perceived risk: Conceptualizations and models. *European Journal of Marketing* 33.1/2: 163–195.

Nidumolu, Sarma. 1995. The effect of coordination and uncertainty on software project performance: Residual performance risk as an intervening variable. *Information Systems Research* 6.3: 191–219.

Pan, Yue, and George M. Zinkhan. 2006. Exploring the impact of online privacy disclosures on consumer trust. *Journal of Retailing* 82.4: 331–338.

Pavlou, Paul A. 2003. Consumer acceptance of electronic commerce: Integrating trust and risk with the technology acceptance model. *International Journal of Electronic Commerce* 7.3: 101–134.

Peter, J. Paul, and Lawrence X. Tarpey. 1975. A comparative analysis of three consumer decision strategies. *Journal of Consumer Research* 2.1: 29–37.

Peter, J. Paul, and Michael J. Ryan. 1976. An investigation of perceived risk at the brand level. *Journal of Marketing Research* 13.2: 184–188.

Roselius, Ted. 1971. Consumer rankings of risk reduction methods. *The Journal of Marketing* 35.1: 56–61.

Schiffman, Leon G. 1972. Perceived risk in new product trial by elderly consumers. *Journal of Marketing Research* 9.1: 106–108.

Shepard, Mark. 2011. *Sentient City: Ubiquitous Computing, Architecture, and the Future of Urban Space*. Cambridge, MA: The MIT Press.

Singh, Jitendra V. 1986. Performance, slack, and risk taking in organizational decision making. *Academy of Management Journal* 29.3: 562–585.

Townsend, Anthony M. 2000. Life in the real-time city: Mobile telephones and urban metabolism. *Journal of Urban Technology* 7.2: 85–104.

Vincent, Mark, and William G. Zikmund. 1976. An experimental investigation of situational effects on risk perception. *NA-Advances in Consumer Research Volume* 03: 125–129.

Waring, Alan, and A. Glendon. 1998. *Managing Risk: Critical Issues for Survival and Success into the 21st Century*. London: Thomson Learning.

Weightman, David, and Deana McDonagh. 2003. People are doing it for themselves. In *Proceedings of the 2003 International Conference on Designing Pleasurable Products and Interfaces*, ACM, 34–39.

Williams, Kevin, Samir Chatterjee, and Matti Rossi. 2008. Design of emerging digital services: A taxonomy. *European Journal of Information Systems* 17.5: 505–517.

Wood, Charles M., and Lisa K. Scheer. 1996. Incorporating perceived risk into models of consumer deal assessment and purchase intent. *Advances in Consumer Research* 23: 399–404.

Youn, Seounmi. 2005. Teenagers' perceptions of online privacy and coping behaviors: A risk–benefit appraisal approach. *Journal of Broadcasting and Electronic Media* 49.1: 86–110.

13

M-Commerce in Smart Cities: Changing Mindsets of Individuals, Organizations, and Society

Himanshu Agarwal and Gaurav Dixit

CONTENTS

13.1 Introduction 167
13.2 Research Methodology 169
13.3 Mobile Commerce: An Overview 169
    13.3.1 M-Commerce Impact: Individual Perspective 169
        13.3.1.1 Access to Information 171
        13.3.1.2 Fast Purchase Opportunity 171
    13.3.2 M-Commerce Impact: Business/Workplace Perspective 171
        13.3.2.1 Ubiquity 172
        13.3.2.2 Dissemination 172
    13.3.3 M-Commerce Impact: Society Perspective 173
13.4 Importance of M-Commerce in Smart Cities 174
    13.4.1 Broad Characteristics of Smart Cities 174
13.5 Barriers to Local and Global Mobile Commerce Adoption 174
13.6 SWOT Analysis of Mobile Commerce 175
13.7 Results and Discussion 175
13.8 Conclusion 177
References 177

13.1 Introduction

Mobile applications (apps) and websites are increasingly being used for routine activities such as online shopping, ordering, booking, gaming, and for accessing e-mails, messages, social networking websites, and other information on the Internet. In this chapter, we study the literature on mobile commerce (m-commerce) and mobile-related topics to analyze the impact of mobile app usage on the mind-set of individuals, societies, and organizations.

M-commerce has started to gain its own space and become a prominent platform for buying and selling products and services over the Internet. Some e-commerce firms are moving away from traditional e-commerce websites and toward mobile-based websites and mobile apps. One reason for this trend could be that m-commerce provides the advantage of accessing the Internet from anywhere and at any time, because of the ease of mobile portability. This trend is visible in the e-commerce industry of India in that some products are now sold through mobile apps only and some e-commerce firms such as Flipkart, Snapdeal, Amazon, Jabong, and Urban Ladder have also started to offer their business through mobile apps. These firms are offering higher discounts for products

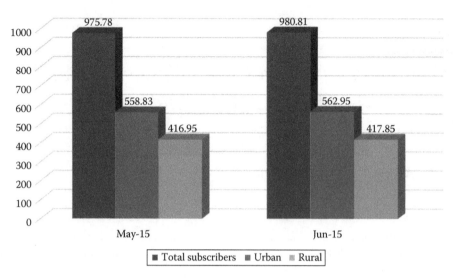

FIGURE 13.1
Total wireless subscribers. (From TRAI, press release no. 47/2015.)

ordered through mobile apps (*Internet Retailer*, 2014). According to the International Telecommunications Union (ITU), there were 3459 million active mobile broadband subscriptions and 7085 mobile cellular telephone subscriptions in 2015. The ITU also estimates that 69% of the world's population of 7.4 billion people will have 3G coverage by the end of 2015 (ITU, 2015a). In India, the total number of wireless subscribers reached 980 million in June 2015, from which the share of urban wireless subscribers is 57.40% and the share of rural wireless subscribers is 42.60% (Telecom Regulatory Authority of India [TRAI], 2015), as shown in Figure 13.1.

India is the second largest Internet-using country in the world, although Internet penetration in India is only 19% (*Indian Express*, 2015). Growth in Internet penetration depends on the adoption of mobile Internet, whereas m-commerce user growth depends upon mobile Internet users. The cost of smartphones is decreasing every year worldwide and telecom companies are also providing different tariffs at very reasonable rates that attract and increase the interest of consumers in using mobiles with the Internet, thus helping to grow the m-commerce markets in India (Ashvin Vellody, Partner–Management Consulting, KPMG) (*Indian Express*, 2015). In India, many in the public and private sector have launched mobile apps after seeing the interest of consumers (i.e., Gmail, Google maps, Indian Railway Catering and Tourism Corporation [IRCTC], Whatsapp, and Facebook).

The potential and feasibility of m-commerce far exceeds that of electronic commerce, given that larger numbers of users have personal mobile phones. The ITU believes that by 2015, the total number of Internet users will pass 3.2 billion users (ITU, 2015).

Personalization and easy accessibility are the main advantages of m-commerce. Mobile phones such as smartphones, android phones, and iPhones have become important devices for Internet users. Consumers use their smartphones for listening to music, watching videos, booking rail/air tickets, sending/receiving files through the Internet, business transactions, and to connect to social networking websites, among many other uses. Many e-commerce firms also report that Internet users are more familiar with mobiles, so all firms have taken this as an opportunity to invest in the field of mobile infrastructure and services.

M-commerce applications are gaining in popularity every day, and more than 75 billion mobile apps have been downloaded to smartphones and from Apple's app store (Statista,

2014). According to recent statistics, in September 2015 the mobile app WhatsApp surpassed 900 million monthly users, who are using the app as a low-cost messaging service compared with SMS (Quora, 2013).

Considering these examples of m-commerce and related apps, it is very easy to say that m-commerce and apps are essential for developing smart cities. According to the ITU, "A smart sustainable city (SSC) is an innovative city that uses information and communication technologies (ICTs) and other means to improve quality of life, efficiency of urban operation and services, and competitiveness, while ensuring that it meets the needs of present and future generations with respect to economic, social and environmental aspects" (ITU, Focus Group on Smart Sustainable Cities, 2015).

In this chapter, we review the existing literature and study the influence of m-commerce on individuals, businesses, and society in many dimensions such as lifestyle and the buying and selling of goods. The review covers 60 journal articles published after 2000.

The chapter is structured as follows: in the second section, the research methodology is described while the third section describes the importance and characteristics of smart cities and the impact of m-commerce on individuals, society, businesses, and workplaces. The fourth section discusses the results, and the final section includes conclusions.

13.2 Research Methodology

Considering the nature of m-commerce research, it is not easy to find and group the literature for any specific domain. M-commerce articles are dispersed across many journals in disciplines such as information technology, management, engineering, computer science, information systems, and business. Hence, various journal databases are shown in Table 13.1 as a bibliography of m-commerce. The literature search was based solely on the keywords "mobile applications" and "mobile commerce," and was also limited to peer-reviewed journals. The search identified 60 m-commerce articles from 35 journals.

13.3 Mobile Commerce: An Overview

The essence of m-commerce revolves around the idea of reaching the individual user/customer perspective, business perspective, society perspective, and workplace perspective. Mobile Internet subscribers can access information from anywhere at any time. This flexibility increases the interest of mobile users in m-commerce apps.

13.3.1 M-Commerce Impact: Individual Perspective

M-commerce allows users to exchange information from anywhere. M-commerce firms also provide customers with the opportunity to purchase products/services online using mobile apps or mobile "lite" websites. In today's world, all banks have developed mobile banking apps and have given a mobile banking option to their customers through which they can transact money in just a few seconds. This increases the trust of customers in the banking system, increases transparency, and saves customer time.

TABLE 13.1

Databases for Mobile Commerce and Apps Journals

Publisher/Online Database	Journal Name
	Journal of Assistive Technologies
Emerald Insight	*International Journal of Web Information System*
	Journal of Systems and Information Technology
	Information Management and Computer Security
	Journal of Enterprise Information Management
	Vine
	Internet Research
	Online Information Review
	Industrial Management and Data Systems
	Info
	International Journal of Pervasive Computing and Communications
	Information Technology and People
	Kybernetes
	Foresight
	Aslib Proceedings
	Logistics information systems
	Aslib Journal of Information Management
IEEE Xplore	*Electronic and Communication Engineering Journal*
	IEEE Internet Computing
	Information Systems Journal
Wiley Online Library	*Thunderbird International Business Review*
	Knowledge and Process Management
	Wireless Communications and Mobile Computing
	Software: Practice and Experience
	Expert Systems
	Systems Engineering
	Journal of the American Society for Information Science and Technology
	Journal of Computer-Mediated Communication
	Tijdschrift voor economische en sociale geografie
Ingenta Connect	*The American Economic Review*
	Journal of Payments Strategy and Systems
	International Journal of Systems Science
	Direct, Data and Digital Marketing Practice
	Social Behavior and Personality: An international journal
	Crossings: Journal of Migration and Culture
Science Direct	*Journal of Retailing and Consumer Services*
	Journal of King Saud University—Computer and Information Sciences
	Electronic Commerce Research and Applications
	Pervasive and Mobile Computing
	Technological Forecasting and Social Change
	Computers in Human Behavior
	Information Sciences
	International Journal of Information Management
Inder Science	*International Journal of Mobile Communications*
	International Journal of Mobile Learning and Organisation

TABLE 13.1 (CONTINUED)

Databases for Mobile Commerce and Apps Journals

Publisher/Online Database	Journal Name
	International Journal of Ultra Wideband Communications and Systems
	International Journal of Wireless and Mobile Computing
	International Journal of Information and Communication Technology
	International Journal of Information Technology, Communications and Convergence
	International Journal of Electronic Business
	International Journal of Electronic Customer Relationship Management
	International Journal of Electronic Democracy
	International Journal of Electronic Finance
	International Journal of Electronic Governance

13.3.1.1 Access to Information

M-commerce provides easy access to information for mobile users and can therefore save time. For example, mobile users are now booking flights and railway tickets through mobile apps compared with traditional online booking systems. By using mobile apps, users can easily confirm the availability of seats and train or flight information, and check passenger name record (PNR) status and live status of trains from anywhere; this is not possible with an off-line ticketing system. The travel industry is booming because of Android phone/iPhone usage, with mobile bookings hitting 40% worldwide (Venturebeat, 2014). In 2013–2014, more than 300,000 tickets were sold online through the IRCTC website and IRCTC mobile app per day, with a peak load of 584,000 tickets per day (IRCTC, 2014). Mobiles have also over-taken the desktop for hotel bookings by travelers in India. Out of the total hotel bookings in India in 2015, 53% were made through mobile phones and in 2014, mobiles contributed to only 29% of total hotel bookings according to Make my Trip (Livemint, 2015).

13.3.1.2 Fast Purchase Opportunity

M-commerce apps are booming and providing the opportunity to mobile users to select services and goods from anywhere. For purchasing goods, a person can take an on-the-spot decision with no need to go to an alternate source (Siau, et al., 2001) (Figure 13.2).

13.3.2 M-Commerce Impact: Business/Workplace Perspective

Mobile apps such as video/speech-enabled apps are the next phase of the m-commerce evolution and allow cost-effective coordination. Modern examples of coordination include

- Arranging meetings
- Making and planning travel plans
- Maintaining and finalizing project plans
- Using a help desk

There is a large difference between working from the office and from outside the office. In the office, everyone is connected with the organization and its resources. Outside the office, making use of the same resources is not easy, can be very time-consuming, and may

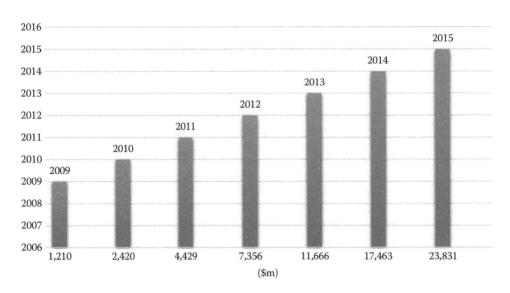

FIGURE 13.2
E-commerce revenues via handsets in the United States, 2009–2015. (From Coda Research Consultancy, 2010.)

have some security issues. Mobile access and mobile apps are the only solution in today's life for faster work. Everyone may connect to their office by using mobile apps whenever they need to.

The latest generation of smartphones makes it possible for employees to use the same communication facilities that they get at their workplace. Employees are able to continue their work when they are away from their office. They can remain in contact with their office and can work from home or while traveling. There are some features that are available in m-commerce but not in traditional electronic commerce (Siau, et al., 2001).

13.3.2.1 Ubiquity

All business firms are able to reach their customers anywhere at any time. Furthermore, users are able to access all information in which they are interested through an Internet-enabled wireless device in the hand.

13.3.2.2 Dissemination

Wireless infrastructure also supports the spreading of information to multiple mobile users at the same time if present in the same geographical region. Most of organizations give various discount offers to mobile app users in the form of discount coupons/apps and promotional offers, or in the form of cash back. For example, Amazon, Flipkart, and Snapdeal gave a discount of 10% cash back and up to an 80% discount only to mobile app users during October 2015 (*Economic Times*, 2015). Both organizations and individuals will benefit from the opportunities provided by mobile apps. For example, "A real estate company would like to provide access to listing information, assess creditworthiness, understand what homes a client can afford, narrow down the choices and map out a plan to visit the potential purchases, while receiving up-to-the-minute alerts about new listings coming on the market.

RESULT: Better customer service, more efficient use of employees' time, financial savings and greater productivity" (Rochford, 2001).

13.3.3 M-Commerce Impact: Society Perspective

M-commerce plays an important role in society. The behavior of consumers changes after adopting mobile apps. Most users adopt m-commerce after taking and analyzing the views of society. For example, 75% of movie tickets are sold through the Internet and mobile apps (*Business Standard*, 2010), while 63% of customers purchase products online from websites or mobile apps that have user reviews (iPerceptions, 2011).

Customer reviews are more trusted than the description that has been given by the m-commerce firm (eMarketer, 2010) (Figure 13.3).

Therefore, society's interest in m-commerce is also increasing because people are getting product reviews on their mobile phones, which was not possible with traditional systems. According to comScore, users are now spending more time on mobile apps compared with other media (Figure 13.4).

FIGURE 13.3
Level of trust in online customer product reviews. (From Power reviews and the e-tailing group, "2010 social shopping"; Provided to e-marketer, May 3, 2010.)

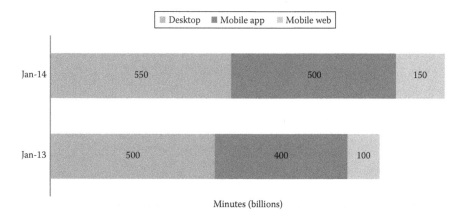

FIGURE 13.4
Digital time spent on growth driven by apps. (From comScore Media Metrix Multi-Platform and Mobile Metrix, United States, June 2013—June 2014.)

13.4 Importance of M-Commerce in Smart Cities

M-commerce and its apps play an important role in developing smart cities. A smart city suggests that individuals and businesses are empowered through increased access to information available on the Internet, are more participatory through the contribution of innovative ideas and solutions, and additionally have an anticipatory government that uses smart technology and devices to better serve citizen's needs (iDA, 2015). For example, m-commerce provides mobile users with easy access to information that can save time. Mobile users are now booking flight and railway tickets through mobile apps rather than traditional online booking systems. A smart city also brings together government, technology, and society to enable a smart economy, smart environment, smart mobility, smart people, smart living, and smart governance (IEEE, 2015).

13.4.1 Broad Characteristics of Smart Cities

1. Smart mobility
   a. Improved accessibility
   b. Safe transportation
   c. More efficient and intelligent transportation systems
   d. New smart activities such as car sharing and carpooling
2. Smart economy
   a. Competitiveness
   b. Entrepreneurship
   c. Productivity
   d. Broadband and Internet access for all citizens
   e. Electronic business processes (e.g., e-banking, e-shopping, and e-auction)
3. Smart governance
   a. Transparency
   b. Public and social services
   c. Participatory decision making
   d. Improved access to services
4. Smart people and environment
   a. Online education system
   b. Ability to utilize ICT-based smart services
   c. Pollution monitoring
   d. Ability to take smart decision by using ICT-based smart services

13.5 Barriers to Local and Global Mobile Commerce Adoption

M-commerce is growing rapidly, both in developed and developing countries. Most m-commerce users are using mobile apps and more than 75 billion mobile apps have been downloaded to smartphones and from Apple's app store (Statista, 2014). Some important barriers to m-commerce adoption include security, screen size, connectivity, unawareness, device inefficiency, and roaming (Anderson, 2012). Mobile users also worry about phone hacking and the possibility of being affected by viruses. They feel more comfortable with and have trust in traditional shopping or shopping from personal computers. Screen size is another barrier to the customer choosing or purchasing a product through a mobile phone. Users experience difficulty in analyzing or viewing the details of products such as footwear and clothes.

13.6 SWOT Analysis of Mobile Commerce (Figure 13.5)

SWOT analysis (strengths, weaknesses, opportunities, and threats analysis) is a framework for identifying and analyzing the internal and external factors that help to achive the objective.
SWOT analysis examines four elements:

- Strengths: internal attributes that facilitate a successful outcome
- Weaknesses: internal attributes that work against a successful outcome
- Opportunities: external factors that use its advantage
- Threats: external factors that fail the project

13.7 Results and Discussion

The research papers were analyzed by topic area, journal, and date of publication. This particular analysis of selected research papers will provide the guidelines for continuing our research on m-commerce, its application, and its challenges.

The article distribution by subject is shown in Table 13.2. Most of the articles are related to m-commerce theory, m-commerce adoption, trust in m-commerce, and m-commerce security issues.

Table 13.3 summarizes the reviewed m-commerce articles that correspond to the subject headings. This will also help researchers in searching m-commerce papers or articles.

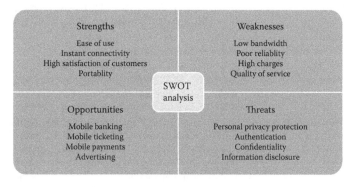

FIGURE 13.5
SWOT analysis of mobile commerce.

TABLE 13.2

Articles Distribution by Subject

Subject No.	Articles by Subject Heading	Number of Articles	Percentage of Subjects
1	Mobile advertising	1	1.666666667
2	Mobile financial applications	10	16.66666667
3	Mobile adoption	10	16.66666667
4	Trust	5	8.333333333
5	Diffusion	1	1.666666667
6	M-commerce in organizations or countries	10	16.66666667
7	Mobile handheld devices	1	1.666666667
8	Security issues	9	15
9	M-commerce theory and research	11	18.33333333
10	Mobile entertainment services	2	3.333333333
Total		60	100

TABLE 13.3

Classification of M-Commerce Articles

Subject No.	Subject Heading	References
1	Mobile advertising	(Yeo and Huang, 2003)
2	Mobile financial applications	(Andrieu, 2001), (Barnes and Corbitt, 2003), (Durkin and Howcroft, 2003), (Herzberg, 2003), (Kreyer, et al., 2003), (Kumar and Stokkeland, 2003), (Lee A., 2003), (Lee, et al., 2003), (Nicolle, 2000), (Pierce, 2002)
3	Mobile adoption	(Chong, Chan, and Ooi, Predicting consumer decisions to adopt mobile commerce: Cross country empirical examination between China and Malaysia, 2012), (Nassuora, 2013), (Sharif, et al., 2014), (Wei, et al., 2009), (Snowden, et al., 2006), (Harris, et al., 2005), (Chong, 2013b), (Chong, 2013a), (Xiang, et al., 2008), (Mahatanankoon, et al., 2005)
4	Trust	(Li and Yeh, 2010), (Sharif, et al., 2014), (Hamed, et al., 2011), (Yeh and Li, 2009), (Cyr, et al., 2006)
5	Diffusion	(Godoe and Hansen, 2009)
6	M-commerce in companies or countries	(Anwar, NTT DoCoMo and m-commerce: A case study in market expansion and global strategy, 2002), (Anwar, 2003), (Bertele et al., 2002), (Buhalis and Licata, 2002), (Denvir, 2000), (Ingram, 2001), (Insa-Ciriza, 2001), (Karkkainen, 2003), (Olla et al., 2003), (Yang et al., 2003)
7	Mobile handheld devices	(Sarker and Wells, 2003)
8	Security issues	(Geng et al., 2002), (Ghosh and Swaminatha, 2001), (Hazari, 2002), (Singh, 2000), (Soriano and Ponce, 2002), (Tan et al., 2003), (Tang et al., 2003), (McDermott, 2000), (Weippl, 2001)
9	M-commerce theory and research	(Laudon and Traver, 2015), (Rochford, 2001), (Jantan and Honeycutt Jr, 2013), (Ocampo et al., 2003), (Olla et al., 2003), (Semrau and Kraiss, 2001), (Barbero, 2001), (Coursaris and Hassanein, 2002), (Friesen, 2002), (Kumar and Zahn, Mobile communications: Evolution and impact on business operations, 2003), (Senn, 2000)
10	Mobile entertainment services	(MacInnes, 2002); (Mok, 2002)

13.8 Conclusion

M-commerce has attracted the attention of society, businesses, and individuals. The research activities of m-commerce have also increased significantly since 2000. This chapter includes 60 journal articles and reports published from 2000 onward. A large portion of this chapter covers the review articles of m-commerce adoption, m-commerce theory, and apps. This chapter will help m-commerce researchers to find valuable articles for future research on m-commerce and also provides a good understanding of m-commerce theories, applications, and security issues.

References

Anderson, A. 2012. 3 barriers affecting mobile commerce adoption. webcredible. Accessed 2015. www.webcredible.com/blog/3-barriers-affecting-mobile-commerce-adoption/.

Andrieu, M. 2001. The future of e-money: Main trends and driving forces. *Foresight, The Journal of Future Studies Strategic Thinking and Policy* 3 (5): 429–451.

Anwar, S.T. 2003. CASES Vodafone and the wireless industry: A case in market expansion and global strategy. *The Journal of Business and Industrial Marketing* 18 (3): 270–288.

Anwar, S.T. 2002. NTT DoCoMo and m-commerce: A case study in market expansion and global strategy. *Thunderbird International Business Review* 44 (1): 139–164.

Barbero, M. 2001. Preparing to ride the wireless wave. *Journal of Business Strategy* 22 (5): 10–12.

Barnes, S.J., and B. Corbitt. 2003. Mobile banking: Concept and potential. *International Journal of Mobile Communications* 1 (3): 273–288.

Bertele, U., A. Rangone, and F. Renga. 2002. Mobile internet: An empirical study of B2c WAP applications in Italy. *Electronic Markets* 12 (1): 27–37.

Buhalis, D., and M.C. Licata. 2002. The future eTourism intermediaries. *Tourism Management* 23 (3): 207–220.

Business Standard. 2010. Use Visa Debit card to buy movie tickets on Bookmyshow. Accessed 2015. http://www.business-standard.com/article/press-releases/now-use-visa-debit-card-to-buy-movie-tickets-on-bookmyshow-com-for-just-re-1-110072600093_1.html.

Chong, A.Y.-L. 2013a. A two-staged SEM-neural network approach for understanding and predicting the determinants of m-commerce adoption. *Expert Systems with Applications* 40: 1240–1247.

Chong, A.Y.-L. 2013b. Predicting m-commerce adoption determinants: A neural network approach. *Expert Systems with Applications* 40: 523–530.

Chong, A.Y.-L., F.T.S. Chan, and K.-B. Ooi. 2012. Predicting consumer decisions to adopt mobile commerce: Cross country empirical examination between China and Malaysia. *Decision Support Systems* 53: 34–43.

Coursaris, C., and K. Hassanein. 2002. "Understanding m-commerce." *Quarterly Journal of Electronic Commerce* 3 (3): 247–271.

Cyr, D., M. Head, and A. Ivanov. 2006. Design aesthetics leading to m-loyalty in mobile commerce. *Information and Management* 43: 950–963.

Denvir, P. 2000. Innovations in mobile telephony: Nokia collaborates with Amazon.com to pursue WAP based m-commerce market. *European Retail Digest* 26: 54–56.

Durkin, M.G., and B. Howcroft. 2003. Relationship marketing in the banking sector: The impact of new technologies. *Marketing Intelligence* 21 (1): 61–71.

Economic Times. 2015. Paytm joins discount wars with Flipkart, Snapdeal. Accessed 2015. http://economictimes.indiatimes.com/industry/services/retail/paytm-joins-discount-wars-with-flipkart-snapdeal-expects-festive-sales-of-rs-1.

eMarketer. 2010. Role of customer product reviews. Accessed 2015. http://www.emarketer.com/Article/Role-of-Customer-Product-Reviews/1008019.

Engadget. n.d. Technology news, advice and features. Accessed 2015. http://www.engadget.com/.

Friesen, G.B. 2002. M-commerce mmm-good? *Consulting to Management* 13 (2): 26–29.

Geng, X., Y. Huang, and A.B. Whinston. 2002. Defending wireless infrastructure against the challenge of DDoS attacks. *Mobile Networks and Applications* 7 (3): 213–223.

Ghosh, A.K., and T.M. Swaminatha. 2001. Software security and privacy risks in mobile e-commerce. *Communications of the ACM* 44 (2): 51–57.

Godoe, H, and T.B. Hansen. 2009. Technological regimes in m-commerce: Convergence as a barrier to diffusion and entrepreneurship? *Telecommunications Policy* 33 (1–2): 19–28.

Hamed, W.S., H.S. Hamza, and I.A. Saroit. 2011. Towards a unified trust model for M-commerce. *Eighth International Conference on Information Technology: New Generations.* IEEE. doi:10.1109/ITNG.2011.170.

Harris, P., R. Rettie, and C.C. Kwan. 2005. Adoption and usage of m-commerce: A cross-cultural comparison. *Journal of Electronic Commerce Research* 6 (3): 210–224.

Hazari, S. 2002. Challenges of implementing public key infrastructure in Netcentric enterprises. *Logistics Information Management* 15 (5): 85–92.

Herzberg, A. 2003. Payments and banking with mobile personal devices. *Communications of the ACM* 46 (5): 53–58.

n.d. History of Ecommerce. Accessed 2015. http://www.ecommerce-land.com/history_ecommerce.html.

iDA. 2015. Smart nation vision. Singapore. Accessed 2016. www.ida.gov.sg/Tech-Scene-News/Smart-Nation-Vision.

IEEE. 2015. *Smart Cities.* Accessed 2016. www.smartcities.ieee.org/about.html.

Indian Express 2015. *IAMAI.* Accessed 2015. http://indianexpress.com/article/technology/tech-news-technology/iamai-says-india-to-have-236-million-mobile-internet-users-by-2016/#sthas.

Ingram, D. 2001. The business case for a mobile economy: Mobile commerce Latin America. *Vital Speeches of the Day* 67: 618–723.

Insa-Ciriza, R. 2001. ECommerce and mCommerce in Southern Europe. *European Retail Digest* 32: 23–25.

Internetretailer. 2014. The 25 most popular mobile commerce apps. Accessed 2015. https://www.internetretailer.com/2014/06/05/exclusive-25-most-popular-mobile-commerce-apps.

iPerceptions. 2011. E-Commerce Industry Report. Accessed 2015. http://finance.yahoo.com/news/iPerceptions-Releases-Retail-iw-1564944333.html.

IRCTC. 2014. Annual Report IRCTC. Accessed 2015. http://www.irctc.com/annualReport_En.jsp.

ITU. 2015a. 3G Mobile-user coverage. ITU. Accessed 2015. https://www.itu.int/en/ITU-D/Statistics/Documents/facts/ICTFactsFigures2015.pdf.

ITU. 2015b. Focus group on smart sustainable cities. Accessed 2016. http://www.itu.int/en/ITU-T/focusgroups/ssc/Pages/default.aspx.

Jantan, M. A., and E. D. Honeycutt Jr. 2013. Current sales training practices in the commercial retail banking industry in Malaysia. *Services Marketing Quarterly* 34 (1): 1–17.

Juniper Research. 2014. *Mobile Banking Users to Exceed 1.75 Billion by 2019.* Accessed 2015. http://www.juniperresearch.com/press-release/digital-banking-pr1.

Karkkainen, M. 2003. Increasing efficiency in the supply chain for short life goods using RFID tagging. *International Journal of Retail and Distribution Management* 31 (10): 529–536.

Kreyer, N., K. Pousttchi, and K. Turowski. 2003. Mobile payment procedures. *e-Service Journal* 2 (3): 7–23.

Kumar, S., and C. Zahn. 2003. Mobile communications: Evolution and impact on business operations. *Technovation* 23 (6): 515–520.

Kumar, S., and J. Stokkeland. 2003. Evolution of GPS technology and its subsequent use in commercial markets. *International Journal of Mobile Communications* 1 (1/2): 180–193.

Laudon, K., and C. Traver. 2015. *E-Commerce 2015: Business Technology Society.* (11th ed., global ed.) Harlow: Pearson.

Lee, A. 2003. Pay as you go. *The Engineer* 292 (7632): 13.

Lee, M.S.Y., P.J. McGoldrick, K.A. Keeling, and J. Doherty. 2003. Using ZMET to explore barriers to the adoption of 3G mobile banking services. *International Journal of Retail* 31 (6): 340–348.

Li, Yung-Ming, and Yung-Shao Yeh. 2010. Increasing trust in mobile commerce through design aesthetics. *Computers in Human Behavior* 26: 673–684.

Livemint. 2015. Mobile overtakes desktop for hotel bookings: MakeMyTrip. Accessed 2015. http://www.livemint.com/Consumer/rE2tOhXQec6FHGuNwgV7PN/Mobile-overtakes-desktop-for-hotel-bookings-MakeMyTrip.html.

McDermott, P. 2000. Building trust into online business. *Network Security* 10 (2000): 10–12.

MacInnes, I., J. Moneta, J. Caraballo, and D. Sarni. 2002. Business models for mobile content: The case of m-games. *Electronic Markets* 12 (4): 218–227.

Mahatanankoon, P., H.J. Wen, and B. Lim. 2005. Consumer-based m-commerce: Exploring consumer perception of mobile applications. *Computer Standards and Interfaces* 27: 347–357.

Mok, W.S.S. 2002. Wireless online games. *The Electronic Library* 20 (2): 113–118.

Nassuora, A.B. 2013. Understanding factors affecting the adoption of M-commerce by consumers. *Journal of Applied Sciences* 13: 913–918.

NDTV. 2015. *Myntra to Shut Down Website, Go App-Only From May 15.* Accessed 2015. http://profit.ndtv.com/news/tech-media-telecom/article-myntra-to-shut-down-website-go-app-only-from-may-15–761894.

Nicolle, L. 2000. Life by phone. *The Computer Bulletin* 42 (6): 20–22.

Ocampo, A., D. Boggio, J. Munch, and G. Palladino. 2003. Toward a reference process for developing wireless Internet services. *IEEE Transactions on Software Engineering* 29 (12): 1122–1134.

Olla, P., N. Patel, and C. Atkinson. 2003. A case study of MMO2's MADIC: A framework for creating mobile Internet systems. *Internet Research: Electronic Networking Applications and Policy* 13 (4): 311–321.

Pierce, J. 2002. Cash is just a phone call away. *The Engineer* 291 (7612): 20–25.

Quora. 2013. How many users does WhatsApp have worldwide. Accessed 2015. https://www.quora.com/How-many-users-does-WhatsApp-have-worldwide.

Rochford, T. 2001. The impact of mobile application technology on today's workforce. iConverse White paper, [March 2001].

Sarker, S., and J.D. Wells. 2003. Understanding mobile handheld device use and adoption. *Communications of the ACM* 46 (12): 35–40.

Semrau, M., and A. Kraiss. 2001. Mobile commerce for financial services-killer applications or dead end? *ACM SIGGROUP Bulletin* 22 (1): 22–25.

Senn, J.A. 2000. The emergence of m-commerce. *Computer* 33 (12): 148–150.

Sharif, M.S., B. Shao, F. Xiao, and M.K. Saif. 2014. The impact of psychological factors on consumers trust in adoption of m-commerce. *International Business Research* 7 (5): 148–155.

Siau, K., E. Lim, and Z. Shen. 2001. Mobile commerce: Promises, challenges and research agenda. *Journal of Database Management* 12.3: 4–13.

Singh, G. 2000. Freedom without compromise: Creating a secure environment on the move. *Computer Fraud and Security* 2000 (12): 11–13.

Snowden, S., J. Spafford, R. Michaelides, and J. Hopkins. 2006. Technology acceptance and m-commerce in an operational environment. *Journal of Enterprise Information Management* 19 (5): 525–539.

Soriano, M., and D. Ponce. 2002. A security and usability proposal for mobile electronic commerce. *IEEE Communications Magazine* 40 (8): 62–67.

Statista. 2014. *Mobile App Usage.* Accessed 2015. http://www.statista.com/topics/1002/mobile-app-usage/.

Tan, J., H.J. Wen, and T. Gyires. 2003. M-commerce security: The impact of wireless application protocol (WAP) security services on e-business and e-health solutions. *International Journal of Mobile Communications* 1 (4): 409–424.

Tang, J., V. Terziyan, and J. Veijalainen. 2003. Distributed PIN verification scheme for improving security of mobile devices. *Mobile Networks and Applications* 8 (2): 159–175.

TRAI. 2014. Total wireless subscribers. Accessed 2015. http://www.trai.gov.in/WriteReadData/WhatsNew/Documents/Press Release-TSD-Mar,14.pdf.

TRAI. 2015. Total wireless subscribers. Accessed 2015. http://www.trai.gov.in/WriteReadData/WhatsNew/Documents/PR-No=47.pdf.

Venturebeat. 2014. Travel industry is booming on smartphones. Accessed 2015. http://venturebeat.com/2014/09/19/travel-bookings-by-mobile-devices-in-u-s-now-at-40-percent-and-growing-report.

Wei, T.T., G. Marthandan, A. Yee-Loong Chong, K.-B. Ooi, and S. Arumugam. 2009. What drives Malaysian m-commerce adoption? An empirical analysis. *Industrial Management and Data Systems* 109 (3): 370–388.

Weippl, E. 2001. The transition from e-commerce to m-commerce: Why security should be the enabling technology. *Journal of Information Technology Theory and Application* 3 (4): 17–19.

Xiang, Y., X. Wu, and Q. Chen. 2008. Personal innovativeness and initial adoption of M-commerce: Toward an integrated model. In *Management of Innovation and Technology. ICMIT 2008. 4th IEEE International Conference on*, pp. 652–657. IEEE

Yang, X., A. Bouguettaya, B. Medjahed, H. Long, and W. He. 2003. Organizing and accessing web services on air. *IEEE Transactions on Systems, Man and Cybernetics* Part A 33 (6): 742–757.

Yeh, Y.S., and Y.-M. Li. 2009. Building trust in m-commerce: Contributions from quality and satisfaction. *Online Information Review* 33 (6): 1066–1086.

Yeo, J., and W. Huang. 2003. Mobile e-commerce outlook. *International Journal of Information Technology and Decision Making* 2 (2): 313–332.

14

The Shift toward a Sustainable Urban Mobility through Decision Support Systems

Valeria Caiati, Salvatore Di Dio, Francesco Ferrero, and Andrea Vesco

CONTENTS

14.1 Introduction 181
14.2 Need for Decision Support Systems in Developing Sustainable Urban Mobility 183
14.3 DSSs for Top-Down Planning and Management 184
    14.3.1 A Simulation-Based DSS for Electric Urban Mobility 184
        14.3.1.1 First Tier: Diffusion of Electric Vehicles in the Target Market 185
        14.3.1.2 Second Tier: Micro Simulation of Realistic Urban Mobility in the Target Urban Scenario 187
        14.3.1.3 Third Tier: Impact of EVs on the Energy Distribution Network in the Target Scenario 187
    14.3.2 A DSS to Improve the Performance of Car-Sharing Schemes 188
14.4 DSSs for Smart Citizens 192
    14.4.1 TrafficO2: A DSS for Sustainable and Environmentally Friendly Trips Based on a Serious Game 193
14.5 Conclusions 196
References 196

14.1 Introduction

The term *smart city* is not an easy one to characterize. There is no universally accepted definition but an authentic multitude of definitions, which tend to highlight different aspects of an issue with many facets. A smart city is "a city well performing in six characteristics, built on the "smart" combination of endowments and activities of self-decisive, independent and aware citizens" (Giffinger et al. 2007). A city may only claim any such status "when investments in human and social capital and traditional (transport) and modern (ICT) communication infrastructure fuel sustainable economic growth and a high quality of life, with a wise management of natural resources, through participatory governance" (Caragliu et al. 2011). Others consider the smart city "as a city in which ICT is merged with traditional infrastructures, coordinated and integrated using new digital technologies" (Batty 2012).

Despite this proliferation of interpretations, the essence of the smart city issue is, for us, relatively simple: the urban population is expected to increase in the coming years to the point that many cities around the world will become megacities, with more than 10 million inhabitants. Furthermore, cities are the places in the world where the bulk of consumption of nonrenewable resources is concentrated; this implies that the innovations that must guide us toward a new model of sustainable development, that is, development that meets the needs of the present without compromising the ability of future generations to meet their own needs (WCED 1987), must be experimented first of all within cities, where they may cause more benefits.

For us, this is the key meaning of urban smartness. Accordingly, the smart city concept addresses the issues of urban development with an emphasis on social, economic, and environmental sustainability (Vesco and Ferrero 2015). Fulfilling the objective of being smart is a long journey and it may only be reached with an open innovation approach, that is, government, industry, academia, and citizens working together to co-create a sustainable future and drive structural changes far beyond the scope of what any one actor could do alone.

The smart city subject encompasses several application areas, among which urban mobility is a central theme. In fact, mobility in urban areas is affected by growing problems caused by increasing demand and inefficient services. These problems, summarized as congestion, more energy consumption, rising noise levels, and air pollution, produce a multitude of consequences on the whole urban system and imply significant economic losses both for the public/private sector and civil society (D'Orey and Ferreira 2014). For instance, road congestion in Europe, which is mainly located in urban areas, costs about 1% of the EU's total gross domestic product annually (D'Orey and Ferreira 2014). There is also an environmental cost related to urban mobility, estimated at 1.1% of gross domestic product in the EU and covering air pollution, noise, and global warming costs (D'Orey and Ferreira 2014). Moreover, given that the demand for mobility in urban areas will increase with the growth of people living in those areas, delivering mobility services to cope with this increasing demand requires the development of effective and, more than ever, sustainable solutions.

The transition toward a more sustainable mobility model not only comprises innovation at vehicle or infrastructure level, but also requires an open innovation approach to services supporting mobility such as monitoring, info-mobility, multimodal travel planning, and integrated ticketing, among the many public/private mobility services. Mobility services such as electric-car sharing, carpooling and bike sharing should be considered, with incentives to provide citizens with new, affordable, appealing, and sustainable solutions. These services indeed have the potential to push and entice citizens to reduce expensive and polluting mobility based on private cars. However, these new services need the right boundary conditions and policies from central and local authorities to penetrate and become an effective alternative.

Interdisciplinary and cross-sectorial expertise, together with information and communication technologies (ICTs), is an enabling factor of sustainable development. When ICTs are not the final goal but a means of the innovation process, they effectively facilitate the transition toward a more sustainable urban mobility. Under this condition, ICTs could effectively help local authorities, solution providers, and investment managers to adopt an integrated approach to the development of a sustainable urban mobility system.

Decision support systems (DSSs) are one of the most powerful applications of ICTs and could play a key role in this endeavor. These systems, which help to analyze complex phenomena, support the institutional bodies and the business sector in many different ways and with many different approaches to contribute to the development of sustainable mobility.

It is worth noting that institutional bodies and the business sector are not the sole key players in the innovation process aimed at the transition toward sustainable mobility. Great importance is placed on the citizen that, thanks to access to information and communications, through adequate engagement techniques and leveraging of custom DSSs, can change his or her habits and contribute to the shift toward more sustainable mobility.

In this chapter we (1) claim that DSSs are instrumental in the sustainable development of urban mobility, as they are useful to each decision maker to better predict, evaluate, and measure the impact of alternative solutions and to take informed and evidence-based decisions; and (2) present a number of DSSs explaining how sustainable mobility targets could be reached through these systems.

14.2 Need for Decision Support Systems in Developing Sustainable Urban Mobility

The development of today's mobility systems is not an easy task because urban mobility is a complex dynamic system. The different elements of the system are linked, meaning that a perturbation in a single element affects the whole system. Therefore, any variation in the system, such as the introduction of new policies or new mobility services, needs to be evaluated by considering the interconnected social, economic, and environmental implications. This issue requires several variables and outcomes to be taken into consideration or, in other words, to take a holistic and integrated approach to the planning and management challenge.

A DSS is designed to increase the effectiveness of analysis because it provides support to all those who need to make strategic decisions in the face of complex problems. Its definition can be deduced from the name itself:

- *Decision*: Indicates the attention paid to decision-making issues.
- *Support*: Indicates that information technology helps in making decisions but does not replace the decision maker, who is the main actor.
- *System*: Highlights that these tools are designed to enable the integration between users, computers, and methods of analysis.

This definition provides evidence that a DSS allows decision makers to predict more efficient initiatives to implement local strategies while reducing the risks associated with the deployment of large-scale innovations in the urban context.

Over the past decades, with the introduction and diffusion of sustainable urban development policies, academia, industry, and government, several DSSs have developed as evaluation tools to support the decision-making process in the field of sustainable urban planning (Gil and Duarte 2013). Due to the complexity of urban systems, there is a large variety of DSSs. Differences are found in several factors, which are, among others, specific sustainability issues, different stages of the urban development process, system scales (i.e., spatial or temporal), and type and number of users involved.

When a DSS for sustainable urban mobility is properly integrated with different modeling and simulation techniques, it becomes an effective tool for the so-called scientific urban management, which means managing urban complexity with a strong scientific approach. Moreover, the implementation of scientific urban management could enable the seamless interaction between all stakeholders involved in the innovation process of urban mobility planning.

Our discussion, until now, addresses DSSs as tools for the classical top-down approach to urban planning and management, where the local authorities, solution providers, and investment managers are the main stakeholders.

However, in recent decades, many methods for how experts and governments could engage citizens in the urban planning processes have been argued (Abdalla et al. 2015), favoring the transition of a city toward a smart and sustainable city. This approach is fostered by the diffused use of collaborative design tools, social media, and new technologies.

Within this framework, DSSs represent a tool that plays a key role in helping citizens (i.e., the users of the urban mobility system) to take decisions on how to commute daily in a more sustainable fashion. These kinds of DSSs typically come in the form of web or mobile apps that empower citizens to change (or not) their habits by proposing different alternatives and enlightening the sustainability implications of the available mobility choices.

14.3 DSSs for Top-Down Planning and Management

This section presents two DSSs developed by the authors to support two stakeholder categories (representing public and private sectors) involved in a top-down approach to sustainable urban mobility planning and management. The typical top-down approach starts from the perspective of the decision maker that looks at the big picture of the whole urban mobility system, focusing on its most relevant problems in order to identify the details that truly matter. The identification of these details enables the definition of possible policies, plans, and infrastructure and technological solutions to optimize the mobility system and to promote the reduction of negative economic, environmental, and social impacts resulting from urban transport.

14.3.1 A Simulation-Based DSS for Electric Urban Mobility

The recent political debate on the design and implementation of effective measures to address important global issues, such as fossil fuel depletion, energy security, and global warming, is causing urban decision makers to ask for new forms of mobility.

Due to its main characteristics and the recent technological developments in the automotive sector, electric mobility has been advertised as the green and sustainable answer to the mobility of the future (DG CONNECT 2012). It also represents a real example of the synergy between ICT and the transport and energy sectors, which is one of the main goals of the European Commission within its European Innovation Partnership on Smart Cities and Communities (DG CONNECT 2012). Furthermore, the governments of developed countries all over the world (e.g., the United States, France, China, Japan, and Germany) and the European Commission have set up ambitious targets for the introduction and diffusion of electric vehicles (EVs) on their roads to meet sustainable development goals by 2020 (Wirgesa et al. 2012).

However, the identification and assessment of the potential impact of electric mobility on the urban system is crucial, since its analysis needs to take into consideration a variety of factors that are linked together. The history of EVs, starting in the mid-nineteenth century, reveals that EVs have been considered a promising technology at repeated time intervals until today (EFTE 2009; Chan 2007; Sovacool and Hirsh 2008). According to Dijk et al. (2013), electric mobility is now at the center of a technological turning point of the automotive sector, benefiting also from various technological developments outside the automotive sector and within the social context of car mobility. Through a deep analysis based on a sociotechnical transition perspective, the authors found that the development of vehicle engine technology is not driven by single factors but is influenced by multiple changes of the whole sociotechnical urban mobility framework. The term *sociotechnical* takes into account not only technological and engineering factors, but also cultural, social, political, and economic aspects (Sovacool and Hirsh 2008).

We designed a tailored DSS in order to understand, encourage, and optimize the diffusion of electric mobility as a new sustainable mobility paradigm. The basic techniques of this DSS include an accurate estimation of the diffusion of EVs, using a modeling approach that takes into account all the enablers and inhibitors to the adoption of the new technology and a careful simulation to assess the response of two main elements of the system: the complex urban mobility system, in terms of real road-network maps and traffic data; and the energy distribution network, considering its real topology and the charging infrastructure. The DSS analyzes the problem through the integration of three tiers of modeling and simulation, implemented as separate modules (see Figure 14.1). The first tier analyzes socioeconomic data to estimate the diffusion of EVs in the target market over time. The output of this tier is used as input by the second tier, which consists of a microscopic traffic simulator to assess the likely effects of real mobility patterns on the state of charge of EVs. The third tier analyzes the impact of electric mobility on the energy distribution network through the charging infrastructure.

14.3.1.1 First Tier: Diffusion of Electric Vehicles in the Target Market

Although a study of EV demand was published more than 30 years ago (Beggs et al. 1981), many studies on the diffusion of alternative fuel vehicles have been conducted in the last 10–20 years. There are two strands of the literature that are relevant to forecasting the market penetration of EVs:

- The first characterizes consumer-level decision; contributions here are mainly based on discrete choice models, often based on stated preferences surveys (Dagsvik et al. 2002; Achtnicht 2009).
- The second uses a diffusion model to predict the uptake of new technologies by the market. In this strand, contributions are mainly based on Bass Diffusion Theory (Bass 1969).

We implemented the first tier in accordance with the Bass Diffusion Model, since it has been widely recognized as one of the theoretical cornerstones of the literature relevant to diffusion of innovation (Cao and Mokhtarian 2004; Becker et al. 2009). The Bass Diffusion Model requires three inputs to forecast the annual number of adopters of a new technology: (1) potential market (M), that is, the number of potential adopters of the technology; (2) coefficient of innovation (p), the likelihood that somebody who is not yet using the product will start using it because of mass media coverage or other external factors; and (3) coefficient of imitation (q), the likelihood that somebody who is not yet using the product will start using it because of word of mouth or other influences from those already using the product.

These parameters may be estimated by the time series of sales of EVs or by adopting the "guessing by analogy" method. Through this method, the parameters are estimated using the time series of sales of another technology whose diffusion process we suppose will be the same as the one that EVs will follow. The analogs used to estimate the parameters of the Bass model are the methane gas vehicle and the natural gas vehicle. In fact, these two

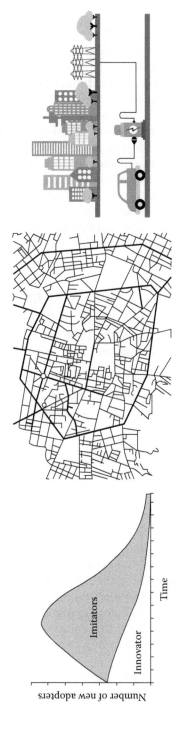

FIGURE 14.1
The three tiers of modeling and simulation building the core of the DSS.

technologies have many similarities to the one we intend to study, for example, category of users, purpose of use, and reliance on the presence of a network of power distributors.

The choice of one method over the other gives the user the possibility of analyzing different diffusion scenarios. However, some preliminary analyses conducted showed that the adoption of the guessing by analogy method is to be preferred in the case of full EVs. This is due to the still-limited penetration of EVs as a percentage of the total market and to the current low annual growth rates.

14.3.1.2 Second Tier: Micro Simulation of Realistic Urban Mobility in the Target Urban Scenario

The second tier is developed around an evolution of the Simulator of Urban Mobility (SUMO 2016). We customized the simulator to also simulate electric mobility, that is, the discharging process of EVs as a function of vehicle characteristics and the simulated driving cycle in a realistic traffic scenario. The simulation is performed on a micro scale, that is, the simulator reproduces the movement of each single vehicle from a source to a destination zone of a real map. The simulator leverages an appropriate model that describes the behavior of individual drivers to simulate the reaction of a driver to a surrounding environment in terms of acceleration, deceleration, and lane changing.

All the details about the complex procedure to make this kind of simulation possible are described by Bedogni et al. (2015). Several data sets are needed to perform it. The first input is the topology of the urban road network, representing the transport supply. In SUMO, the road network is a directed graph composed of nodes indicating the position of intersections and edges representing the road infrastructure. In addition to this basic structure, the network contains further traffic-related information such as the number of lanes of each edge, the shape and speed limit of every lane, the right-of-way regulations, the connections between lanes at junctions, and the position and logic of the traffic lights. Road networks with related information can be imported to the simulator from different sources such as OpenStreetMap (OSM 2016), a crowd-sourced platform that creates and makes available to everyone free geographic data for cities worldwide.

The second input required is the traffic demand; it is commonly stored in an origin–destination matrix that describes the traffic intensity between the source–destination couple available in the urban scenario. An adequate traffic assignment technique defines the choice and volume of the route to get from the origin zone to the destination zone. The third input is the characteristics of EVs such as mass, weight, friction factor, and battery pack, to correctly simulate the discharging process.

The second tier is therefore able to simulate, in realistic traffic conditions, the state of charge (SoC) of the share of EVs (input from the first tier) in order to direct them to a charging station when necessary and to calculate the SoC when they reach the destination. This precise information is the input to the third tier of the DSS to assess the energy demand due to electric mobility. It is worth noting that the simulator traces any charging event by considering the time and geo-localization of the request.

14.3.1.3 Third Tier: Impact of EVs on the Energy Distribution Network in the Target Scenario

The third and final tier allows the general assessment of the qualitative and quantitative impact of EV charging on electricity distribution. It describes the charging infrastructure geo-referenced coherently with urban maps and classified in two types: fast-charging stations and residential standard-charging stations. While the first are typically located at the roadside and used by vehicles that need to charge their batteries to continue their trip, the second are located near homes and parking lots and are typically used at the destination of a trip. Both stations can be configured in terms of number of columns and charging process features.

The EV recharge model is interfaced with the mobility simulator (the second tier), in order to exchange data in both directions. First, the simulation of battery recharge takes data of EV arrival at recharge stations and of their residual SoC. Then, it returns the final SoC when the EV leaves the charging station, depending on the elapsed time and the type of charging.

However, other data are necessary to quantify the distribution of energy demand, according to the habits, activities, and decisions taken by vehicle owners such as the driver's logic used to decide when, where, and how much to charge the EV battery. These behavioral models are the focus of our future work.

The approach we propose to build up a DSS for electric-based urban mobility represents an emblematic example of how the cross-sectorial scientific expertise of the research world, supported by the use of ICTs, could allow decision makers (e.g., local administrations, energy distributors, and mobility providers) to adopt an integrated approach to smart city planning. In fact, the DSS could be used for several purposes, all aimed at encouraging the diffusion of EVs in urban areas.

Using information on the discharging/charging process of EVs and data related to driving cycles in a realistic traffic scenario, distribution network operators could estimate the increase in electric power demand due to EV activities and examine the influence on standard load shapes. These analyses will be useful when taking important decisions about load management techniques and in planning the locations of the charging infrastructure and corresponding capacities. The DSS could also help local administrators in defining and optimizing urban mobility policies and traffic regulations based on the analysis of EV impacts on air quality and noise levels.

14.3.2 A DSS to Improve the Performance of Car-Sharing Schemes

Car-sharing is an innovative and sustainable mobility concept. It represents a potential solution for cities that try to take measures to reduce the wasteful use of cars and their environmental impact, marking an important shift from vehicle ownership to service use (Prettenthaler and Steininger 1999). Having become popular worldwide in the 1990s, the overall car-sharing service has grown rapidly in recent years, reaching several million customers and counting a fleet of some tens of thousands of vehicles (Le Vine 2014). Furthermore, consolidated projects on car-sharing services have been implemented in more than 600 cities in over 18 countries (Shaheen and Cohen 2013). The car-sharing market also witnessed a growing interest in delivering the service from various types of organizations, such as for profit (Greenwheels 2016; Communauto 2016) and not-for-profit operators (Carma 2016), public transport operators (Flinkster 2016; Transdev 2016), car manufacturers (Daimler 2016; BMW 2016), and citizen networkers (Getaround 2016; Drivy 2016; Tamyca 2016).

As more players enter this new market, the competition among them is intensifying. Along with the strong interest in this innovative type of mobility, all car-sharing players have to be prepared to face the challenges and threats of this new market.

A clear need thus arises for a valuable decision-supporting tool, able to help car-sharing providers develop efficient strategic and operational planning as well as continuously monitor the performance of the service.

Starting from this context analysis, we have developed a DSS that is specifically designed to be a valuable solution to support the strategic decisions of the operators and improve their business performance.

The DSS was developed thanks to strong cooperation by private companies that operate in the green economy sector and provide innovative and environmentally sustainable car-sharing services in Italy. The cooperation with real players allowed us to build the DSS using real data (about 6000 clients and 2 years of rentals) to design a DSS that easily adapts to different car-sharing services (i.e., station based or free-floating; traditional or EVs). The DSS is a web-based tool that supports the car-sharing provider with specific infographics based on historical data showing the evolution of the car-sharing service. A simple dynamic graphic interface allows easier understanding of complex data and information. In addition to the representation of historical data related to the service performance, the DSS provides mathematical models for demand forecasting, operational decisions, and service optimization. The DSS is composed of three sections that reflect the demand and supply characteristics of car-sharing systems: (1) the client section, (2) the service section, and (3) the relocation section.

The first section collects and analyzes client data sets and displays a series of information through different infographics. This information could be relevant for developing marketing strategies and implementing better planning of the service. Splitting by age and by number of car rentals made in a given period for all users registered to the service, it was possible to apply an appropriate clustering algorithm that creates distinct groups of clients. Through a reliable cluster analysis, the DSS could in fact help the car-sharing provider to differentiate the profitable clients from the nonprofitable ones. Consequently, the provider could develop a more focused marketing campaign customized to each of the identified customer groups. As an example, Figure 14.2 shows the result of a clustering analysis, performed by means of the *k-mean* algorithm. The analysis of the data set clearly identifies four classes of users.

Furthermore, this first section also collects and maps data related to the geographic distribution of clients and information related to the popularity level of each zone of the operational area of the car-sharing service. In fact, in order to develop an accurate demand model, it is necessary to discretize the operational area in zones comparable with micro geographic units with homogeneous socioeconomic characteristics, since the dislocation of activities and services within the operational area influences demand distribution. Through the visualization of these data, DSS users could have instant feedback about the existing spatial distribution of clients. This information could be used to find the optimal distribution of car-sharing vehicles within a given zone, matching car-sharing demand and supply. More specifically, by taking into account the starting point of the customers and their preferences about departure and arrival zones, the car-sharing provider could take important decisions in terms of strengthening or weakening existing zones and extending or restricting the operational area.

The second section gives the user an at-a-glance overview of the performance of the car-sharing service. All the data are presented in easy-to-understand histograms. First, it gives information about the number of car rentals in a given interval of time since the beginning of the service. Second, as shown in Figure 14.3, it provides an overview of the service usage data with specific statistical measures on a zone-by-zone basis. These measures are related to the number of arrivals; the number of departures; the workload number, which identifies the most-used zones since it is calculated as the sum of departures and arrivals in each zone; and the car needs number. This last information allows the car-sharing provider to understand if a zone is used mainly as a starting point and thus potentially needs

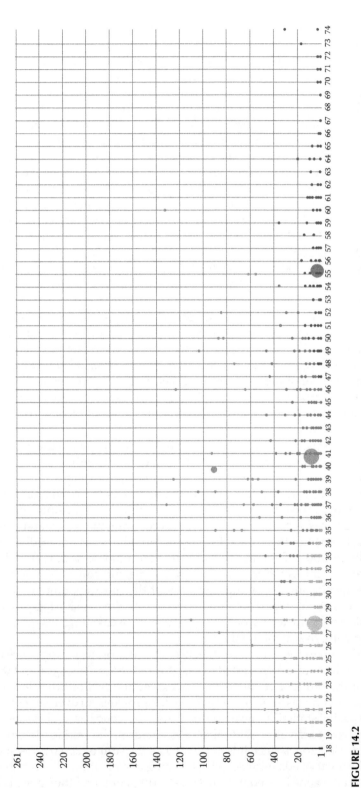

FIGURE 14.2
Result of the clustering analysis; points are the clients, with client age along the x-axis and total number of rentals of each client along the y-axis; the circles are the representative cluster users.

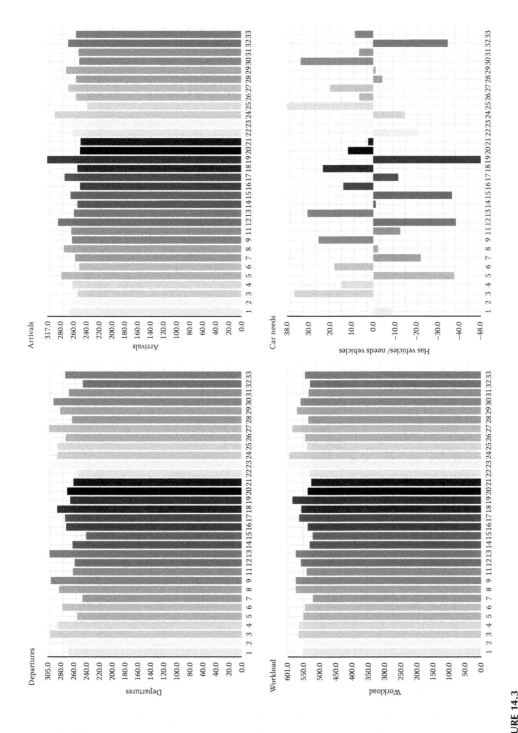

FIGURE 14.3
Performance dashboard. The x-axis defines the zone identification number.

a greater number of vehicles, or alternatively if it is used as a point of arrival and therefore already has vehicles. In other words, it could indicate a potential shortage or accumulation of vehicles at certain zones. In this way, it gives, through a simple view, a first input to the planning of its relocation strategy.

Built to be regularly updated (e.g., weekly or monthly), the service section is a sort of performance dashboard that displays the most important information to decision makers so that they can monitor and manage the service more efficiently.

The first two sections were developed as data analysis systems (Power 2002), which means that they collect, analyze, and display in an intuitive manner all current or historical data about the clients and the service performance. Furthermore, the use of a dynamic graphic interface allows users to query data in real time, evaluate the performance of the analyzed system, and consequently make decisions. The relocation section goes a step further than the first two sections. It is an extension of the data analysis system since it processes the data collected using a forecast model for the prediction of future demand. The result of this modeling technique is an intuitive tool that supports the decision-making process related to relocation strategies. Relocation is defined as an activity that is performed by the car-sharing operator staff to prevent or minimize vehicle imbalance issues, moving vehicles between zones having vehicles in excess and zones having a lack of vehicles. In order to efficiently rebalance the resources of the service, it would be useful for the car-sharing operators to know the number of vehicles required to meet the demand for each of the most-stressed zones. For this purpose, we have implemented an algorithm in our tool, able to predict this number by using different historical data sets related to the service usage of each zone. Setting a specific time slot (hour and day of the week), the tool gives information about the probability of a zone receiving a request for a rental. This leads to the implementation of efficient relocation strategies that maximize the number of satisfied requests and reduce logistics costs.

This DSS represents a powerful tool, generated by the fruitful collaboration between the business and research communities. The first one made the data sets available in order to optimize its overall performance in a more efficient way, while the second one provided the scientific methodologies to analyze and visualize the data sets to have a better understanding of the business and operational aspects and support the diffusion of this new type of sustainable mobility.

If the current DSS supports the decision making of an operator running the service, one of the main goals of our future work is the development of a tool that supports the service design process of a car-sharing company that wants to enter a new city, both in the case of the absence or coexistence of other car-sharing providers in the same environment. The tool will aim to determine the fleet size, which is an important asset in order to meet customer demand and optimize the service within the covered area, and to choose the service model that best suits the environment in which it will operate. In addition, it will be a useful tool for the evaluation of different service-planning alternatives on the basis of cost structures and revenue streams.

14.4 DSSs for Smart Citizens

The transition toward sustainable urban mobility not only depends on the implementation of top-down policies and initiatives. Since mobility is a basic human activity (Gil et al. 2011), sustainable improvements in the urban mobility system can come directly from a bottom-up perspective. In this context, the bottom-up perspective can be seen as one taken by citizens that make sustainable or unsustainable transport choices every day to satisfy their mobility needs.

The decision-making process that leads to the travel mode choice is affected by a wide variety of factors, such as individual lifestyles and daily habits, socioeconomic characteristics, circumstances of the journey (e.g., travel distance or weather conditions), and quality of available transport services and infrastructures.

In a time of scarce resources, it seems possible to influence citizens' decisions about travel mode choices without any infrastructural transformation (Di Dio et al. 2015). In fact, the rapid and increasing market penetration of smartphones and other personal mobile technologies, supported by the effective use of ICTs and social networks, could enable the citizens' transport behavior-change process, helping cities to reach their sustainability goals. In other words, to make the transition toward sustainable mobility feasible, it is important that citizens have all the necessary information to change bad habits and take better decisions on how to move in the city, thus driving a real change.

Over the last few years, a growing interest has emerged in developing mobility applications (apps) as tools for making cities smart (Schaffer and Reithinger 2014; Weissman and Villalobos 2012). Usually, they are multimodal trip planners available on mobile devices that give users the information they need to plan their journey and move around the city, using both origin and destination as starting points and desired departure/arrival time. They also combine data from different transport operators in order to provide information about real-time data and schedules, total travel time, availability of every means of transport (e.g., buses, underground, and bike-sharing stations), and up-to-date information on weather, traffic conditions, and potential disruption to the mobility services (e.g., interruptions, roadside works, and maintenance).

However, in order to change travelers' behaviors, we need to develop solutions acting as DSSs for travelers and inducing more sustainable behavior regarding the use of urban transport (Di Dio et al. 2015).

In the following, we describe a DSS aimed at providing a series of information, both of a qualitative and a quantitative nature, about the sustainability of each travel choice and educating citizens about the consequences of their decisions on the urban mobility system.

14.4.1 TrafficO2: A DSS for Sustainable and Environmentally Friendly Trips Based on a Serious Game

Several cities in the Mediterranean region are facing serious urban mobility issues, influenced by different socioeconomic and demographic changes (Debyser 2014). These issues become more complex considering the scant investment powers of the local authorities and the lack of good development policies introduced in the past (Di Dio et al. 2015). Within this framework, innovative ways of urban mobility planning based on changing the behavior of citizens have increasingly gained significance.

Palermo is one of the Italian cities that in recent years has experienced a paradigm shift in the way they think about urban mobility planning. It is the most important city in Sicily, in the south of Italy, with a population of about 680,000 inhabitants in an urban area of about 160 km^2. As a center of the main directional and administrative function of the island, the city attracts students and workers from the whole of Sicily as well as large numbers of tourists all year round, becoming a complex urban environment.

However, the social and economic context of the city does not allow it to meet all the needs required in such a dynamic situation, causing different, heavy consequences on urban systems, among which is the mobility system. According to TomTom's annual Traffic Index, based on 2014 data, Palermo is the ninth most traffic-congested city in the world and the most congested among Italian cities, with a congestion level (i.e., increase in overall travel time when compared with a free-flow situation) of 42% (TomTom 2015). The analysis also found that commuters in the city of Palermo lost up to 24 minutes per day (based on two 30-minute peak period trips per day). But vehicular congestion caused by the indiscriminate use of private transport is not the only problem with the mobility system of Palermo. The city is characterized by the lack of an underground transport system; a scarcity of interchange-based parking lots, which are also poorly connected to the city center; and a bus fleet that is one of the oldest in Italy, with a supply (seats per kilometer per inhabitant) below the Italian average. Moreover, all these infrastructural problems were joined by a lack of urban mobility policies for many years. Only in March 2013, the municipality adopted a new general urban plan for traffic management, which provides a series of plans and interventions for the urban mobility structure. However, the political dynamics in urban planning, supported by strategic plans and technical decisions, must be only a part of a wider instrument aimed at achieving sustainable mobility. In order to be really effective, the necessary modifications of urban structure have to be accompanied by a social and cultural change, achievable by a series of bottom-up initiatives that share the same ambitions (Di Dio et al. 2015).

The TrafficO2 initiative is a social innovation project which aims "to reduce vehicle traffic flow and pollution without making any modifications to the urban structures and without applying substantial modifications to mobility policies" (Di Dio et al. 2015). The strategy, described in Figure 14.4, is to foster local communities to change and make their mobility habits sustainable through specific information and tailor-made tangible incentives for

FIGURE 14.4
Strategy of the TrafficO2 initiative.

each responsible choice made by the users, with the help of a technology-driven (mobile app) serious game.

The project has been ideated and developed by PUSH, a not-for-profit innovation laboratory based in the city of Palermo, and funded by the Italian Ministry of University and Research in the framework of the 2012 tender "Smart Cities and Communities and Social Innovation."

The mobile app acts as a DSS for urban commuters, providing them with comprehensive information on traffic issues to make an informed choice between sustainable transport modes available in the city (i.e., walking, bike, public transport, carpooling, car-sharing, and so on). However, urban commuters are not the only actors directly involved in the system. The project also creates commercial value for local retail businesses, which could actively participate in the project by subscribing to the platform and becoming stations (i.e., local business station [LBS], star sponsor station [SSS]) for each sustainable transport system. This means that their locations become visible on the map in such a way as to be selectable by users as departure and arrival points at which to check in. In this way, local businesses involved in the platform invest in an innovative advertising and communication technique, since they receive more visibility and obtain detailed information on their customers.

Through a survey integrated in the mobile app, each user could describe his or her personal mobility habits and preferences on transport choices. This description represents the starting point of the decision-making process of the user, being the base of the user's mobility behavioral change process and giving the possibility to monitor his or her improvements toward more sustainable travel behavior. Then, the mobile app acts effectively as a DSS, supporting users to plan their journeys in the most sustainable way. Using global positioning system (GPS)-based technology and a specific algorithm for motion recognition, it allows users to configure their trips, choosing the starting point and the destination matching the closest stations on the map. After that, the app calculates the best overall routes between origin and destination for each of the previously mentioned sustainable travel modes. The user can make a well-informed travel decision thanks to a list of data about the selected trip: the calories burned, carbon emissions, travel time, and economic costs. The integration of all these data into a travel planner app has an important cultural and educational power, informing citizens through quantitative values about the economic, environmental, and social consequences of their travel decisions. In fact, the initiative has engaged about 500 active users to date, and changing their habits has saved 55.160 g of carbon dioxide.

Furthermore, urban commuters are encouraged to use the TrafficO2 app and to change their habits, thanks to their involvement in an interesting gaming strategy. The users have in fact the possibility to earn so-called O2 points for each travel choice. The O2 points awarded are proportional to the carbon emissions of each mobility system and are also influenced by a weather factor. These points can be used to challenge other users via the mobile app and play for prizes made available by the 98 LBSs and SSSs affiliated with the platform. Within this context, the sponsors get more effective media exposure, attracting new customers and loyalizing them through gift and discount coupons for an amount of about 10 euros. They also have access to detailed statistics on user ratings of prizes and games.

The example of the DSS we have proposed represents a successful case study of how the diffusion of mobile technology and the effective use of ICTs could be the enabling factors of virtuous communication actions aimed at providing information and establishing a direct dialogue with citizens. This involves citizens in the transition toward a sustainable urban mobility system without changing the characteristics of the context.

14.5 Conclusions

Urban mobility is affected by growing problems caused by increasing demand and inefficient services. These problems, summarized as congestion, more energy consumption, rising noise levels, and air pollution, produce a multitude of consequences for the whole urban system and imply significant economic losses both for the public/private sector and civil society. This chapter has highlighted that the transition toward a more sustainable mobility model not only comprises innovation at vehicle or infrastructure level, but also requires interdisciplinary and cross-sectorial expertise together with effective decision-making support. The chapter has presented a number of DSSs with a discussion on how sustainable mobility targets could be reached through these systems to support the claim that DSSs are instrumental to the sustainable development of urban mobility. We strongly believe that DSSs empower local authorities, urban planners, and solution providers to better predict and measure the impact of alternative smart city initiatives on the path toward the triple sustainability targets. At the same time, DSSs in the form of simple, fancy, and effective apps for smart user devices allow citizens (i.e., the users of the urban mobility systems) to make informed, conscious, and evidence-based decisions for their commute, hence positively contributing to the achievement of sustainability targets.

References

Abdalla, S., Elariane, S., and El Defrawi, S. 2015. Decision-making tool for participatory urban planning and development: Residents' preferences of their built environment. *Journal of Urban Planning and Development* 142(1):1–13.

Achtnicht, M. 2009. German car buyers' willingness to pay to reduce CO_2 emissions. Accessed April 4, 2016. ftp://ftp.zew.de/pub/zew-docs/dp/dp09058.pdf.

Bass, F. 1969. A new product growth model for consumer durables. *Management Science* 15(5):215–227.

Batty, M., Axhausen, K.W., Giannotti, F., Pozdnoukhov, A., Bazzani, A., Wachowicz, M., Ouzounis, G., and Portugali, Y. 2012. Smart cities of the future. *The European Physical Journal* 214:481–518.

Becker, T. A., Sidhu, I., and Tenderich, B. 2009. Electric vehicles in the United States: A new model with forecasts to 2030. Accessed April 4, 2016. http://odpowiedzialnybiznes.pl/public/files/CET_Technical%20Brief_EconomicModel2030.pdf.

Bedogni, L., Gramaglia, M., Vesco, A., Fiore, M., Harri, J., and Ferrero, F. 2015. The Bologna Ringway dataset: Improving road network conversion in SUMO and validating urban mobility via navigation services. *IEEE Transactions on Vehicular Technology* 64(12):5464–5476.

Beggs, S., Cardell, S., and Hausman, J. 1981. Assessing the potential demand for electric cars. *Journal of Econometrics* 17(1):1–19.

BMW. 2016. Drivenow. Accessed April 4, 2016. https://de.drive-now.com/en/.

Cao, X., and Mokhtarian, P.L. 2004. The future demand for alternative fuel passenger vehicles: A diffusion of innovation approach. Accessed April 4, 2016. http://www.tc.umn.edu/~cao/AQP_Cao.pdf.

Caragliu, A., Del Bo, C., and Nijkamp, P. 2011. Smart Cities in Europe. *Journal of Urban Technology* 18(2):65–82.

Carma. 2016. City car share. Accessed April 4, 2016. https://citycarshare.org.

Chan, C.C. (2007). The state of the art of electric, hybrid, and fuel cell vehicles. *Proceedings of the IEEE* 95(4):704–718.

Communauto. 2016. Round-trip and one-way carsharing. Accessed April 4, 2016. http://www.communauto.com.

D'Orey, P.M., and Ferreira, M. 2014. ITS for sustainable mobility: A survey on applications and impact assessment tools. *IEEE Transactions On Intelligent Transportation Systems* 15(2):477–493.

Dagsvik, J.K., Wennemo, T., Wetterwald, D.G., and Aaberge, R. 2002. Potential demand for alternative fuel vehicles. *Transportation Research Part B: Methodological* 36(4):361–384.

Daimler. 2016. car2go. Accessed April 4, 2016. https://www.car2go.com.

Debyser, Ariane. 2014. Urban mobility: Shifting towards sustainable transport systems. European parliament research service. Accessed April 4, 2016. http://www.europarl.europa.eu/RegData/etudes/IDAN/2014/538224/EPRS_IDA(2014)538224_REV1_EN.pdf.

Flinkster. 2016. Flinkster—Carsharing. Accessed April 4, 2016. https://www.flinkster.de.

DG CONNECT. 2012. ICT for the fully electric vehicle, research needs and challenges ahead. Accessed April 4, 2016. http://cordis.europa.eu/fp7/ict/micro-nanosystems/docs/brochure-ict-for-fev-2nd-edition-2011_en.pdf.

Di Dio, S., Lo Casto, B., Micari, F., Rizzo, G., and Vinci, I. 2015. Mobility, data, and behavior: The TrafficO2 case study. In *Handbook of Research on Social, Economic, and Environmental Sustainability in the Development of Smart Cities*, edited by Andrea Vesco and Francesco Ferrero, 382–406. Hershey, PA: IGI Global.

Dijk, M., Orsato, R.J., and Kemp, R. 2013. The emergence of an electric mobility trajectory. *Energy Policy* 52:135–145.

Drivy. 2016. Rent the cars next door. Accessed April 4, 2016. https://en.drivy.com.

EFTE. 2009. How to Avoid an electric shock. Electric cars: From hype to reality. Accessed April 4, 2016. http://www.transportenvironment.org/sites/te/files/media/2009%2011%20Electric%20Sh ck%20Electric%20Cars.pdf.

Getaround. 2016. Rent great cars from people nearby. Accessed April 4, 2016. https://www.getaround.com.

Giffinger, R., Fertner, C., Kramar, H., Kalasek, R., PichlerMilanović, N., and Meijers, E. 2007. Smart cities: Ranking of european medium-sized cities. Accessed April 4, 2016. http://www.smartcities.eu/download/smart_cities_final_report.pdf.

Gil, A., Calado, H., and Bents, J. 2011. Public participation in municipal transport planning processes: The case of the sustainable mobility plan of Ponta Delgada, Azores, Portugal. *Journal of Transport Geography* 19:1309–1319.

Gil, J., and Duarte, J. 2013. Tools for evaluating the sustainability of urban design: A review. *Urban Design and Planning* 166(6):311–325.

Greenwheels. 2016. Access to a car whenever it suits you. Accessed April 4, 2016. https://www.greenwheels.com.

Le Vine, S., Zolfaghari, A., and Polak, J. 2014. Carsharing: Evolution, challenges and opportunities. Accessed April 4, 2016. https://www.acea.be/uploads/publications/SAG_Report_-_Car_Sharing.pdf.

OSM. 2016. Accessed April 4, 2016. http://www.openstreetmap.org.

Power, Daniel J. 2002. *Decision Support Systems: Concepts and Resources for Managers*. Santa Barbara, CA: Greenwood Publishing.

Prettenthaler, F. E., and Steininger, K. W. 1999. From ownership to service use lifestyle: The potential of car-sharing. *Ecological Economics* 28:443–453.

Schaffer, S., and Reithinger, N. 2014. Intermodal personalized travel assistance and routing interface. In *Mensch und Computer*, edited by Michael Koch, Andreas Butz, and Johann Schlichter 343–346. Munich: De Gruyter.

Shaheen, S. A., and Cohen, A. P. 2013. Carsharing and personal vehicle services: Worldwide market developments and emerging trends. *International Journal of Sustainable Transportation* 7(1):5–34.

Sovacool, B., and Hirsh, R. 2008. Beyond batteries: An examination of the benefits and barriers to plug-in hybrid electric vehicles (PHEVs) and a vehicle-to-grid (V2G) transition. *Energy Policy* 37:1095–1103.

SUMO. 2016. Accessed April 4, 2016. SUMO—Simulation of Urban Mobility. http://www.dlr.de/ts/sumo/en.

Tamyca. 2016. Find the right car. Accessed April 4, 2016. https://www.tamyca.de.

TomTom. 2015. Traffic index: Measuring congestion worldwide. Accessed April 4, 2016. https://www.tomtom.com/en_gb/trafficindex.

Transdev. 2016. Autobleue. Accessed April 4, 2016. https://www.auto-bleue.org/en.

Vesco, A., and Ferrero, F. 2015. *Handbook of Research on Social, Economic, and Environmental Sustainability in the Development of Smart Cities*. Hershey, PA: IGI Global. doi:10.4018/978-1-4666-8282-5.

WCED. 1987. *Our Common Future*. Oxford: Oxford University Press.

Weissman, D., and Villalobos, M. 2012. Mobility apps. Accessed April 4, 2016. http://escholarship.org/uc/item/4v40t1q5.

Wirgesa, J., Linderb, S., and Kesslerc, A. 2012. Modelling the development of a regional charging infrastructure for electric vehicles in time and space. *European Journal of Transport and Infrastructure Research* 12(4):391–416.

15

Low-Carbon Logistics Network for Smart Cities: A Conceptual Framework

Harpreet Kaur and Surya Prakash Singh

CONTENTS

15.1 Introduction..199
15.2 Literature Review of Smart City Logistics Networks...............................200
    15.2.1 Review of Indicators of Smart Cities...201
    15.2.2 Review of City Logistics Models for Smart Cities 201
    15.2.3 Review of Technology-Enabled Logistics Networks for Smart Cities 202
15.3 Problem Description..203
15.4 Low-Carbon Logistics Networks for Smart Cities...................................205
15.5 Case Study 207
    15.5.1 Case Study 1 207
    15.5.2 Case Study 2 209
15.6 Conclusion and Future Scope of Work 211
References 211

15.1 Introduction

The logistics network of any firm (manufacturing or service) involves procuring raw material from suppliers and then distributing the finished goods inventory to warehouses or markets. The logistics network also involves the distribution of either the raw material or finished goods inventory through different modes of transportation using various carriers. Such logistics networks cause carbon emissions or other pollutants that affect the environment of a city or country. It has been estimated that carbon emissions caused by industry contribute more than 30% of the total carbon emitted to the atmosphere, thus making the environment unsafe for healthy living. Apart from government organizations, civil bodies have started providing awareness about the drawbacks of large carbon emissions in the atmosphere. Therefore, government bodies have proposed the concept of smart cities with the objective to make the city, in the presence of industrialization, a place for healthy living without hampering the business growth of industry. Undoubtedly, industry emits carbon to the atmosphere and, to a large extent, various checkpoints have been set by governments to minimize carbon emissions from industry. However, the amount of carbon emitted during transportation needs to be controlled. Logistics takes place either inland (involving roadways and railways) or offshore (involving waterways), and nearby cities or regions are affected. Therefore, the concept of building smart cities cannot be fulfilled unless the logistics network of business firms become low-carbon logistics. Such a concept evolved due to rapid climate change in the past few decades, which started pushing government bodies and environmental agencies toward developing and designing smart cities, not only within their country but across the globe. In particular, large cities in any country are polluted to a large extent by the rapid growth of industrialization, which causes high carbon emissions due to large numbers of manufacturing industries. Thus, to make a city smart, it is essential to integrate the manufacturing industry with its logistics network located in the city, keeping possible carbon emissions to a minimum. The term *smart* considers three main aspects of sustainability: people, profit, and planet. Therefore, this chapter provides a conceptual framework for a smart city where the manufacturing industry relies heavily on procuring raw material and distributing finished goods, develops a low-carbon logistics distribution network to minimize carbon emissions when procuring items from various suppliers, and transports finished goods to the warehouses located in a city to keep it sustainable and smart. The conceptual framework provides a low-carbon logistics network solution for industrial buyer-supplier raw materials/goods distribution of manufacturing units located in a city to make the entire city sustainable, thus making the city smart. To demonstrate the application of the proposed conceptual framework, two case studies are provided from emerging and developed economies. In the first case study, a manufacturing firm and its associates (raw material suppliers and warehouses) are located in a large city. To lower the city's carbon emissions, the distribution (inbound and outbound) logistics network is designed to keep carbon emissions low and hence make the city smart. Inbound logistics include distribution from suppliers to manufacturing firms and outbound logistics include distribution from manufacturing firms to warehouses. Similarly, in another case study, a multinational manufacturing firm operates in a country and has global suppliers. The firm procures raw material from these global suppliers through various modes of distribution, that is, roadways, waterways, and railways. The inbound distribution is designed to ensure a low-carbon distribution network to reduce the region's carbon emissions.

The rest of the chapter is organized as follows. A literature review of the application of low-carbon concepts is provided in Section 15.2. The description of the stated problem for a smart city is shown in Section 15.3. The conceptual framework for a low-carbon logistics network for smart cities is presented in Section 15.4. Section 15.5 provides two cases studies from emerging and developed economies, followed by the conclusion.

15.2 Literature Review of Smart City Logistics Networks

It has been estimated that about 65% of the global population will be urban by 2015. Also, business organizations tend to locate their plants and warehouses around urban areas to harness the advantages of better connectivity, market availability, and nearness to suppliers. In the past three decades, government bodies all over the world have initiated the development of metropolitan and urban regions to enhance the living and working environment of citizens and to promote business conditions. Therefore, to provide safer (i.e., pollution-free) living and working conditions, government and industry has come together. Hence, policy makers and city planners have also led industries operating in these regions to adopt low-carbon or sustainable business practices. Sustainability is an important paradigm for smart cities to capture the interdependence of environmental and economic dimensions. The procurement of raw material and the distribution of finished goods are essential activities of all firms. These involve multiple suppliers and multiple warehouses where raw materials and finished goods are transported, using all possible modes of transportation and carriers. It has been observed that freight transportation carriers are only 10%–20% in number as compared to passenger vehicles. But these carriers contribute to 16%–50% of carbon emissions owing to their size and the loads they carry (Dablanc, 2007). Hence, city logistics and freight transportation are addressed in the literature as an integral aspect of the smart city.

Due to government regulations and self-commitment to the environment, manufacturing firms have realized that, in order to operate in these smart cities, their inbound and outbound logistics networks have to be sustainable. Therefore, distribution networks have to be designed to not only keep transportation costs low but also to keep carbon emissions low. This can be done by utilizing transportation carriers and routes that produce less carbon emissions. This section provides a review of recently published papers in which logistics networks and the smart city concept have been proposed.

15.2.1 Review of Indicators of Smart Cities

In a seminal work by Hensher and Puckett (2005), the importance of buyer–supplier interactions to reduce freight transportation costs in a city was emphasized. The authors also emphasized the need for logistics performance among several agents of the supply chain rather than each focusing solely on profitability. Performance of logistics is a function of reduction in traffic congestion, which is the major issue in city logistics. This issue can be overcome by better interactions between different supply chain levels. Similarly, Yu and Liao (2008) have explored the role of governance in the integration of local suppliers with manufacturing firms. A comparison was done between local and international firms and their transactions with local suppliers in China. Their study elaborates the role of government in encouraging investment in smart cities. The role of government to design its policies to facilitate transaction-specific investments and long-term relationships with international manufacturers is emphasized. Lombardi et al. (2012) modeled the performance of smart cities' carbon emissions as an important smart city component. In the same year, Russo and Comi (2012) identified several indicators for designing and assessing city logistics based on their analysis of several European cities. These indicators include traffic congestion, mobility, safety, noise, and pollutants emitted into the environment. Sustainability performance is measured using these indicators. The study revealed that high cost investments are not necessary to achieve environmental goals in the cities. Recently, Jong et al. (2015) also identified sustainability as an important indicator for urban development, policy-making, and business practices in smart cities. A variety of terms related to smart cities are studied by authors, such as *sustainable city*, *smart city*, *resilient city*, *low-carbon city*, *eco city*, and *knowledge city*. Jong et al. observed in their study that all of these terms are used interchangeably, and that the key objective of these cities is to establish an optimal balance between economic, social, and environmental activities. Therefore, there is a need to address carbon calculations in city logistics to make a city smart. Anand et al. (2015) also reviewed several city logistics models and evaluated their environmental, economic, and safety aspects. It was observed that delivery vehicles were major sources of freight problems. Therefore, the choice and design of vehicles must be also addressed while modeling city logistics. The following section provides a focused review of city logistics models for smart cities.

15.2.2 Review of City Logistics Models for Smart Cities

Crainic et al. (2009) proposed models for integrated city logistics systems for urban freight transportation. One model suggests the integration of supplier, carrier, and route selection for a two-tiered distribution system. The optimal selection of routes and the scheduling of vehicle departure to curb traffic congestion in cities caused by freight vehicles are proposed. Cattaruzza et al. (2014) reviewed vehicle routing for city distribution considering multiple levels and multiple trips. The study revealed that a huge cost is involved in the distribution of goods within a city. The optimization of vehicle routing can lead to a significant reduction in transportation costs incurred by a firm. Masson et al. (2015) also developed a model based on European Commission directives (2007) for the need of city logistics systems for both goods and passengers. Here, the authors proposed a mixed urban transportation model to facilitate efficient urban mobility for both goods and passengers in the city by avoiding traffic congestion and reducing emissions produced at the same time. However, this arrangement is not favorable for large-scale industry procurement or the procurement of hazardous materials. Höjer and Wangel (2015) investigated sustainable smart city practices and development over the past decade. The need for stricter regulations and policies is suggested by the authors to overcome regulatory challenges faced by these bodies. Recently, Lee et al. (2016) proposed an integrated framework for parcel delivery in the just-in-time (JIT) system, considering energy conservation in logistics. The authors showed a significant reduction in the total transportation costs incurred and the emissions produced during distribution. However, the proposed framework was developed for only one mode of transportation. Multimodal distribution networks are not considered in the proposed framework. The evaluation of sustainable activities is also a major concern for government bodies and carbon emission regulatory bodies. The following section presents a focused review of technology-enabled logistics networks for smart cities.

15.2.3 Review of Technology-Enabled Logistics Networks for Smart Cities

In this era of globalization, global supply chain networks are much more complex when dealing with multiple global suppliers and markets. Logistics is one of the time-consuming processes in the global supply chain network. Hence, there is a need for transparent knowledge sharing among different supply chain partners. Addressing this issue, Smirnov et al. (2009) suggested the use of technology in flexible vehicle routing for a production firm. The technology enables all the involved partners to have clear information about the mobility of goods and disruptions in the global logistics network. Although the use of such online monitoring tools reduces the transportation risks involved, it doesn't ensure the sustainability of the system, which is an important aspect of smart cities. Montreuil (2011) identified current logistics practices used throughout the world as unsustainable. In order to make the entire process more sustainable, multilevel integration is considered essential for sustainable smart city logistics. The authors suggested the development of physical Internet vision and the need to further research and joint collaboration between government, industry, and academia for sustainable logistics practices. There is a lot of published work emphasizing the need to redesign vehicles and integrate technology in smart city logistics. Balakrishna (2012) proposed the application of widely used smartphones and their applications to ensure smart mobility. Smart mobility is the availability and accessibility of information through various technologies in sustainable logistics systems. However, large-scale deployment of these technologies and their integration into conventional logistics systems is a huge challenge for business organizations in smart cities. It is a common perception that these advanced technologies can only be afforded by large-scale enterprises. Kawa (2012) proposed a cloud computing–based model for small- or medium-scale enterprises to provide easy access, cost-efficient data collection, and better management of logistics systems. Bijwaard et al. (2011) and Nowicka (2014) proposed cloud computing adaptations for city logistics by interconnecting mobile devices and sensors based on the cloud computing model to achieve transparent, real-world data.

It has been widely discussed in the literature that smart cities require efficient infrastructure, technological modifications in the processes, information technology integration, and the use of hybrid vehicles using alternative fuels to emit less carbon. However, the importance of strategic changes to the existing systems, rather than redesigning whole new systems, is not given much attention. There is some research on the significant reduction of carbon emissions in industrial operations by a few strategic changes, however, although the adaptation of this concept to smart city logistics is not reported. Most of the published work did not integrate the logistics network of manufacturing industries with the idea of keeping the city smart. As discussed previously, these published works to a large extent provide a description of either the smart city concept or some models of logistics networks without relating these to sustainability. Hence, the integration of business activities is necessary to make city logistics more sustainable. Table 15.1 provides a summary of the reviewed literature on smart city logistics.

Based on the literature review carried out, it can be seen that a lot of work on sustainability in city logistics has been reported and carried out to make logistics networks more sustainable and efficient. However, most of the work is focused solely on distribution networks, ignoring the effect of load and the selection of suppliers/carriers for a manufacturing firm. Also, numerous models have been developed that focus on carbon reduction in several manufacturing operations dealing with various issues such as lot-sizing, supplier selection, scheduling, and facility layout. However, carbon lowering in the manufacturing industry focuses on procurement, supply chain, and logistics networks and does not integrate with the idea of making cities smart, especially where the manufacturing industries and their prominent suppliers are located. This chapter provides a conceptual framework to integrate the low-carbon logistics network of a manufacturing industry procuring items from suppliers located in the same city to make the city smart. Thus, the chapter is an attempt to propose a framework for a smart city through the low-carbon logistics network of in-house manufacturing industries.

15.3 Problem Description

The manufacturing industry is located in a city, and tries to procure required items from nearby suppliers to manufacture products to meet the market demand. However, the suppliers have a limited capacity to meet the demand raised and have limited modes of transportation with varying carrier capacity and carbon emissions. Procurement in the manufacturing industry involves procurement processes such as ordering cost, inventory carrying cost, procurement cost, and transportation cost. At the same time, carbon emissions are also associated with ordering, keeping extra inventory, and using transportation with fixed and variable emissions for delivery. The variable carbon emissions depend on the load the carrier is carrying and the delivery point, that is, the buyer's location, the mileage on the vehicle used, and the vehicle load (quantity).

TABLE 15.1

Summary of Reviewed Literature on Smart City Logistics

| | Low-Carbon Logistics Dimensions Addressed in the Past | | | | | | | | |
| | Logistics | | | | | | Type of Load Carried | | Sustainability Aspect |
Published Work	Network Design	Carrier Selection	Vehicle Scheduling	Vehicle Design	Policy-Making	Online Monitoring	Goods	Passengers	
Hensher and Puckett (2005)		✓	✓				✓	✓	
Smirnv et al. (2009)	✓					✓	✓		✓
Dablanc (2007)	✓	✓			✓		✓		✓
Uckelmann (2008)				✓	✓		✓		
Crainic et al. (2009)	✓		✓				✓	✓	
Trentini and Malhene (2010)	✓						✓	✓	
Masson et al. (2015)									
Bijwaard et al. (2011); Kawa (2012); Nowicka (2014)						✓	✓		✓
Montreuil (2011)	✓	✓				✓	✓		
Balakrishna (2012)	✓			✓		✓	✓	✓	
Russo and Comi (2012)	✓						✓	✓	
Cattaruzza et al. (2014)	✓						✓		
Jong et al. (2015); Hojer and Wangel (2015)					✓				✓
Lee et al. (2016)	✓						✓		✓

15.4 Low-Carbon Logistics Networks for Smart Cities

This section provides a conceptual framework for designing a smart city while considering the main issue of carbon emissions caused by the manufacturing industry and its associated suppliers/organizations located in a city. The proposed framework provides a low-carbon logistics solution for the entire network of city industries in order to make and keep the city smart while considering all the parameters of sustainability, such as people, profit, and planet. The proposed framework, involving various parameters to integrate the logistics of a city industry with the smart city concept, is shown in Figures 15.1 and 15.2.

Figure 15.1 shows two different parameters, where parameter type 1 takes care of industry cost issues while parameter type 2 takes care of carbon emissions caused by the industry and its suppliers located in a city. The cost parameter is an industry concern, and the industry primarily deals with cost minimization. Similarly, the carbon emissions parameter is a city concern, and government and environmental bodies mainly focus on the minimization of carbon emissions in the environment due to the rapid industrialization taking place in the city and the entire country. Integrating both types of parameter will not take care of industry issues but will cater to the needs of city, nation, and society at large. The integration provides a low-carbon logistics solution for manufacturing industries dealing with the procurement of various items from their suppliers located in a city, to maintain industry interest as well as environmental standards in order to design a smart city.

Figure 15.1 shows two sets of parameters: cost parameters and carbon emissions parameters. Cost parameters are considered to ensure a logistics network that requires the lowest transportation cost while carbon emissions parameters are considered to ensure that the logistics network optimizes the routes having minimum carbon emissions. These two sets of parameters provide an optimum trade-off between transportation cost and carbon emission cost. Similarly, Figure 15.2 shows various carbon

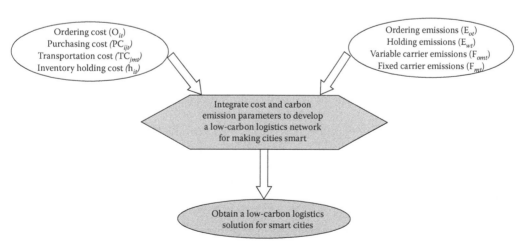

FIGURE 15.1
Sustainable procurement and logistics flowchart.

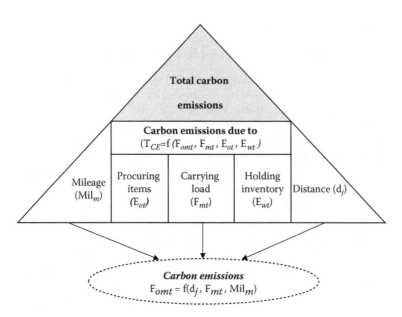

FIGURE 15.2
Building blocks for total carbon emissions calculation.

emissions caused by the carrier and inventory and also provides the calculation process for carbon emissions caused by the logistics involved in the ordering and delivering of items. The carbon emissions calculated from these parameters are minimized so as to minimize the overall cost. Two equations can be used to calculate carbon emissions. Equation 15.1 represents the computation of carbon emission from the carrier used for the logistics, and is directly proportional to the distance being covered, the mileage of the vehicle used for the raw material or goods transportation, and the quantity (amount of raw material or finished goods) being transported. It can be seen from Equation 15.1 that a good mileage carrier will lead to reduced carbon emissions and hence fewer carbon emission costs. Similarly, carbon emissions will increase for longer travel. Since the carrier type and its condition is also one of the factors that affects carbon emissions, the emission factor is considered to account for this. Considering all these factors, variable carrier emission (F_{omt}) can be calculated using Equation 15.1. Furthermore, total carbon emitted (T_{CE}) is determined using Equation 15.2. Equation 15.2 simply puts together all the carbon emissions caused by fixed carrier emissions (F_{mt}), variable carrier emissions (F_{omt}), ordering emissions (E_{ot}), and holding emissions (E_{wt}). The total carbon emitted (T_{CE}) is used to calculate the carbon emissions cost. Finally, the carbon emissions cost calculated using T_{CE} and the total transportation cost due to ordering cost (O_{it}), purchasing cost (PC_{ijt}), transportation cost (TC_{jmt}), and inventory holding cost (h_{it}) is considered to optimize the low-carbon logistics network when designing the smart city framework.

$$F_{omt} = \left(d_j \,/\, \text{Mil}_m \right) * \left(\text{emission factor} \right) * \left(\text{quantity loaded} \right) \tag{15.1}$$

$$\text{Total carbon emission} \left(T_{CE} \right) = F_{mt} + F_{omt} + E_{ot} + E_{wt} \tag{15.2}$$

15.5 Case Study

The concept of a smart city integrated with a low-carbon logistics network for the manufacturing industry is described using two case studies. These case studies are taken from emerging and developed economies, where some aspects of the conceptual framework have been implemented to design the smart city while considering the fact of rapid industrialization of the manufacturing units in a city or country.

15.5.1 Case Study 1

This is a case of a logistics network for a manufacturing company (M_1, M_2, and M_3) operating in several different locations in a large Indian city and procuring different types of raw material from various nearby sources (S_1, S_2, S_3, and S_4) to manufacture goods to meet local demand. All units of the manufacturing firm must procure raw material in a timely manner and then distribute it to warehouses (W_1, W_2, W_3, W_4, and W_5) situated in the market area. This is shown in Figure 15.3. Due to local government and environmental regulations, the company has also to redesign its procurement and distribution network so as to minimize the carbon emissions generated during transportation, procurement, and holding of the raw material and finished goods inventory. All units can procure items through all possible existing routes using different transportation modes such as small-, medium-,

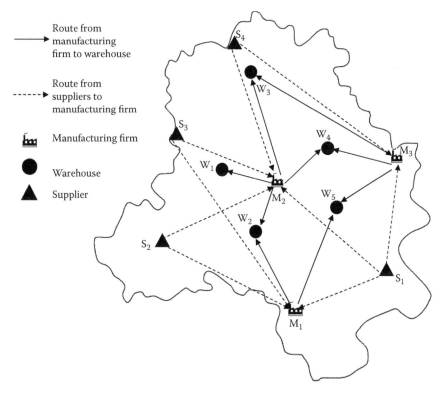

FIGURE 15.3
Distribution network for local city manufacturing units.

and large-sized trucks with varying capacities. These different transportation modes emit different carbon emissions to the city environment. In order to meet government regulations to minimize carbon emissions so as to save the carbon credit and minimize logistics costs, the company needs to optimize the logistics network. For this, the details of the carbon emissions from each transportation mode (i.e., carrier) must be used. The proposed conceptual framework can be applied in this case to optimize the low-carbon logistics network of the manufacturing units in a city to make and keep the city smart. The distance (d_j) data for all manufacturing units from the suppliers and then to all warehouses are taken into account. The distance (d_j) information is used to calculate the carbon being emitted to the city from each carrier type. All carriers having different mileage (Mil_m) and carrying capacities emit different quantities of carbon (F_{omt}). The carbon emission (F_{omt}) is calculated using Equation 15.1. Similarly, carbon is being emitted while procuring (E_{ot}) and holding extra inventory (E_{wt}). Each carrier also emits carbon, which is considered as fixed carbon emission (F_{mt}). Considering all this information, total carbon emitted (T_{CE}) for each route, that is, from suppliers to manufacturing units and from manufacturing units to warehouses, can be easily calculated by applying Equation 15.2. Based on the total carbon emitted (T_{CE}), carrier capacity, supplier capacity, and demand raised/required at the manufacturing units, the low-carbon logistics network within the city can be minimized, keeping to the minimum level for emission of carbon. The low-carbon network not only makes the logistics smart but also makes the entire city a smart city. In this case, the low-carbon optimum logistics network is represented in Figure 15.4 by bold and dashed lines.

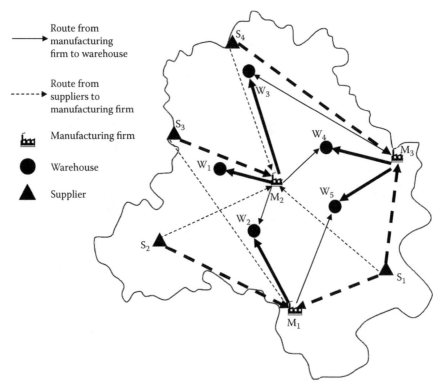

FIGURE 15.4
Low-carbon logistics network for local city manufacturing units for smart cities.

The bold dashed lines represent the low-carbon routes from all suppliers (S_1, S_2, S_3, and S_4) to manufacturing units (M_1, M_2, and M_3), and the bold continuous lines represent the low-carbon logistics routes from manufacturing units (M_1, M_2, and M_3) to all warehouses (W_1, W_2, W_3, W_4, and W_5).

15.5.2 Case Study 2

This is the case of an international automobile firm (M) procuring raw material from five different global suppliers (S_1, S_2, S_3, S_4, and S_5). These global suppliers are in different countries and can supply through inland (roadways and railways) and sea transportation (waterways) routes. For inland transportation, existing railways or roadways can be used to procure raw materials from suppliers. Similarly, water transportation can be used to procure materials from suppliers located in other countries. In this case, raw material is transported to six nearby ports (P_1, P_2, P_3, P_4, P_5, and P_6) by the suppliers and then supplied through waterways to the buyer firm. Hence, the suppliers can use more than one mode of transportation for supplying raw materials. The possible routes for procurement from the suppliers are shown in Figure 15.5. The firm is bound to restrict carbon emissions during procurement due to government emission regulation policies. Carbon emissions produced by each mode of transportation are different depending on the distance traveled (d_j), mileage (Mil_m), and load carried by the respective transportation modes. These variable carbon emissions (F_{omt}) can be calculated using Equation 15.1. However, fixed carbon emissions (F_{mt}) associated with each transportation mode must also be taken into account. Comparative emissions of different modes of transportation are shown in Table 15.2.

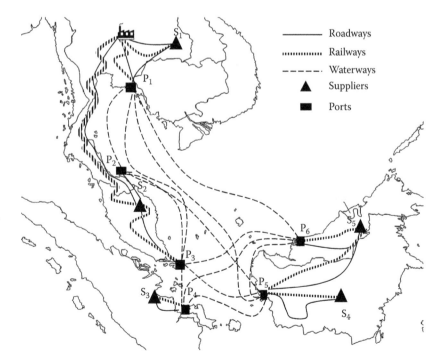

FIGURE 15.5
Possible roadways and waterways between manufacturers and global suppliers.

TABLE 15.2

Scale Distribution of Various Parameters for Roadways, Railways, and Waterways

Parameters	Roadways	Railways	Waterways
Emissions (kg/ton-km)	High	Medium	Low
Capacity	Low	Medium	High
Transportation cost (/ton-km)	High	Medium	Low
Mileage (km/L)	Medium	High	Low
Lead time	Medium	Low	High

Carbon emissions are also caused while procuring (E_{ot}) and holding extra inventory (E_{wt}). Hence, lead-time information is useful in calculating the amount of inventory to be kept. Therefore, it is necessary for the manufacturing firm to calculate the emissions for each route using Equation 15.2. The manufacturing firm must optimize the logistics network to procure raw material from suppliers, minimizing total carbon emissions while considering carrier capacities, supplier capacities, and lead time. The optimal low-carbon international logistics network for automobile firm (M) is shown in Figure 15.6. Among all possible networks, the low-carbon international logistics network is shown as a shaded region. The optimized logistics network establishes a trade-off between emissions caused, load ordered, lead time, and cost incurred. For example, supplier S_5 is considered for bulk orders placed well in advance. The logistics network of supplier S_5 includes waterways and railways. Both these modes of transportation produce fewer emissions and have more lead time and carrier capacity than roadways. Hence, a trade-off is established between

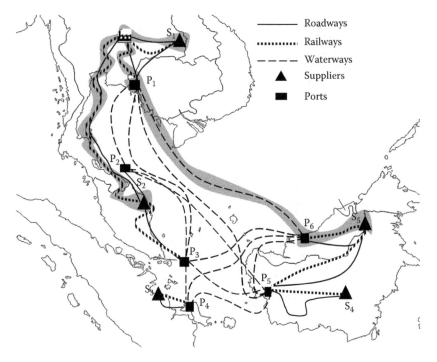

FIGURE 15.6
Low-carbon international logistics network of a manufacturing firm.

cost, emissions, and lead time. Similarly, supplier S_1, connected to the manufacturing firm by roadways, is chosen as one of the optimal networks. Although roadways are associated with high carbon emissions, supplier S_1 is located nearby, resulting in a shorter lead time and used only when raw material is urgently required.

Supplier S_2 is also selected to supply raw material to the manufacturing firm. S_2 is connected to M by all three modes of transportation. However, railways are chosen as the optimal mode of transportation for S_2 as rail transportation takes less time than roadway and waterway transportation. Another possible route is a combination of railways and waterways ($S_2 \longrightarrow P_2 \longrightarrow P_1 \longrightarrow M$), for which the lead time is greater because of additional loading and unloading time at ports P_1 and P_2.

15.6 Conclusion and Future Scope of Work

The chapter provides a conceptual framework to design a smart city concept by taking into account the needs of the industry and environmental issues. The proposed framework attempts to provide a low-carbon logistics network for the manufacturing industry and/or associated suppliers, and its sister concern of minimizing carbon emissions due to the procurement process, carrying of items, and delivering items through multiple transport modes in a city. The proposed concept can also be implemented for a large-sized residential or commercial township focusing on low-carbon transportation with a view to keeping a city smart.

References

Anand, N., Duin, R., Quak H., and Tavasszy, L. 2015. Relevance of city logistics modelling efforts: A review. *Transport Reviews*, 35 (6), 701–719.

Balakrishna, C. 2012. Enabling technologies for smart city services and applications. In *2012 6th International Conference on Next Generation Mobile Applications, Services and Technologies (NGMAST)*, Paris, edited by Al-Begain, K., 223–227. Washington, DC: IEEE.

Bijwaard, D. J., van Kleunen, W. A., Havinga, P. J., Kleiboer, L., and Bijl, M. J. 2011. Industry: Using dynamic WSNs in smart logistics for fruits and pharmacy. In *Proceedings of the 9th ACM Conference on Embedded Networked Sensor Systems*, edited by J. Liu, P. Levis, and K. Römer, 218–231. New York: ACM.

Cattaruzza, D. et al. 2015. Vehicle routing problems for city logistics. *EURO Journal on Transportation and Logistics*, 5, 1–29.

Crainic, T. G., Ricciardi, N., and Storchi, G. 2009. Models for evaluating and planning city logistics systems. *Transportation Science*, 43(4), 432–454.

Dablanc, L. 2007. Goods transport in large European cities: Difficult to organize, difficult to modernize. *Transportation Research Part A: Policy and Practice*, 41(3), 280–285.

European Commission, Directorate-General for Energy and Transport. 2007. *Towards a New Culture for Urban Mobility*. Luxembourg: Office for Official Publications of the European Communities.

Hensher, D. A., and Puckett, S. M. 2005. Refocusing the modelling of freight distribution: Development of an economic-based framework to evaluate supply chain behavior in response to congestion charging. *Transportation*, 32(6), 573–602.

Höjer, M., and Wangel, J. 2015. Smart sustainable cities: Definition and challenges. In *ICT Innovations for Sustainability*. M. L. Hilty and B. Aebischer, eds. Cham: Springer International Publishing, pp. 333–349. Available at: http://dx.doi.org/10.1007/978-3-319-09228-7_20.

Jong, M., Joss, S., Schraven, D., Zhan, C., and Weijnen, M. 2015. Sustainable–smart–resilient–low carbon–eco–knowledge cities: Making sense of a multitude of concepts promoting sustainable urbanization. *Journal of Cleaner Production*, 109, 25–38.

Kawa, A., 2012. Supply chain configuration in high-tech networks. In *Intelligent Information and Database Systems: 4th Asian Conference, ACIIDS 2012*, Kaohsiung, Taiwan, March 19–21, 2012, Proceedings, Part I. In J.-S. Pan, S.-M. Chen, and N. T. Nguyen, eds. Berlin: Springer, pp. 432–438. Available at: http://dx.doi.org/10.1007/978-3-642-28487-8_45.

Lee, S., Kang, Y., and Prabhu, V. V. 2016. Smart logistics: Distributed control of green crowdsourced parcel services. *International Journal of Production Research*, 1–13. DOI: 10.1080/00207543.2015.1132856.

Lombardi, P., Giordano, S., Farouh, H., and Yousef, W. 2012. Modelling the smart city performance. *Innovation: The European Journal of Social Science Research*, 25(2), 137–149.

Masson, R., Trentini, A., Lehuédé, F., Malhéné, N., Péton, O., and Tlahig, H. 2015. Optimization of a city logistics transportation system with mixed passengers and goods. *EURO Journal on Transportation and Logistics*, 2, 1–29.

Montreuil, B., 2011. Toward a physical Internet: Meeting the global logistics sustainability grand challenge. *Logistics Research*, 3(2), 71–87.

Nowicka, K. 2014. Smart city logistics on cloud computing model. *Procedia: Social and Behavioral Sciences*, 151, 266–281.

Russo, F., and Comi, A. 2012. City characteristics and urban goods movements: A way to environmental transportation system in a sustainable city. *Procedia: Social and Behavioral Sciences, 39*, 61–73.

Smirnov, A., Levashova, T., and Shilov, N., 2009. Knowledge sharing in flexible production networks: A context-based approach. *International Journal of Automotive Technology and Management*, 9(1), 87–109.

Trentini, A., and Mahléné, N. 2010. Toward a shared urban transport system ensuring passengers and goods cohabitation. *Tema. Journal of Land Use, Mobility and Environment*, 3(2), 37–44.

Uckelmann, D. 2008. A definition approach to smart logistics. In *Next Generation Teletraffic and Wired/Wireless Advanced Networking*, edited by S. Balandin, D. Moltchanov and Y. Koucheryavy. 273–284. Berlin Heidelberg: Springer.

Yu, C.M.J., and Liao, T.J. 2008. The impact of governance mechanisms on transaction-specific investments in supplier-manufacturer relationships: A comparison of local and foreign manufacturers. *Management International Review*, 48(1), 95–114.

Index

Actor-network theory (ANT), 23
Airtel Money services, 117
ANT. *see* Actor-network theory (ANT)
Authenticity, 18

BCR. *see* Benefit-to-cost ratio (BCR)
Behavioral issues, 17
Benefit-to-cost ratio (BCR), 144–145
Bhartiya City Integrated Township, 36
Big data, in smart cities, 106–107
Bombay Electric Supply and Transport, 117, 122
Building energy consumption
    CO_2 emissions reduction, 145
    daylight level optimization
        lighting power density (LPD), 141
        and light pipe, 139–141
        and light shelves, 135–139
        orientation, 129–131
        visual light transmittance (VLT), 131–133
        window-to-wall ratio (WWR), 133–135
    methodology, 129
    overview, 127–129
    and techno-economic evaluation, 141–145
        benefit-to-cost ratio (BCR), 144–145
        initial capital cost, 142–144

Car-sharing schemes, 188–192
Cashless transactions/payments
    cloud-based model for, 118–122
    limitations, 123
    literature review, 116–118
    merits, 122–123
    overview, 115–116
Causal loop diagram (CLD), 96–97
China *vs.* India, manufacturing sector, 73–76
City logistics systems, 201–202
CLD. *see* Causal loop diagram (CLD)
CLIOS. *see* Complex, large-scale, interconnected, open, and sociotechnical (CLIOS) model
CO_2 emissions reduction, 145
Communication issues, 17
Complex, large-scale, interconnected, open, and sociotechnical (CLIOS) model, 128
Crime and disaster issues, 17
Crowdsourcing, 16
Cultural issues, 17

Daylight level optimization
    lighting power density (LPD), 141
    and light pipe, 139–141
    and light shelves, 135–139
    orientation, 129–131
    visual light transmittance (VLT), 131–133
    window-to-wall ratio (WWR), 133–135
Decentralized wastewater treatment system (DEWAT), 41
Decision support systems (DSSs)
    and car-sharing schemes, 188–192
    for electric urban mobility, 184–188
    electric vehicles (EVs) and, 184–188
    overview, 181–183
    purpose of, 183–184
    for smart citizens, 192–195
    TrafficO2 game, 193–195
Delhi Mumbai Industrial Corridor (DMIC), 34
DEWAT. *see* Decentralized wastewater treatment system (DEWAT)
DIN. *see* Director identification number (DIN)
Director identification number (DIN), 65
DMIC. *see* Delhi Mumbai Industrial Corridor (DMIC)

Economic indicators, 45
Ecosystem, of smart village, 86
E-filing tax systems, 59–63
EGMM. *see* E-government maturity model (eGMM)
E-government maturity model (eGMM), 56
Electric urban mobility, and DSSs, 184–188
Electric vehicles (EVs), 184–188
Electronic government/e-governance/ e-government, 53–54. *see also* Smart governance
    barriers and challenges, 54–55
    information systems and, 55–57
Electronic passports (e-passports), 64
Electronic ticket-issuing machine (ETIM), 118, 122
Electronic transaction, 53–54
Energy Conservation Building Code (ECBC), 141
Energy management, and smart village, 88
Entertainment, 15–16
Environmental indicators, 45

E-Sahyog, 63
ETIM. *see* Electronic ticket-issuing
    machine (ETIM)
EVs. *see* Electric vehicles (EVs)

FFM. *see* Five-factor model (FFM)
Five-factor model (FFM), 26

GDP. *see* Gross domestic product (GDP)
Governance, and smart cities
    classification, 11–18
    concept of, 10–11
    entertainment, 15–16
    human issues, 16–17
    overview, 9–10
    political issues, 16
    public participation, 16
    research methodology, 11
    security issues, 17–18
    sustainability, 15
    technological issues, 18
    urban development, 15
Governance model, of smart village, 89
Gross domestic product (GDP), 15, 72

Hardware and software incompatibility, 18
Human Development Index, 151
Human issues, 16–17

Income tax returns (ITRs), 59–63
India
    vs. China, 73–76
    industrial policies in, 72–73
    urban context, smart cities in, 109–111
Industrial policies, in India, 72–73
Information-based services, 153
Information systems, and electronic
    government, 55–57
Infrastructure development, 15
Initial capital cost, 142–144
Integrated solid waste management (ISWM),
    34, 41–42
Integrated township planning
    concept development and
        methodology, 37–42
        commercial areas, 39
        decentralized wastewater treatment
            system (DEWAT), 41
        integrated solid waste management
            system, 41–42
        mixed-use development area, 39
        public and semi-public buildings, 39–40
        recreational areas, 40

residential area distribution, 38–39
        road system, 40–41
        solar energy generation, 42
        sustainable water management, 41
        transportation facilities, 42
        zoning, 38
    concept of, 32–33
    economic indicators, 45
    environmental indicators, 45
    layout plan and 3-D model, 42–43
    literature review, 34–37
        and Bhartiya City Integrated Township, 36
        and Magarpatta City, 35–36
        policies, 36–37
    mobility planning, 44
    overview, 32
    principles of, 33–34
    social indicators, 45
    sustainability indicators, 44–45
    and sustainable development, 34
Internet of Things (IOT), 108
Investments, and smart village, 88
IOT. *see* Internet of Things (IOT)
ISWM. *see* Integrated solid waste
    management (ISWM)
ITRs. *see* Income tax returns (ITRs)

Land acquisition, and smart cities, 110
Layout plan and 3-D model, 42–43
Leadership in Energy and Environmental
    Design (LEED), 131
LEED. *see* Leadership in Energy and
    Environmental Design (LEED)
Legitimacy, of smart cities, 111
Leisure and recreation, 16
Lighting power density (LPD), 141
Light pipes, 139–141
Light shelves, 135–139
Low-carbon logistics network cities
    case studies, 207–211
    and city logistics systems, 201–202
    description, 205–206
    overview, 199–200
    problem description, 203–204
    review of indicators of, 201
    technology-enabled, 202–203
LPD. *see* Lighting power density (LPD)

Manchester Digital Development Agency
    (MDDA), 86
Manufacturing sector, and smart economy
    India *vs.* China, 73–76
    industrial policies in India, 72–73

overview, 71–72
research methodology, 76–77
MCA21 Project, 65
MDDA. *see* Manchester Digital Development
    Agency (MDDA)
Mission mode projects (MMPs), 50
Mixed-use development area, 39
MMPs. *see* Mission mode projects (MMPs)
Mobile commerce (m-commerce), in smart cities
    barriers to, 174–175
    business/workplace perspective, 171–172
    dissemination, 172
    importance of, 174
    individual perspective, 169–171
    information access, 171
    overview, 167–169
    purchase opportunity, 171
    society perspective, 173
    SWOT analysis of, 175
    and ubiquity, 172
Mobile phone/cloud–based cashless travel
    model, 118–122
Mobility planning, 44
M-PESA, 117
Multifaceted risk mapping
    for technology-assisted consumer
        contact, 160
    for technology-facilitated consumer
        contact, 161
    for technology-free consumer contact, 162
    for technology-generated consumer contact,
        161–162
    for technology-mediated consumer
        contact, 161

National Building Code (NBC), 131
National Capital Region (NCR), 34
NBC. *see* National Building Code (NBC)
NCR. *see* National Capital Region (NCR)
NEO-PI. *see* Neuroticism-Extraversion-
    Openness Personality
    Inventory (NEO-PI)
Neuroticism-Extraversion-Openness
    Personality Inventory (NEO-PI), 26
NGOs. *see* Nongovernmental
    organizations (NGOs)
Nongovernmental organizations (NGOs), 59

Oyster cards, 117

Passport seva project, 63–64
PayTM, 117
PayUMoney, 117

PEOU. *see* Perceived ease of use (PEOU)
Perceived ease of use (PEOU), 59
Perceived risk, 157
    dimensions of, 157–159
Personal innovativeness in information
    technology (PIIT), 59
PIIT. *see* Personal innovativeness in information
    technology (PIIT)
Political issues, 16
Privacy issues, 17–18
Public and semi-public buildings, 39–40
Public participation, 16
Public utilities, and information-based
    services, 153

QR. *see* Quick response (QR) code
Quick response (QR) code, 121, 123

Recreational areas, 40
Residential area distribution, 38–39
Risks
    definition, 157
    perceived, 157
        dimensions of, 157–159
Road system, and integrated township, 40–41

Security issues, 17–18
SFD. *see* Stock and flow diagram (SFD)
Simulator of Urban Mobility, 187
Smart cards, 122–123
Smart cities
    big data in, 106–107
    concept of, 106
    controlling, 110
    and decision support systems (DSSs)
        and car-sharing schemes, 188–192
        for electric urban mobility, 184–188
        electric vehicles (EVs) and, 184–188
        overview, 181–183
        purpose of, 183–184
        for smart citizens, 192–195
        TrafficO2 game, 193–195
    definitions of, 150–152
    and digital services
        categorizations/classifications of, 154–157
        vs. service, 153–154
    dimensions, 150–151
    energy efficiencies and sustainability, 110
    and governance
        classification, 11–18
        concept of, 10–11
        entertainment, 15–16
        human issues, 16–17

overview, 9–10
political issues, 16
public participation, 16
research methodology, 11
security issues, 17–18
sustainability, 15
technological issues, 18
urban development, 15
in Indian urban context, 109–111
and Internet of Things (IOT), 108
and land acquisition, 110
legitimacy of, 111
literature review, 25–26
low-carbon logistics network for
case study, 207–211
and city logistics systems, 201–202
description, 205–206
overview, 199–200
problem description, 203–204
review of indicators of, 201
technology-enabled, 202–203
mobile commerce (m-commerce) in
barriers to, 174–175
business/workplace perspective, 171–172
dissemination, 172
importance of, 174
individual perspective, 169–171
information access, 171
overview, 167–169
purchase opportunity, 171
society perspective, 173
SWOT analysis of, 175
and ubiquity, 172
overview, 1–2, 24–25, 150
public utilities and information-based
services, 153
research methodology, 26
success factors, 108–109
and system dynamics (SD)
causal loop diagram (CLD), 96–97
limitations, 102–103
literature review, 94–96
overview, 93–94
results and analysis, 99–102
stock and flow diagram (SFD), 97–99
Smart citizens, DSSs for, 192–195
Smart economy, 3, 24, 151
and manufacturing sector
India *vs.* China, 73–76
industrial policies in India, 72–73
overview, 71–72
research methodology, 76–77
Smart environment, 4–5, 25, 152

Smart governance, 4, 25, 152–153. *see also*
Electronic government/e-governance/
e-government
barriers and challenges, 54–55
and e-filing tax systems, 59–63
information systems and, 55–57
literature review, 52–57
electronic government and electronic
transaction, 53–54
smart city, 52–53
and MCA21 Project, 65
and Ministry of Finance, 59
overview, 49–52
and passport seva project, 63–64
research gap, contribution, and scope, 57–58
research methodology, 58
Smart living, 4, 25, 152
Smart mobility systems, 3–4, 25, 152
Smart people, 3, 25, 151
Smart village
definition of, 85–86
ecosystem of, 86
and energy management, 88
governance model of, 89
growth strategies, 89
and investment scenario, 88
issues and challenges in India, 86–88
literature review, 84–85
overview, 83–84
performance measure of, 89–90
Social indicators, 45
Social issues, 17
Social media, 16
Solar energy generation, 42
Special Investment Region Act, 110
Stock and flow diagram (SFD), 97–99
STOPE. *see* Strategy–technology–organization–
people–environment (STOPE)
Strategy–technology–organization–people–
environment (STOPE), 56
Strengths, weaknesses, opportunities, and
threats (SWOT) analysis, 175
Sustainability indicators, 44–45
Sustainable development
and integrated township planning, 34
Sustainable water management, 41
SWOT analysis. *see* Strengths, weaknesses,
opportunities, and threats (SWOT)
analysis
System dynamics (SD)
causal loop diagram (CLD), 96–97
limitations, 102–103
literature review, 94–96

overview, 93–94
results and analysis, 99–102
stock and flow diagram (SFD), 97–99

Techno-economic evaluation, 141–145
  benefit-to-cost ratio (BCR), 144–145
  initial capital cost, 142–144
Technology-enabled logistics networks, 202–203
Technology/technological issues, 18
  -assisted consumer contact, 156, 160
  -facilitated consumer contact, 156, 161
  -free consumer contact, 156, 162
  -generated consumer contact, 157, 161–162
  -mediated consumer contact, 157, 161
Tourism, 16
TrafficO2 game, and DSSs, 193–195

Transportation
  and integrated township, 42
  and logistics, 15

UK Environmental Industries Commission, 110
Urban development, 15
U.S. Green Building Council (USGBC), 127
USGBC. *see* U.S. Green Building Council
  (USGBC)

Virtual Environment software, 129
Visual light transmittance (VLT), 131–133
VLT. *see* Visual light transmittance (VLT)

Window-to-wall ratio (WWR), 133–135
WWR. *see* Window-to-wall ratio (WWR)